A YEAR IN WHO WE ARE

Brian L. Coatney

Published by:
Christ, Our Life Ministeries, Inc.

A YEAR IN WHO WE ARE

Published by Christ, Our Life Ministries, Inc.
P.O. Box 43268
Louisville, KY 40253-0268

Printed in the U.S.A. by
Thoroughbred Printing
904 N Broadway
Lexington, KY 40505

Foreword

My good friend of 38 years, Brian Coatney, has done it again. Brian first began writing years ago, but like all who hear from God, he has been powerfully transformed by the Spirit of Wisdom into a literary master, and in my opinion, will someday be listed with the Greats. Of course his main reference is a masterpiece in itself, as he says, "How can you go wrong when your material is the Bible?"

This book of daily devotional insights had its beginnings when Brian began his excellent Internet blog. Every day he faithfully offered the reader manna from Heaven. His daily, crafted meals offered food for those who hunger and thirst after the righteousness of Christ, and also to those who want to mature into the full stature of Christ, as Paul describes in his Ephesians letter: "Be filled with all the fullness of God."

Brian uses his own personal experiences along with his Biblical insights to weave together a tapestry of truth unlike any other. The Word of God as Brian presents it will "put fire in your bones" as well as introduce you to the same wisdom that resides in him.

Brian's insightful writings speak loud and clear into the hearts and minds of God's family. If whole-heartedly received, his insights will spiritually advance and transform any seeker into God's wise masterpiece.

Know that Brian did not get to know and hear from "the still small voice" easily. No master is transformed without pain. So by faith, Brian learned how to seek Wisdom first and daily "practice the presence of God" in his own life, and now he shares with the Lord's people the wisdom he has gained from his journey of faith.

Brian is a poet himself, so by his own poetic medium, I offer this poem from an old hymn. It perfectly describes Brian's walk with the Lord.

Say, canst thou drink of that dark cup,
Where tears of anguish flow
And, e'er the baptism of fire,
Be first baptized in woe?

Before the voice of God doth speak,
"As man speaks to his friend,"
A great strong wind perchance may break
The rocks and mountains rend.

Still wilt thou stand before the Lord,
And for His promise wait?
The earth may quake, and shattered hopes
Leave thy life desolate.

Within thy heart His fire must burn,
Consuming all the dross;
Till, midst the ashes of a world,
Stands nothing but the Cross.

Then, in the calm, "a still small voice"
Shall speak, yea, speak to thee;
Wrapped in the mantle of God's truth,
And power thy lips shall be.

Be blessed as you partake of the Spirit's rich wisdom and the many insightful "Pearls" found in this tremendous devotional. Dare to go to the depths with Brian and find a daily diet of Spirit food. As Proverbs says, "The lips of the righteous feed many."

Sylvia D. Pearce

Sylvia D. Pearce

Acknowledgements

Many people have contributed to this book by influencing or mentoring me over the years. My mother, Constance Boxley Coatney, gave me my first Bible-story book, and my grandmother, Anna Leslie Boxley, set a firm standard for absolute fidelity to the Lord, which I didn't follow for a season, but remembered later with deepest respect. My mother-in-law Mimi Anderson and my sister Sylvia Coatney Boldt led me into my first taste of the Holy Spirit's anointing. Mimi later began talking about union with Christ and gave me books by the great missionary statesman Norman P. Grubb. I found these books inaccessible until my resolutions to serve the Lord started falling apart. Then the books made sense, and Norman's personal friendship over the approximately fifteen years I knew him cannot be measured.

Mimi also introduced me to Dan Stone, who faithfully came to Hopkinsville to lead a "day apart" once a month in the mid-1970s. Through Mimi, I also met Sylvia Pearce and her family in 1979. Sylvia has influenced our family beyond words, and she and Scott, her husband, along with their children, have been a family to us, as well as being commissioned together by the Lord in the outreach of the Gospel.

Sylvia introduced me also to Louis Tucker, who along with Barry Craig, helped me a lot in dealing with failure. Along the way, she also introduced me to the writings of two greats of old, Jacob Boehme and William Law, as well as introducing me to my dear friend, Alan Parker, who has been one of the great mentors in my life.

In 2010, our friend, Nancy Gilmore, said, "Brian, you should start a blog." Nancy also posted my blog on her site for several years. The blog has run continuously these seven years, and in the last four years, I have posted the daily readings that comprise this book, honing them each year. The idea to write a book like this came a few years into the blog when I reflected on my longtime admiration of Oswald Chambers. I wanted to produce a volume like that—short daily readings that dig deep. The Internet is a great outreach, but many of us like to sit with a book as well, and thus the printing of this volume.

A few longtime readers, plus some more recent, ardent readers have encouraged me countless times with their comments. Tim Langdon from Alaska has read the blog since its inception. Along came Nicholas Pujdak, our artist friend from the Los Angeles area, where he befriended an old mentor, Bill Bower, who is famous for saying, "Put the heat on God." Nicholas has been every blogger's dream for years now. Others cheering me on include of course Sylvia, Louie and Tracey Lewis, Richard Krupa, Suzy Lovell, Lanny Howe, Jenny Fienning, Roel Velema, Byron Shore, Brenda Luttrull, and Patsy Lovejoy.

Jenny Fienning took on a special role in reading through the manuscript for typos and clarity of thought. My wife, Tandy, did the same thing, so I had two of the best. Tandy also steers and helps create every aspect of the book's content and appearance. And our grandson, Wesley Coatney, helped with formatting.

We all know what a wise wife means to any man, and the cost of two people learning to walk in wisdom together in the love of Christ. Together we have lived and died, through forty-six years of marriage, that which makes the miracle of this book possible. The book is our testimony. It does not make us who we are; we would be who we are if there were no book. But the Lord commends us to share with readers the roots of our adventures, and thus we have done that here, for everything is known from its roots and no other way.

The book is also dedicated to our children and grandchildren, not out of sentiment, but out of respect for the challenges that each generation faces. Those whom we bring into the world and build an outer family tree from, need us to cheer them on with the faith of the inner tree—the Tree of Life—as they too build their trees and do the same.

And we know that the greatest miracle of all is the Lord Himself, who saved us through His Son, Jesus Christ, and witnesses to us of that salvation by the Holy Spirit in the Wisdom, Power, Might, and Glory of God.

Brian Coatney
November 2017

Why the Law?

An astonishing amount of energy goes into court-houses and jails. Litigation and punishment are productive unto justice, but for fruit bearing, they do not help except as a motivating shock. On the helping side, many professions aim to prevent or treat what we come to find out disappears in the new birth simply because the old man died for the new man to be birthed. This is not to slight anyone serving unto the Lord but to highlight our death and burial in Christ. Anything and everything that was wrong with us got crucified in Christ when He died, and the church will finally see that God never intended to fix the old man but crucify him, to start over with a new birth, in which we live by the Spirit. This means a supernatural life, not a natural life reformed. In that day no one will try to be like Christ.

This is why Paul says, "understanding this, that the law is not laid down for the just but for the lawless and disobedient, for the ungodly and sinners" (1 Tim. 1:9 ESV). The law cannot reform people but only give a faint measure of how far we fell. Though not glory, the law is necessary to expose the wheel of wrath already in the lost person, which wheel is fueled by Satan, whose nature is behind all sin, for Satan authors sin, with the human as the slave.

Thus, the human is not evil but is dominated by evil, and the law is the first form of correction, not to change a person but to be the Spirit's instrument of conviction that one is falling short of the glory of God. The first remedy is salvation, which means agreeing with the need for a savior. I finally abandoned trying to improve my old man and agreed with God that my old man died in Christ and was buried in Him.

Jesus Christ must save us, and nothing and no one else. His blood cleanses from sin, and His Spirit is the agent in manifesting Christ in us. Who is the "us"? It is those who are raised as new creatures in Christ!

The Four Kinds of Suffering

Suffering comes in four kinds, two that we do not have to keep enduring. First, no one needs to remain lost. The wages of sin is death (Rom. 6:23). To be lost is a fearful state; getting saved is the remedy. The Bible is a book of lost and found stories—stories of redemption. When we recognize our need for a savior, there He is—Jesus Christ the Lord. The Gospel is the good news of how to escape the wages of sin and the sin-boss, Satan, who stole us and operated us in our lost condition (2 Tim. 2:26).

Second, suffering continues until seeing the revelation of "not I but Christ" (Gal. 2:20) and walking in the Spirit (Gal. 5:16). Every Christian I've met has battled by trying to keep the law, which cannot work. God does not even mean it to because He created us powerless to keep it. The idea that we can operate independently is the devil's lie to keep the woeful sense of wretchedness going for those attempting to live independently. But trying to be like Jesus is a sin. Deliverance comes by seeing "not I but Christ."

The third suffering is not sin related. James tells us to count it all joy when experiencing temptations and trials. This is a constant jolt and challenge to the mindset that considers suffering an indication of a life not pleasing to God. But temptation and trials are what God *means*, though He does not tempt us but uses the convenient agent, the devil. God establishes us, and often has a purpose that we may not understand. But we can rest, wait, and endure.

The fourth suffering is voluntary, the intercessory kind—a bodily calling to fulfill a commission. Focus is on the commission and not letting its cost deter us into thinking that it is payback for sin. Completion of the commission is the point. The cost is not to be compared with the privilege of serving.

In the World but not of It

It is easy to shun the world as evil. Yet the world is the setting in which to excel and earn a living, so the mystery is how to be in the world but not of it. We are here, so now what?

The issue is inner—how we see. It does not work to anxiously seek success, questioning God's provision or whether others will esteem us: the needy consciousness never knows enough. Here is the lie: "I cannot go forth and succeed and make a living." However, Paul says in 2 Thessalonians to avoid the idle, and in Ephesians to work in order to help those in need, so the first thing one has to do is to trust "Christ in you" to function at a basic level.

Sin has damaged that ability. Even in the "successful," sin does its damage through lack of rest—not ceasing from one's own works. Therefore, our foremost job is this: "it is no longer I but Christ"—free of anxiety despite the constant bombardment of thoughts and feelings. These, if taken as an identity, keep us bound in condemnation and perpetuate the lie. Those who are practiced know to laugh off the lie; it is not our spirit core where we are one with Christ.

Clarity releases energy formerly tied up in condemnation and efforts at control. Then, temptation is seen for what it is. Instead of being fooled, life is lived on the deep level of God's keeping. In the moment, we love the person at hand. You discover what it means to be a steward; your gifts are given by God to seek the good of others. Ultimately, you are intended to reproduce yourself so that others see themselves as who they are and in turn become stewards.

The remnant looks small, but the mustard seed will win the world. It already has to those of faith, who get perplexed but do not despair while watching one seedling after another spring to life in the resurrection power of Jesus Christ.

Love Requires Opposites

Norman Grubb often said, "The universe is protons and electrons loving each other." Glue holds everything together, and love is the glue, manifesting in opposites that attract in dance and delight. However, in a fallen world, when a love enterprise fizzles or crashes, the seeker quests again to find the lost treasure in some person, place, or thing. The problem is that we are self-for-self apart from union with Jesus Christ. He alone is love, and the scripture says, "God is love." God is the one self-for-others person in the universe; apart from Him, no love exists nor can.

Reliance on emotions will not work, for Jesus said, "God is spirit, and they that worship Him must worship Him in spirit and in truth" (John 4:24). Apart from knowing that, the seeker can only continue the freakish fantasy search for what turns out every time to be self-for-self. How then can a person love? It can be only one way: the believer loves by faith, putting love beyond emotion and reason. The Spirit of God Himself in us is love, and the director of its flow, first to God, then toward others. Then we are able to say, "What is best for that person?"

This can only happen by faith, but faith seems unreal at first—contrary to what looks real. This is because we have been used to believing what is seen and felt outwardly. That leads to pain, which is conditioning for the inner world of faith. If I want to know that I love a person, or know that my involvement with an enterprise is holy, it must be by faith. That is how God means love to operate in His sons. Therein is stability that comes up inside by the witness of the Spirit after faith has stood sufficiently without that witness.

Yet even standing without the witness comes from God. Appreciation of vessel-hood is never so great as when it must be "not I but Christ" before "the life I live in the flesh I live by the faith of the son of God."

Sometimes the Cup Is the Point

I didn't make coffee at home this morning because there is a coffee machine at the end of a quiet hall in a building on campus. The thought of a cup there, fifty cents by the way, offered a special moment before slipping into the office to do this blog. Grabbing four quarters from the car, I headed across the parking lot, two of the quarters for a second cup later.

At the end of the hall, I dropped in my two quarters and heard the machine hum and rev up, followed by the sound of the coffee dispensed. But I hadn't heard the pop and thud of the cup dropping down. Opening the flap, I watched disappointedly as the coffee went down the drain, never to be enjoyed. Sometimes the cup is the point. We are vessels of Christ to express Him and offer Him to the world. Without us, He is coffee down the drain. Fortunately I remembered an office on another hall where the staff has a coffee pot. Perhaps I could beg a cup. Sure enough, the pot was there, with hot coffee waiting, and a stack of cups.

Christ needs every cup, each one in his body—you in the moment of your living. Not a drop is wasted. Being a vessel is a topic I never tire of talking about. We could talk all the old surrender talk about yielding ourselves as cups, and Romans Chapter 6 says, "present your members as slaves of righteousness (6:19). People labor that way too much, as if it is a constant process that never really happens anyway. However, the business of being a cup is delightful and easy. It's certainly more so than trying to be the coffee, or thinking, "A cup needs to surrender but never does."

I'm enjoying my coffee, and you know what? I'm enjoying the cup more than usual. God loves cups, and He loves His coffee in a cup and serving it that way.

Knowledge Is Dependent upon Love

Knowledge as information to the brain makes us able to invent and operate technologies. It cannot stand alone but needs awe of God as the creator. Otherwise, knowledge will be sterile and mechanical.

Having glimpsed the beautiful truth of creation, the next discovery is grace: all we have is given, not earned. But the Fall sank us into the wheel of works, from which we must be saved—saved from boasting of an identity based on comparison to others.

Grace is indispensable even in a sinless realm. With or without sin, God is the creator and giver—we eternally the receivers. But grace starts with admission of sin and Christ as the savior from sin. He atoned for sin through His blood, as the Lamb of God, and keeps us from sin by His indwelling Spirit.

Once we know that we only receive, "God is love" becomes our central passion. Love yearns and unites as Paul says to the Philippians. Knowledge is made safe and used for others—not for self-exaltation over others.

Knowledge without love cannot succeed ultimately. It will look learned and in control but will destroy everything in its path eventually. Love is what makes knowledge safe. When love operates knowledge, the outcomes are sweet. The question becomes, "What is best for that person?" This is true knowledge. "For you are all partakers with me of grace…I yearn for you all with the affection of Christ Jesus. And it is my prayer that your love may abound more and more, with knowledge and all discernment, so that you may approve what is excellent, and so be pure and blameless for the day of Christ" (Philippians 1:7-10).

Depression Can Lead to Knowing "Dead to Sin"

Depression has its good aspect because God uses it. It is His invitation for us to say, "I want more than a Savior to forgive my sins." Yet the more one pursues this, the worse the self appears. I concluded, "I am nothing like what the Bible says I am to be."

We did not know that the problem is sin, not just sins. Sins are the products, sin the producer, so the sin producer must be cut off. No wonder Paul says, "Do you not know that you are dead to sin?" Have you thought, "That can't be right because I can still sin"?

But dying to sin means breaking our old union to the sin spirit. Sin is a person just like righteousness is a person, so before we were Christians, we were slaves to sin, needing to "escape from the snare of the devil, having been held captive to do his will" (2 Timothy 2:26). Dead to sin means dead to the devil's enslavement. This is far more than thinking of sins only on the level of commandments and particular sins. This gets to the producer level, like when one cuts down a plant that grows back unless it is dug out by the roots.

We had to die to sin, but there was no way unless we could die in Christ, who Himself did not need to die to sin but did so with us in Him on the Cross, so that we could die. Romans Chapter 6 tells this story: basically God unzipped Christ on the Cross and put us into Him.

Ignorance of this comes from the deception that the self can improve, but self-improvement is the big lie. The self *can't* improve. It needs to die to its slavery to sin and Satan, and get resurrected as a new creature, in which Christ Himself does the living as us. The Cross accomplished this because when the body of Christ died, the devil lost a body to live in. We died. Then when Christ rose, we rose too as new creations, Spirit operated.

God's Plan Looks Terrible at First

God's greater plan doesn't look like it at first. Disaster appears. However, out of ruin God brings the greatest life. Joseph is a perfect example. His coat set him apart in favor from his angry brothers; his dreams further incited them. You know the story. Joseph thought his life was over, yet his faith did not die. Soon came unexpected favor from his master, Potiphar, followed by the lust-driven aim of Potiphar's wife, who when refused, cried rape.

Joseph could have quit faith but didn't, and God favored him in jail with administrative wisdom. Finally, he supernaturally interpreted Pharaoh's dreams, gaining national favor, and Egypt became the world's breadbasket during the famine that followed. Joseph's family would migrate to Egypt and grow into a nation. This is intriguing. Why would God lead Abraham to the Promised Land, only to have his offspring move to Egypt to eventually become enslaved? Yet God had a plan to bring about the Exodus back to the Promised Land.

Joseph's place in his suffering was not to foresee all this. He didn't. He knew that he needed to be faithful and operate in the favor that God shined on him in his misery. This turns suffering into glory. The broad master plan appears later. While enduring suffering, our preparation for a calling takes place in obscurity and solitude, alone with God.

When the public moment arrives, we are grounded in the Cross. This kept Joseph from retribution later against his brothers. He could have sold his brothers into slavery but instead, love ruled: "Do not be distressed, or angry with yourselves, because you sold me here; for God sent me before you to preserve life" (Gen. 45:5). He reiterates this when he says, "So it was not you who sent me here but God." This response is miraculous, followed by "You meant it for evil, but God meant it for good" (50:20). This takes us past what others have done to us: the worst things are what God has meant to prepare us for the best things.

You Don't Have to Be Lonely

Loneliness is epidemic since the Fall. Adam gave into Eve's solicitation, with both lonely ever since. We think, "I am lonely, and the answer is to be around people." This never works, but the dream goes on. The lie of loneliness is that you must be with somebody, even if both are bored, wondering what others are doing.

Connections offer hope: family, friends, dating, mating, sports, clubs, and even work. The hunger is universal and God-made, but when connection is on a human level only, the result is only human—and this is the enemy's deception.

Marriage is the most often tried avenue. It is God's creation, but let's look at marriage. God created Eve as Adam's companion. Did she meet his need? The Bible does not offer hope that romance and marriage satisfy loneliness. When Jesus shocked His disciples with the standard for marriage—that a man not put away his wife except for fornication—His disciples answered, "If the case of the man be so with his wife, it is not good to marry" (Matt. 19:10).

Attraction wears off, sex loses its fizzle with that person, and off one goes searching for a new rush—one doomed to the same fate. The cycle repeats in futility. No wonder the Bible says that we are vessels and temples not meant to be filled by any created thing, but only by God, the Creator, made known through Jesus."

God boxes us in. Jesus' disciples caught this, and though they had the magic, they knew that it was Jesus who had it, and they, therefore, when with Him. They persevered with Him, so He drew them ever more into the mystery of how He operated from union with His father. Then He called them branches in the same union.

Joined to the tree of life, loneliness cannot hang around because life is Christ plus nothing. Solitude is pleasant, and when extended beyond measure is endured without loneliness. There is no need to believe in loneliness anymore.

Dead to Dysfunction

Let the past go and enjoy God's grace. Put the past into Christ and say, "I am no longer a victim of dysfunction, no longer helplessly in bondage because of a dysfunctional family." You are in a new family: "because ye are sons, God hath sent forth the Spirit of His Son into your hearts, crying Abba, Father" (Gal. 4:6).

This saves endless rehearsing of the past that goes nowhere from a fleshly point of view. In fact, how could any family not be dysfunctional—full of blame and guilt? That is what sin is, and all have sinned; and all have sinned against others, especially where people live close together. Of course abuse is abuse. The intent is not to callously say, "Just forget it." The Holy Spirit brings up pain so that the Cross can be the healing instrument. Apart from that, no approach to healing can work. Only the blood of Christ and the Spirit of Christ cleanse and bring peace where Satan used anger and hurt to perpetuate bondage.

Knowing one's own sins helps in letting go of self-righteousness and forgiving others. What if through the Cross, no one ever needs to attribute anything in life ever again to the actions of family or past abusers. God takes us out of that family and past and into a new family in which God is our father. No dysfunction exists there. Our inheritance means a new blood line—Christ's, in which we receive everything from Him.

Some may protest that we need therapy to process past hurts. This might be true for denial and repression. But to continue dredging up memories may turn into refusal to leave the devil's lie. The Gospel calls us to settle into the reality of our new bloodline in Christ. No longer do we trace any effect upon us from the first Adam but instead from the last Adam. This releases others and also holds out hope for them. We do not minimize our earthly families. No. We acknowledge them and responsibilities for provision and support, but now from who we are.

January 11

God Is Love

William Law aptly said, "Love is willed action for others." Emotional man, sentimental man, hormone man—all flee at this. Only the spirit man can stand firm and enter into joy. Feelings appear first but also exit first, making them unsuitable for love's staying power. Thoughts are the same, and of course hormones. A decision is required, for no one can will to love on his own or possess his own love. What the world considers love is an attachment that adversity eventually shakes loose. Love is a gift, and the volitional part is receiving. A branch does not generate the life of the tree; it expresses the life of the tree. We are made to contain and express God's love so that God and the human appear as one, but with the roles clear: the eternal creator making Himself known in finite human form.

To see this is to cease trying to love, which would be going under the law again and bringing back the lie of independent self, with its accompanying manifestation of self-effort. But since we are made in the image of God, we possess the faculty of desiring, which fuels the will into seeking and finding. Finding is by faith, which says, "God *is* loving that person perfectly by me." Lack disappears except on a soul and temptation level.

When feeling inadequate to love, disregard all negative feelings and thoughts: move by faith into whatever expression of love the Spirit brings forth. The solidity of love is that love is God, and so what faith expresses is divine love, not temporal love. It is tempting not to see love. When things do not appear to line up, should we dig for "issues"? Maybe a lie is hidden in the love—a little leaven. My friend Sylvia Pearce says that if you "speak the truth, the lie will untangle itself." It is the truth that heals. In the Holy Spirit, there is no condemnation; and repentance, when needed, becomes refreshing and freeing—not an exercise in the introspective twins, guilt and blame.

January 12

The Spontaneity Factor

Dan Stone talked about envying the spontaneity of lost people, which he too enjoyed in his carefree days before the Gospel. Like Paul, he said, "I was alive once apart from the law" (Rom. 7:9). After Dan got converted, he spent years trying to be like Christ, all the while secretly jealous of the non-Christians who lived spontaneously.

But it wasn't the Gospel that ended Dan's spontaneity, or ours. It was thinking that Christians are under the law—the lie that there is an independent self who can keep the law. After years of wearing down, Dan discovered that a Christian lives spontaneously by trusting Christ within to keep His own law. He saw God's use of the law to condition us away from self-effort and into Christ's life in us as our supply. Then life becomes spontaneous. It is the spontaneity of the Spirit in us that quickens us in daily life.

There will be suffering but not a sense that God's word is a tedious chore. John tells us, "His commandments are not burdensome" (1 John 5:3). At first, experience does not line up with this. Getting into the Law as a young adult Christian, I read that verse and said, "That's a lie!" Then I thought, "Wait a minute; this is the *Bible*! John just said that God's commandments are not burdensome, and I've impulsively blurted, 'That's a lie!' Who's right—John or me?"

Seeing the new birth resolves the apparent contradiction. John assumes the new creation man in union with Christ and the believer abiding as a branch. Only this overcomes evil because no man has the power over his own body and the enemy's pulls to misuse it. That power comes in seeing the body by faith as a cleansed temple housing Christ, who lives there by His Spirit—even in an earthly, mortal tent. He keeps His temple and makes it a beautiful place of manifestation for His own life. It's like being at home, which is the spontaneity.

Kierkegaard on Boredom

In *Either/Or* by Soren Kierkegaard, he calls man's basic problem boredom. This seems odd since sin would normally come to mind. But Kierkegaard takes an indirect angle on sin. When Adam got tired of God, he got bored and craved diversion. The earth looked so palpable to Adam that he wanted to be of it, whereas God meant him to be lord over it, and in it, but not of it. This was Adam's test— that he not descend into being primarily a sensual being.

When God is not enough for a man, what is left? External earth proves to be a fallacy, a bitter delusion leading to slavery since nothing only of the earth feeds the spirit in an eternal way. Kierkegaard likens this slavery to children with a governess. It is not enough for a governess to be moral, a good educator, and an activities planner. A governess who cannot entertain the children will fail because they will become bored, leading to their bad behavior.

Adam was to be continually enthralled with God and not yield to the lie of boredom. But when not enthralled, the lie of busyness appears—a form of being self-absorbed. Then busyness becomes a virtue. What day goes by that you won't hear a conversation among people talking about how busy they are, with its implied self-importance. It even becomes an identity. It hardly matters what one is doing as long as one is busy.

There is much to do, and James says, "faith without works is dead," but notice that it is the faith that produces the works, not the need to validate an independent self. False busyness eventually drains one of energy. Spirit rest, on the other hand, increases energy. The miracle comes, and energy from rest then produces the works the Father intends for us as His vessels. Boredom cannot exist in this mindset: "They shall run and not be weary" (Isa. 40:31).

Endnote: An easy way to get introduced to *Either/Or* is the readings from it in *A Kierkegaard Anthology* Ed. Robert Bretall Princeton: Princeton UP. 1946. Print.

Kierkegaard on the Progression of Boredom

Kierkegaard says that Adam was bored with God; therefore, Adam wanted Eve. Then he and Eve were bored, so they had children and were bored. Eventually the whole world was bored and built the Tower of Babel. Why? Separated life is restless—trying not to confront the fact that there is no rest at center because fear and condemnation steal the enjoyment of life. Externals invade into the place designed for internals. Had God allowed the Tower of Babel, what would it have taken next to fill the emptiness?

The Roman Empire tried circuses and gladiator battles—more military campaigns, more conquered nations, more roads, more engineering, and more civilization. The public craved more entertainment and diversion—finally in more debauched and brutal forms. Nothing is enough. There must be more adrenalin, a new relationship, new analysis about failure, and new programs, but ultimately there is more brutality and over-the-edge behavior.

Yet contentment is easy. We are to be content with food and clothes (1 Tim. 6:8). I remember leaner times, looking at apparent lack, and simply taking that verse by faith. The simple person can enjoy anything, being already whole and complete. The world adds nothing to who we are, because Christ is our life (Col. 3:1-3).

To know that God created people and things to contain and express His glory, one does not feed on the forms but on Christ as the inner food of everything. When stressed, see the image of God in others. Call them to return by Christ to their Creator. To anyone who receives, the Cross reverses the Fall by birthing that person as a new creation—a place where boredom cannot exist.

Endnote: *Either/Or. A Kierkegaard Anthology* Ed. Robert Bretall Princeton: Princeton UP. 1946. Print.

From Earthly Father to Heavenly Father

My earthly father left home when I was eleven, never to return. He pursued the idea that he could become a god through reincarnation. Hurt and anger resulted, but I forgave him, believing for his salvation. However, I still lived convinced that, as a son of my earthly father, I inherited a link to his dysfunction, one that caused me to walk as an incomplete man. When beset with turmoil, I could always say, "That's the influence of my father." Nothing could break that link, or so I thought. Oddly, I believed for his salvation, yet did not see the completeness of my own.

Manifestation of our word comes in unexpected ways. The Spirit of God, in His way and time, bears witness in us, making our faith into a genuine "I see." For me, this occurred after my faith dwindled to an ember in the wake of embarrassing depression, suicidal obsession, and humiliating dependencies. At the bottom, God's still small voice said, "Stop obsessing about your family and look at Me." I hesitated, but obeyed. What was there to lose? A glimpse of light came—the first in a long time.

We think at the bottom that God's word to us will be harsh. Yet, His conviction is of the truth, not the lie, and He convicted me unexpectedly of righteousness at the time I thought I should be convicted of sin. This came about through John 16: 8-11: Astonishingly, the Holy Spirit put His finger directly on me that He was convicting me of righteousness. Tears came; this word seemed impossible, but the Spirit pressed down on me to agree, so I did. The result was the awareness of God's presence and goodness.

Then, I say, *then*, I began to experience the genuine sorrow of repentance. What an indirect route. As Paul says, "The goodness of God leadeth thee to repentance" (Rom. 2:4). Condemnation fled away, and I knew the "repentance without regret" Paul speaks of in 2 Corinthians 7:10. Life was new.

January 16

Coming Home

Becoming aware of my own sin stopped the blame toward my earthly father. He didn't cause me to rebel. Everyone rebels no matter what father and mother have done. It is our own self-centeredness, which at root is slavery to sin and the sin producer, Satan. The offenses of others drive us to desperation and need for healing. Healing comes in seeing that God's response to sin is not condemnation and never has been. Condemnation comes from the enemy, and God means condemnation to drive us to Christ's deliverance. Gratitude then flows: "If that is what it took, Lord, to see the Cross, then I am glad You did not listen to pleas to stop short."

Deliverance means release from all connection to sin passed through the generations, *leading back to the first Adam*. Through union in Christ's death, burial, and resurrection, a new blood line opened up in the *last Adam*, and we only receive from Him now. Paul calls this the true circumcision—from enslavement to sin and sin's producer, Satan. This does not eradicate instantly the memories of one's enslaved life. But where do these memories come from? They do not come from God except filtered through the glory of God's washing them away in the blood, plus the gift of a new, supernatural life in Christ that stops dwelling on old things, except as new testimony. Memories for the sake of blame and guilt drop away. The Holy Spirit reveals how Christ's death ended the sting. His burial declared them dead, and His resurrection brought a new life untouched by them. His ascension put us on the throne with Christ, retaking the world one person at a time.

Satan repeatedly brings up offenses as if nothing could have extinguished them or replaced them. The world says about tragedy, "They will never get over it." If this is true, then Christ did a lot but not enough. Such an idea is an insult to Christ, and Hebrews Chapters 9 and 10 drive that home.

Believing for My Father's Salvation

I felt troubled when my father fell into a coma that would lead to death within days. When my sister, Sylvia Boldt, called me that he had passed, it was February 1996, and I pulled off the shelf *Streams in the Desert-1*, given to me at Margaret Lester's house by Jane Rogerson and Diane Pearce. The reading for February 22nd brought the witness of the Spirit.

A young man with questions on how to "*take the Lord for needed help*" received this reply from a sage, old woman: "You've got to believe that He's done it and it's done." The reading continues, "The great danger with most of us is that, after we ask Him to do it, we do not believe that it is done, but we keep on helping Him, and getting others to help Him; and waiting to see how He is going to do it."

As I read this, I believed that the Lord had indeed saved my father. Later that day, my boss sent me in the truck with a load of hardwood to Raleigh, NC. Even before I got into the truck, I had the overwhelming awareness, with tears that buckled me over, that my father and mother had reconciled in heaven (she having departed gloriously in 1985).

As I drove toward Raleigh, the Holy Spirit fell upon me with a picture of the thief on the Cross; He showed me a picture of my father at the last instant of his life grabbing the outstretched hand of Jesus reaching toward him.

Hymns flowed in my mind, with lyrics including, "Grace that is greater than all our sin." The Spirit stayed on me a good part of that drive. This was the Lord manifesting what I did not hear from my father's lips. God is not limited by a coma.

Our God is a good God; He saves to the uttermost, at the uttermost time, and in the uttermost ways. He does beyond all that we ask or think. He is a God who manifests Himself to those that believe.

Spirit to spirit

Good Bible minds debate whether man is bipartite or tripartite, some thinking that spirit and soul both refer to our immaterial part. Some overlap at first appears reasonable, but the New Testament moves from soul to spirit as our center. The Old Covenant of separation is superseded by the New Covenant removing separation from God, who reveals our spirit-to-Spirit union with Him through Jesus Christ. Spirit bursts onto the scene as the dominant focus. In both God and man, the self operates by desiring, willing, and knowing.

The afterlife as well is emphasized, with eternity at stake. This could appear to minimize the body, in contrast to the Old Covenant where life was in the here and now before an indeterminate Sheol, but the New Testament also liberates the body. First, it liberates it by letting it be temporal with the promise of a new, celestial body. This mortal body is free to be released in faith.

Second, the uncleanness of the body, accented in the Old Testament, gives way to what the writer of Hebrews calls "bodies washed with pure water" (Hebrews 10: 22). The New Testament reveals the secret to all uncleanness as indwelling sin in our bodies and not our bodies themselves. Paul explains this by revealing what circumcision and baptism really are—the cutting off of our bodies from indwelling sin (Satan) through the Cross.

The *KJV New Testament Lexicon* at Crosswalk.com includes a second definition of the Greek word *pneuma* as: "the spirit, i.e. the vital principal by which the body is animated" and two amplifications: "a. the rational spirit, the power by which the human being feels, thinks and decides" and "b. the soul." A subsequent entry for pneuma reads this way: "a spirit, i.e. a simple essence, devoid of all or at least all grosser matter, and possessed of the power of knowing, desiring, deciding, and acting." Spirit joined to spirit has taken over! Soul and body now follow their orders.

Getting Soul in Perspective

The word *soul* comes from the Hebrew *yuchv* that transliterates to the Greek word *psuche*, and means "the breath of life," "the vital force which animates the body," "life," and "the seat of the feelings, desires, affections, aversions (our heart, soul, etc.)."

The lexicon suggests some overlap and freedom to use spirit and soul interchangeably, but a shift occurs under the New Covenant: the Spirit of God moves from above the ark in the Holy of Holies, to man as God's temple. Before this, the law's condemnation made intimacy foreboding, and only pioneers of faith found it. The Old Covenant was a "blazing fire" and "darkness and gloom and whirlwind" (Heb. 12:18). Familiarity with God known by Noah, Abraham, David, and the prophets was the exception.

In contrast, the soul, as breathed out of God and connected to earth, told of present, animate life. Yet, pioneers of faith did believe beyond the Old Covenant and saw the heavenly city from afar, as well as the resurrection, but the total unveiling of this mystery would come through Christ and the New Covenant. The New Testament writers clarify these mysteries, with heaven and hell as vividly conscious future states, and this present life as transitory preparation for eternity, during which God conforms believers to the image of Christ by forming Christ in us (Gal. 4:19). Union with God—spirit to Spirit—becomes preeminent: "he that is joined to the Lord is one spirit" (1 Cor. 6:17).

The rest of a man follows suit like dominoes. All of a man is joined to the Lord. Soul is still immaterial—connected with earthward things like emotions and thoughts (the kind of feelings and logic based on body chemistry). But now there is a clear seat in man, *spirit*, joined to the Holy Spirit for living life. The reflexive needs of soul and body become slaves of righteousness. Christ manifested through the whole man is what pleases God, manifesting His self-for-others nature to the world.

The Truth about Power

The great enemy of faith is trying. Trying supposes that we can make a thing happen or prevent it. We think we have control, but we do not. This is because God created Adam and Eve powerless even *before* the Fall. He means to be the power in our powerlessness—so that the two work as one. Why would we need our own power?

However, the serpent deceived Eve into thinking that she could have her own power. Then Adam, seeing her dark countenance and sensing the presence of evil, still chose Eve over God, deliberately sinning, whereas, Eve fell through deception. They were now powerless over sin, meaning Satan. They were powerless to keep Satan out of themselves, for God created them to be vessels, not self-operators. Since nature abhors a vacuum, Adam and Eve could not remain empty when the Spirit left them.

Satan entered them and hid, his goal being to make us think that we are independent selves rather than dependent selves. The most hideous shock in the world comes when God reveals to us that we have not been free persons but slaves of sin—powerless over the spirit of error at work in us as unbelievers. Even as Christians we are powerless over the spirit of error in our external members if we yield our members to unrighteousness. Not walking in the Spirit opens the door to anything.

We are always powerless: this is not a product of the Fall, but rather our eternal condition as creatures. Even in eternity, Christians will be powerless, for powerlessness is not about sin or addiction, but about our created state as vessels to express the life of God—His power manifesting in our weakness. God means this. It is therefore a mistake to see weakness as sin. The problem is never weakness, but refusing to walk in the Spirit.

You Don't Have to Remain a Sinner to Be Humble

Everybody excepting Jesus is born a sinner and needs a savior. The Bible is plain on that. The death, burial, and resurrection of Jesus solve the dilemma. Now what? Are you one of those Christians who thinks that sinning is the key to humility? Those who answer yes fear that to give up sin would make them perfect and therefore arrogant, thus making sin to be the key to humility. That is a strange idea since the Bible commands us to be holy.

Jesus was humble and perfect, so it should not require sin for any human being to be humble. The biblical picture of a Christian is that sin is forgiven, and the abiding Christian overcomes sin by walking in the keeping of God's Spirit. The Christian life is Christ living it, and He does so by His Spirit for anyone who will take it.

To deny this means saying that the blood of Christ does not really cleanse completely, and that the Spirit of the Lord does not provide all of the holiness that God requires. The focus, therefore, is not on what we do, but on what God has done. Then we pop back into the picture.

Now let's posit the washed, clean, abiding Christian. Either that is possible or it is not. The Bible declares that it is, and so all that remains is for faith to agree. To say that the Bible is true but hedge on what it offers is double-minded and unstable, keeping an excuse for sin.

How then is it that you are humble? One might argue, "I needed to be forgiven of sin, so that is why I will forever be humble." There is more to it than that. God created us as vessels to contain Him and branches to express the vine. The issue is source. God is the source, and humans the expressers. There is humility in just being an expresser. Let's not forget too that God's nature is humility. There is an eternal Cross in His heart, now abiding also in ours.

Contentment

The mind of Christ is joined to my spirit in a union in which the Lord does the keeping, all the while that He means for the world to have its fallen impact against us, including the assaults of the devil. But as spirit people, we no longer live by the dictates of flesh that is destined for the grave; we live according to the Spirit that quickens our mortal bodies and supplies our minds with every remedy for the suffering we endure.

The unspeakable good news is that we are relieved from the sin consciousness that formerly dominated when we clung to the flesh as our reality; and far from spurning our vile bodies, as Paul calls them, we count them vile only because they are mortal—of corruptible material and not the substance of the new body in the wings, that will join up later with our spirits, now already resurrected.

Yet our bodies are washed with pure water (Heb. 10:22)—our bodies are now the wonderful seat of right appetite and potential to express the life of God, for we are not angels but humans, though not in the form that God created us when Adam had a glorious body greatly different from the body after the Fall.

Having given ourselves to Christ, we have already made that eternal decision about who gets to live in us and express the fruit of the Spirit in the whole man: spirit, soul, and body. Yes, even in our bodies in a world of temptation and pulled by various appetites, we belong to Jesus Christ and are His sanctified branches. Our branches were never evil of themselves, merely attached to the wrong vine.

The Holy Spirit makes us content in our hearts, enabling us then to know the joy of the Lord, living as good stewards of the mortal body and of whatever possessions God gives to us, so that in both of these—the body and our possessions—we glorify God in much or little, showing forth contentment.

January 23

The Facts of Faith

Faith sounds ethereal, but it is actually practical. First, something must be available. Our faith is worthless if Jesus did not rise from the dead. We might as well eat and drink, for tomorrow we die (1 Cor. 15). Yet a historical Jesus cannot save a person if Jesus remains only historical and not received. The Gospel is union with Christ. Christ died to sin, Paul tells us in Romans 6, and our union with Him started in being crucified with Christ, expelling the enemy from our bodies since a spirit must have a body in order to manifest. Satan is out of us and Christ is in us. Therefore, the devil is no longer our master, and we are dead to sin. This must be *desired* and *taken* in order to be experienced. The truth is that to be a Christian means to be dead to sin. Take that; it's true. Nothing ever takes us unless we take it.

But those who think that the world was saved at the Cross apart from individuals receiving the good news, err, because they dispense with the clear Bible word about taking, as if people just automatically are a thing that they do not even choose to be. This would make everyone a Christian, for does not Paul say in 2 Corinthians 5 that in Adam all die and that God reconciled Himself to the world by Christ?

Yet to remain on this level, not acknowledging what else Paul says, makes everyone already a Christian whether one chooses to be or not; and does not Paul equally say, "Be ye reconciled"? If this is not true, one need not take Christ; He is already taken without the taking, which is to say that I am operating from the energy of food that I have not eaten, as if bread may sit on the plate rejected, and yet supply me needed energy. We can never get away from taking, for God made us to take, and that is how we are taken by Him. Then you are one with all that He is.

January 24

Elihu Is the Bridge to the Cross with Job

Elihu was the prelude to God coming in the whirlwind to Job. He is God's special agent to clarify the lie of independent-self tempting Job. Therefore, Elihu says, "your righteousness is for a son of man" (35:8)—conveying the subtle undertones that Satan's worst attack has been underway against Job without Job's awareness. Job is tempted to think that the self can produce its *own* righteousness, which is the trap that could get to Job more than all he had been through so far.

Elihu also addresses Job's disturbance over the prosperity of the wicked, telling Job that he must "wait" even though God has not brought judgment to the wicked (35:14). It is dangerous to flirt with ideas about how we would do things as opposed to how God *is* doing things. How little we know and how much God knows. God knows everything about matters of repentance or judgment and is not hurried to explain details.

What God *does* tell us through Elihu is that "One who is perfect in knowledge is with you" —the ancient version of "Christ in you." Elihu adds, "God is mighty but does not despise any." This is merciful news—that God desires repentance so that people would see their "transgression" and how they in pride have "magnified themselves" (36:4-9).

Elihu says that God opens the ears of those wishing to listen. This is good reason to not judge the wicked ourselves and instead to wish better for them. Thus, Job has a decision to make. Elihu says that Job is being pulled toward judging the wicked by seeing them from a place of his own anger, starting to shrink back from "the greatness of the ransom" (36:18). God's view is always through the Cross, so of course we will experience the Cross to stay with God's view. The wait to see the fruit in others seems interminable and too painful, but how rewarding it is when patience has her perfect work in us (James 1), and the harvest grown in faith finally manifests.

January 25

Man Has Always Been a Temple

Before Christ ascended, God's glory inhabited the room behind the curtain in the tabernacle (and later the temple)— entered only once a year by the high priest to take the annual atonement blood behind the curtain to put it on the Ark. But under the New Covenant, the perfect propitiation was made by Christ, never to be repeated, superseding the Old Covenant and bringing about the reformation that makes Christians temples of God.

Imagine walking around containing and expressing God. That is what a temple does. This means more than asking Jesus into your heart and thinking of Him as a small Christ in a big, independent self. The idea that most Christians have of Jesus in them is anemic—not the biblical idea of union, where man is joined to God spirit-to-Spirit as one, and where man is a vessel, temple, and branch.

The idea of union is connection of the closest kind where two are as one while enjoying face-to-face fellowship. This is a mystery only the Trinity can supply the key to. Man was created to be the temple of God and has always been a temple, but was stolen by the evil one who entered the temple when Adam fell and promptly hid, leaving man to think of himself as independent. However, independence is a lie, and that is why on the Cross, God unzipped Jesus and put us into the body of Christ on the Cross to be crucified with Christ, thus cutting us off from the evil one.

We died with Christ and rose with Him as new creations—living, human temples. This is why the new birth is more radical than most know. God "delivered us out of the power of darkness, and translated us into the kingdom of the Son of His love" as Paul says in Colossians 1:13. The devil stole us in Adam's fall, but God redeemed us back in Christ as His sons. Like Father, like son, and no wonder, for the Son manifests as us.

The Truth about Being Lost

Who we are is a deep subject and the unfolding of it no small matter to talk about, but there has to be a simple approach that gets the discussion in focus. The foundation of knowing what a human is comes from the biblical assertion that we are containers possessing freedom to choose our indweller. The function of choice is independent because freedom has to be that way. *Doing*, however, is not that way. No one does anything except by the one living inside, which is to say that nobody is independent. Again—freedom has the quality of independence, while *action* does not. A person does what his master dictates.

Paul wrote to Timothy, speaking of those who need to "escape from the snare of the devil, after being captured by him to do his will" (2 Tim. 2:26). Paul wrote the Ephesians speaking of our lost estate: "And you were dead in the trespasses and sins in which you once walked, following the course of this world, following the prince of the power of the air, the spirit that is now at work in the sons of disobedience— among whom we all once lived in the passions of our flesh" (2:1-2). John even says, "it is evident who are the children of God, and who are the children of the devil" (1 John 3:10).

This is all strong language indeed. What it means is this: not only did I commit sins as a sinner, I was under the control and indwelling of the sin spirit. It is no wonder that being lost is such a dire state and that it takes such transformation to see the condition from which God rescued us. No one takes easily to this truth because it is humbling to see that we were vessels of the devil before we were vessels of Christ. That hits hard. It sounds nice that Christ lives in us as Christians, but not so nice that Satan lived in us and controlled us prior to salvation. But if we are vessels when we are saved, we were vessels when we were lost— always vessels.

The "Not I" Revelation

The truth of who we were before Christ came to live in us was hard to see but finally necessary if we are ever to truly get the blame off of the human self as if the problem is being human. This is why Paul is so clear in Romans Chapter 7: "So now it is no longer I who do it, but sin that dwells within me." This takes the blame off the human self, not off the human choice to believe the lie of independence, but off the human self. The self is not defective or evil; it is not shameful or despicable. Rather, it is a wonderful and beautiful thing to be a human self. The problem never was the self, but the choice to believe the lie inherited in Adam, coming from the liar who captured Adam, and thus us.

This is why Christ had to shed His blood and also take us into His body to be crucified with Him, so that in His death, we would be cut off from the evil one and joined spirit-to-Spirit in union with Jesus Christ, having died with Christ and risen with Him as new creations, never again to be indwelled by the spirit of error as our master. Sin may deceive a Christian, but sin may never again own a Christian.

Therefore, sanctification is completed. Our transformation on a consciousness level corresponds to seeing the totality of what God did in Christ. Can a Christian sin? Yes, but it is not necessary. If a Christian sins, it is not who the person is any more but a diversion from one's identity in Christ and ownership by Him.

This is why we are to focus on identity and not on particular works. If you focus on your identity and the One who is keeping you, God will settle you in your faith. Sins will drop away, soul and spirit will become clear, and temptation and the enemy will have been exposed. Even more, walking in the Spirit will become your norm.

January 28

Sit Here and Rest

No matter how ornate a chair is, it becomes an ordinary thing. Once we've sat down, our thoughts go elsewhere. The chair largely becomes an under layer of consciousness. On a basic supporting level, the chair is the strong member since it holds us, whereas, the one sitting is the weak member.

Faith operates like this. God created us to be the weak member. To operate strength, we must take strength by faith, and strength is a person. It is God Himself. To think of strength as an attribute reflects how incredibly thing-oriented the Fall of Adam made us and how unconsciously we lived in the lie of attributes that we can acquire by practice.

But God is the one person in the universe, and we are persons in a created and derivative sense. To see this is to rejoice in human weakness and revel in God's strength "made perfect in weakness": "When I am weak, then I am strong" (2 Cor. 12:9, 10). Strength becomes like a chair. We sit down in God and rest, mostly forgetting God as we go about living, while He sinks to the under layer of our consciousness. That makes us the outward expression of His power in what we do throughout a day.

Does that mean that we do not commune with God or bring up specific matters to Him? How silly; of course we do. Yet in the main, life is lived in a regular way—supernaturally normal. Since God is the eternal self-for-others, life is a stream of the same as us. Others may even think we are just the way we are—not knowing it is Christ as us. They want to sit on us because they feel safe using us for chairs.

Those who don't know how to rest seek you to rest on, not knowing that they are resting on the One in you. This opens the door for them to see Christ in themselves and learn to rest. It can be very common and certainly not glamorous to be a chair for others, but how lovely it is.

January 29

Sexuality

God is sexually complete within Himself, or else sexuality is only a created thing. Theologians correctly state that God is complete within Himself though they do not much explore God's intrinsic sexual completeness. We may not understand this, but plainly it is true, or mankind has blackmail potential toward a needy deity. Jesus said that in the resurrection we will not be married in the earthly sense but be like the angels. It sounds gender neutral but isn't, for male and female will not be separated as in the Fall, but like flowers, and glorified. In the resurrection, to be human is to be a complete sexual person who does not live in unfulfilled longing. There is the eternal sense of coupling within of the male and female essences of the Godhead—the kind of eternal and sexual union that breathes of ecstasy, purity, and union.

Why else does the Bible say that husband and wife become one flesh? The view is union—two made one. Paul thus appeals to the Corinthians to see their oneness with God through Christ: "But the one who joins himself to the Lord is one spirit with Him" (1 Cor. 6:17). We are so accustomed to the wrong use of sex that the right is startling to get used to. The truth about sex is that it is the fountain and energy of the Godhead; it is self-for-others, spirit level, and the glory of union with Christ and His Shekinah. To know this is to be able to abstain from self-sex, pornography, obsessive fantasies, fornication, and adultery. The sexuality of the Godhead swallows up the dark side, and the flower child emerges as the complete, whole human, lacking nothing as James says (1:4). A man can marry or not marry in this life with such completion. No wonder "The Song of Solomon" is the greatest poem ever written—a poem that is erotic to the ultimate, yet it is holy and never defrauds or entices to lust. It takes back everything stolen in the Fall and celebrates the resurrected version.

The Seldom Heard Truth of Romans 5

Everything grows from a root. When Adam sinned, everyone born of Adam sinned. It does not seem fair that a baby born today should be born already having sinned, but this is fact.

Though Eve fell first, sin or righteousness is reckoned to us through our father. Dan Stone always said, "Romans 1-4 talks about sins, *plural*; Romans 5-7 talks about sin, *singular*." Thus, the producer had to be eliminated, or the products would keep growing up from the root.

Romans 5 takes sin beyond our individual acts as Adam's descendants and traces back to the root. When Adam fell, sin entered, and everyone since then dies because of Adam. Paul gives proof. Death was the assigned result for only one specific sin—Adam's disobedience. No other sin by any other person carried that sentence because the law had not been given yet. Between Adam and Moses everyone died for only one reason—Adam's sin, which everyone sinned when he fell.

Sometimes I line ten people up along a wall to illustrate this—the first being Adam and the last being Moses. Adam is the *only one* to violate the particular law carrying the sentence of death to the human race, so he dies. However, between person number one and person number ten, everyone else dies as well because of Adam. Through him, in came sin, death, and condemnation.

God, however, is a "much more" God on the grace side. There is no comparison, since anyone by faith has the freedom now to get birthed into the Last Adam—Jesus Christ. Christ is the replacement Adam. As devastating as our losses were by being born into the first Adam, the benefits are immeasurably more glorious when born into the last Adam, namely Christ. These benefits include righteousness, eternal life, and no condemnation. In Adam, we sinned. In Christ, we are made perfect.

Entrance to Union

In Romans 5:20. Paul announces that God's purpose with the law is "that the offense might abound." Instead of aiding us to doing right, law exposes our inability to keep it. Without the law, we would not know failure. We would not discover that God created us as containers to express His indwelling life with only one obedience—that of faith.

This fact got lost at the Fall when sin entered through Adam. However, something far more sinister than individual acts of sin occurred in the garden. Sin is a spirit not of ourselves. Ephesians says that we "walked according to the course of this world, according to the prince of the power of the air, the spirit that now worketh in the children of disobedience" (2:2). This means that Satan not only tempts us to sin, but worked *in* us to do the sinning before we became Christians. When Adam sinned (and all sinned therefore) the spirit of error entered the human vessel and became the disguised inner operator, projecting his thoughts as ours so that we thought we were just ourselves wanting our own way. We did want our own way, but it was really Satan wanting his own way in us.

Therefore, to die to sin, God must remove the Satanic spirit and replace it with Christ as permanent indweller, making us dead to sin. Christ died not only *for* sin, but *as* sin, so that He could die as the first Adam. This is Romans 6. When Christ died, sin left His body and therefore ours, and the lifeless body went into the grave. But a dead body, though dead to sin, cannot live; so the Spirit raised Him up as us. The "new nature," so often referred to by Christians, is actually Christ Himself.

Satan has been put out and can only gain admittance into the outer man through the deception once again that we can keep the law. Otherwise, we go on with life as spontaneously as we did when Satan lived in us, except that now it is really He living His life, but as we.

The Concept of Master in the Bible

Because of the Fall, we start out thinking that we do our own good or evil. This is the standard view of being human, even for agnostics and atheists. The difference is that agnostics and atheists see the world as random and material, instead of being created by a personal God who holds everyone accountable. The Bible asserts that God created man in order to live in him and express Christ. The definition of being human is containing and expressing the indwelling life of our creator and master. That might even be palatable to the agnostics and atheists except for assertion of God's authority; God and man cannot both be master.

A master creates the possibility of rebellion. Where there is no master, no rebellion can occur. But there is a master, which Paul says in Romans 6: we always serve a master, whether we like it or not. When unsaved, sin was our master; we were instruments of sin. But those who died in Christ were buried in the baptism of His death and rose as the newly created man serving a new master. This master died for us so that we could live again—this master Himself being the tree of life, God Himself. The pivotal concepts are two: God created us in order to express Himself as us, while at the same time in a relationship with us.

If you know that you are dead to sin, and that you are an instrument of righteousness, that all the power you need to resist sin is in you as the new man, then you laugh at the devil, who would have you still believe that the old man did not die when Christ died. But the old man did die in Christ, making you now a slave to your new master, as Romans 6 describes; so it is supernaturally natural to see our bodily members as His instruments. No one can really live according to the nature of God unless it is God expressing His own nature as the person—spirit, soul, and body (1 Thess. 5:23). That is the fullness of being born again.

Getting Clear on the Self

We died to sin. Failure to recognize that keeps sin needlessly operational (Rom. 6). Consider this: Christians do not have two natures. Yes, there are two natures, but neither of them is the human self. To think that sin is the human self keeps self-hatred alive (Rom. 7:17). If one has an old nature, there is ample reason to give sway to that nature when temptation feels overwhelming, even providing an excuse to sin. However, neither is righteousness the human self. Our mission is not to swing the scales over to a better self or a self that improves with God's help.

He who knows that he is dead to sin is not fooled by temptation and does not take condemnation for it. He says, "I died with Christ and am the new man, with but one master. Jesus cut me off from Satan (who is the old nature) when I died in Him." He is the new indwelling master and the new nature. Sin was never the human self but an invader; and righteousness is never the human self, but is Christ Himself—by us.

Apply this to the common theme of addiction or self-righteous pride, and why Christians can still experience these. It is from not *knowing* that we are dead to sin. No sin has any right or necessity to manifest in the new man. The Holy Spirit is the keeper from sin and the Spirit that produces fruit. Yet addictions in those who do not know how to walk in the Spirit can actually serve as friends. Addictions violently tear off the mask of a dignified self, supposedly able to control itself, which is the real sin behind all other sins. Paul lists "self-control" among the fruit of the Spirit in Galatians 5:23, meaning that only one person in the universe possesses self-control—God.

Think of that: only God can control Himself. Everyone else fakes it, living a lie that might not show itself for a while but eventually will, for no one can live according to the nature of God unless it is God expressing His own nature—by you.

From Old to New

Christians often refer to the "old man" or "old nature" as if referring to themselves. It is a strange combination, however, to be a new creation with an old nature. The nature of something would logically seem to be one thing and not two. Nature gets down to what a thing is, or in this case who a person is. Once you are joined to the Lord as one spirit, it makes sense that the new man is who you are. Otherwise, the result is a messy, complicated view of the Christian as both old and new on the identity level, which gets translated to really mean an unreliable car with some great new parts but still an unreliable car!

Usually, when Christians talk about an old nature, they mean the flesh, with negative emphasis on the body. Although sin must have a body to operate through, it does not follow that the body is sinful. Paul tells us that the body is dead because of sin (Rom. 8:10), but he also goes on to say that the Spirit gives life to our mortal bodies, meaning that we are not at the mercy of sin's pulls upon the outer man.

Yes, mortality remains, meaning that we walk by faith, not by sight. However, residing in perishable bodies, while being new creations on the inside, does not imply that the body is without special purpose. God's command in Romans Chapter 6 is to present our bodies as instruments of righteousness. Without the body, we could not connect with unbelievers in empathy like Jesus connected with us when He was made flesh. The world needs to see victory lived out in quickened, mortal bodies buffeted by the ailments of this temporal life and the pulls of the devil—even victory over the lie that we are still the old man or helpless subjects to sin.

Ours is not a life of, "touch not; taste not; handle not" and forging "doctrines of men" (Col. 2:21, 22). Washed with pure water (Hebrews 10:22), our bodies are sanctified as well because Christ's blood and body did a complete work.

The Law Is Holy and Good

Those were great days when we lived vibrantly alive before the law entered. Coming and going as we pleased, we thought little except about our next plan to enjoy life. Paul knew days like that—days when life moved along almost effortlessly with anticipation of more good to come. Then one day, Paul discovers God's law, and he realizes that he repeatedly transgresses that law. Denial springs up as he struggles to hold on to his former life, but confronted with God's law, he has to admit sin and the need to change.

Maybe with some adjustments, much can remain the same, plus compensatory good behavior can make up for failures. So thinks Paul in his first wriggling, and so think we in ours. Certainly some winking at the law or a milder interpretation of it will allow room to move more easily and escape conviction that we are caught in sin.

The more we try to keep the law, the more we do the very things the law speaks against. Perhaps the law is sin since it serves as the occasion for constant sinning. But in a moment of honesty, Paul acknowledges that the law is not sin (Rom. 7:7), but holy and good (Rom. 7:12). The culprit is not the law, but sin. Sin somehow uses the law to cause sin.

At first this sounds contradictory. How can sin use God's holy law in someone wanting to keep the law? Paul at first doesn't know the answer. He only knows that he would not know the power of sin apart from the law that corners him. Furthermore, the power of sin rages so greatly that he says, "For sin, taking occasion by the commandment, deceived me, and by it slew me" (Rom. 7:11).

No longer can he affirm himself as a good man going wrong in disobeying some of God's laws. He sees himself as utterly self-seeking and dies to all hope of holding himself up as good. Optimism flees, hope for self-improvement dies, and hope for escape by any human means disappears. What will he do?

Paul's Romans 7

Sin deceived Paul by making him think he could keep the law and improve himself. He did not start out knowing this; only by revelation did he see it when he could not find any other way through. Before that, Paul thought sin was part of his "I" and that keeping the law would get sin out of him. Dying to that deception meant becoming convinced of his utter captivity to sin. He was "held" (Rom. 7:6), "slain" (Rom. 7:11), and "exceedingly sinful" (Rom. 7:13). In desperate honesty, he admitted, "For we know that the law is spiritual: but I am carnal, sold under sin" (Rom. 7:14).

Then Paul sees, "it is no more I that do it, but sin that dwelleth in me" (Rom. 7:17, 20). He does not yet solve the mystery, but he does, through a process of elimination, conclude that the problem is neither the law, nor his "I." Sin is the culprit. The inference is that Satan is Mr. Sin, though Paul does not come right out and say it here. Yet he still could not escape even though the lie stood exposed. As a vessel trapped by indwelling sin, he needed a new master since a vessel has no nature of its own but expresses the nature of its indwelling master. In Christ we died to the law and Satan's deception of independence, for sin's power comes from using the law to deceive us into the lie of independence.

Paul cried out, "Who shall deliver me from the body of this death?" (Rom. 7:25). He turns the powerlessness of his vessel into an asset: just as sin came from another—Satan—so deliverance comes from another—Christ, the one who is life itself and upon whom we set our minds. "The mind set on the Spirit is life and peace" (Rom. 8:6). The battle against sin is over on our part except to be Spirit minded. In the Spirit, all takes care of itself. Temptations to specific sins are never about the sin itself but about walking in the Spirit that cannot sin. Yes to the Spirit is always the keeping.

It's the Same for Everyone

James says that Elijah was "a man of like nature with ourselves." Miracle powers do not keep anyone from being human. If anything, they make a man suffer when others do not yet know how to live supernaturally in a natural world. At first the suffering is grief over feeling like a minority when God's full provision is so easily available to anyone. The suffering then turns to grief over what others do not see yet, to their own needless pain. Finally, there is the suffering of retaliation from those who cannot stomach grace.

Thankfully, there is detachment from the natural world since we are in it but not of it. It is a strange thing to see where others are, entrenched in the lie of trying to be like what Christ already is in them. While being human like others are—meaning having a soul and body to go along with our spirit—we do not interpret the world by soul and body since we have entered into rest (Hebrews 4). Therefore, we point the way for others on walking by faith in the liberty of the sons of God.

The one pointing the way is living among men as a man whose spirit is in the heavenlies. That is the way it is for now, and so we are touched by what happens to others. This does not mean unhealthy attachments or addictive connection to others whereby we are enslaved to them or they to us; it means simply that we are not untouchable, we are touchable. We relate to living as a saint in a fallen world.

It is also juvenile and satanic to elevate others to a special place, exempting them from the full human experience. That would make them no longer ordinary humans whose faith gets exercised like anyone else's. Faith is the common currency of humanity that transforms anyone into a resting saint, manifesting the fruit of the Spirit (Gal. 5) plus a daily course of miracles crafted by God for each person's situation. Wherever you are is wherever your adequacy and miracles are.

Spirit Life

The world continually analyzes and defines big issues. Only when issues are considered in light of the eternal can there be any meaning. Otherwise, ideals end up limited to the temporal level of "eat and drink, for tomorrow we die" (1 Cor. 15:32). It is strange, even alien, to hear experts debate conflicts that never get related to being made new creations in Christ. The operating thought in the world is independence, even from God, or rather especially from God. Romans 1 identifies this as exchanging the glory of God for the worship of creation. Doing good gets redefined in human terms relative and manageable to what flesh on its own supposedly can attain. The Christian life, however, is defined by the Spirit, who is the operating agent in the life of a Christian. Not to have the Spirit of God means not to belong to Him (Rom. 8). The Christian life cannot be defined in terms of behavioral objectives and imitation carried out on a mere human level. Such is the essence of religion, which always leads to frustration and failure—the works of the flesh (Gal. 5).

Failure, however, is the junction where one either leaps into the supernatural, keeping life of the Spirit or else redefines faith in terms of approving what flesh already does that was once condemned, but is now embraced since humanity cannot rise above it. This is where the Cross comes in. Jesus Christ manifested the full expression of the Cross, which is the nature of God, and no one can walk in that love without the indwelling of Christ Himself. The supernatural life cannot be imitated. When the Spirit of God, however, lives in us, love must eventually come forth because a branch must be traced back to its origin in the vine. It may take a while for the carnal mind to wear out, but finally, as the Apostle John says, one who is born of God cannot sin. Will you take that now or wait until heaven? All the fruits are in the Spirit now (Gal. 5).

How Do We Know Who We Are?

How do we know who we are? It takes a miracle. Methods fail, and they are supposed to—because they are natural, and the natural or carnal man can only do what flesh does. Faith, though, is not a method; it is the God created capacity in us of receiving. A branch receives, a cup receives. That is the offense, namely that life is only in God and must be received only from Him.

When we were of the world, we sought to receive from other humans. That is the world, with its mixed up, devilish craving for acceptance by others (Eph. 2). Receiving by faith, however, means starting from emptiness, which looks frightening until the self runs dry of energy to sustain itself. Then grace appears sweet.

Having nothing left with which to try, means that only a miracle will satisfy and bring the sought relief—the relief of being kept. The thought of going back to old ways to keep one's self is dark and exhausting. Now, God must do the job or else. This is God's trick—the leap of faith that says, "I don't know what's ahead, but I know what I can't go back to." It's a leap even before the witness of the Spirit comes. God knows the timing on that to ensure that faith gets tested.

The day comes when a supernatural mirror appears (it has been there all along) and one simply looks away from the self to the Lord. There is ease in this, where one is made supernaturally natural. One sees the true self—the new man, and it is nothing like the image that the self formerly constructed. This image is too good to be true and originates in the one who births us by resurrection and not by anything else.

Paul calls this the mind that is set on the Spirit, for the mirror of identity is in the Spirit. Self-talk failed. However, when looking away from the self, the new man appears in the mirror—a self that does not take work to maintain because it runs on God-sustained faith.

Count It All Joy

James says, "count it all joy, my brethren, when you meet various trials." Notice the appeal to the will, rather than to emotion or reason. The will abides where the believer's spirit is joined to the Spirit of God—the place where peace transcends every situation. Here, the will is detached enough to see what attracts or repels the soul and body, providing the ability to maintain identity and assess truth apart from all storms. One may not understand what God is doing, but faith knows that He is doing a work that can only be completed by suffering.

It would feel nicer if resolution came quickly, but that does not often happen, calling for perseverance in faith. The Holy Spirit fruit of patience takes over, which is the nature of God. No wonder Peter says that God has made us "partakers of the divine nature" (2 Pet. 1). James does not say, though, that understanding is impossible; it just might take a while. It is at God's discretion. No one can know anything unless God knows it in him, so although reason is part of our humanity, it is but the expresser of truth, not the originator of it.

Waiting sets up trusting for wisdom, and wisdom's first trait is the fear of the Lord, which is not cowering in fear or shrinking back from God. Wisdom means approaching God in reverence and respect to inquire what He is up to. The one who steadfastly trusts for wisdom will win the crown. Time *is not* of the essence, but waiting *is* of the essence—until God gives insight, and give it He will. It is always good exercise to affirm that God is making things known and getting things done in His perfect timing. It is the wisdom of the Cross, which never makes sense to the natural or carnal mind. The doorway to understanding is not saying, "Why does God allow trials?" It is saying, "God, what are you up to? I will stick fast until You show me!"

Every Man Can Wear a Crown

Death is the equalizer. Rich and poor alike leave the same earth behind and go to the same heaven. Every flower fades in a mortal world, so it is good to reflect and not consider one's self too busy to think about the life to come. This is not to indict wealth or extol poverty but to aim at the eternal. Doing so gives grit in trials and temptations. This life is to forge what is real and what will not burn up like wood, hay, and stubble when this life is over.

There is a crown of life for those who do. Crowns are for those who rule, and by the Spirit of God we learn to reign now while things are difficult, so that we will always know in eternity that we faced the worst and stood by faith in God's keeping.

This does not mean that God is the tempter. He means us to be tempted, and to respond in faith, but His nature has no evil in it and can only generate good and what draws us to good. God does not tempt anyone, but neither does He protect us from being tempted. Norman Grubb used to say, "We're in Satan's camp; he has a right to shoot at us." This sounds scary, and reason wants to say that God, as a loving parent, should protect His children like an earthly parent would keep little children from harm. This is true except that God's ways are higher than ours, and God knows that only by overcoming the evil one will we mature from children to young men to fathers, as John declares (1 Jn. 2).

Therefore, God placed Adam in a garden that was paradise, yet temporarily roamed by God's enemy. Man, as the new regent, had to face the enemy. He failed as we know, but God's plan stood fast: the last Adam, Jesus Christ, would defeat the enemy—and by living in us cause us to do the same. "He who is in you is greater than he who is in the world" (1 Jn. 4:4).

Transcending the Appearance of Finality

What Christian has not looked and felt a fool when taking a stand to see life come out of death? When Jesus looks at you and tells you He can do something, He means it, and His invitation is the faith of your faith to watch the miracle unfold. Jairus, a synagogue ruler accustomed to preferential treatment, learned this. When his twelve-year-old daughter hovered at the point of death, he humbled himself to come to Jesus (Luke 8). He took the risk. It is the same risk today. A wrenching need in someone close can be what brings any person to Jesus.

In the story, a woman with an issue of blood came behind Jesus and touched His garment. After Jesus took the time to engage her, a messenger arrived saying that Jairus' daughter had died. Would Jairus resent the intruding woman, or Jesus stopping for her? This would be the deeper need—not to judge God and the bleeding woman. Jesus had not passed her by or become time-conscious. Jairus was tempted to accept defeat and give in, but he found a quickening spark of faith. This is always the way when appearances show the darkest side of things.

Jesus prompted him: "Do not fear; only believe, and she shall be well" (8:50). The beauty of the story is that it transcends the appearance of finality. Death is not the final say with Jesus, giving hope to anyone when appearances say, "It's over." Do not take the scorn, depression, and self-examination of what ifs. Find the word spoken by Jesus to you about your situation, no matter how great the tension. You may not see how Jesus is right, but you will have the right person on your side.

From Lust to Love without Sinning

In temptation, a man is "carried away" (James 1:14). This comes from one's own lust, which means strong desire, even "enticement." However, there is no sin yet because lust has not conceived. Therefore, hard as it is to believe, cravings are not sin. Lust is immediately dubbed as sin by many, despite what James says, leading them to mistake temptation for sin, with the result of a sin consciousness.

James sets the context as wealth and power, with not a word about sex. This expands lust beyond hormones alone. Notice that the three temptations of Jesus are not about sex, yet Jesus was tempted in *all* points, Hebrews says, so that includes sex. The overall lesson is that temptation toward self-for-self is present in any situation.

The antidote is that "every perfect gift is from above." By whatever avenue lust entices us, God draws us the opposite way toward love. As alarming as cravings are when we are not used to them, they do not mean that sin has yet conceived. Choice stands ready to interpret and respond from the Spirit. Lust can move to sin, but it can as easily be seen as crucified and the servant of love. The power of any attraction is not the point but how faith uses opposites to manifest glory. Because life is built on opposites, expect strong negatives to be awakening moments.

Do not panic and think that the enticement has captured you already or that you inevitably will give in. If you are perfectly kept, you can hold out forever and even learn to laugh at the enticement.

Since temptation is a form of suffering, the process is unpleasant. The Cross leads to the expression of Spirit life now where sin formerly ruled, as you, the spirit person, stand apart from your temptations and know your real self. My friend Bill Bower says, "I *am* a spirit, I *have* a soul, and I live *in* a body." That's it! Stand apart from cravings now and respond from the standpoint of who you are. The new man has fresh life every moment.

Throw off That Dirty Garment

God "brought us forth by the word of truth" (James 1:18). How beautifully procreative this is. Not by imitation, but by birth, does God bring forth His desired family of sons. Creation of the new man takes place by "the word implanted" (1:21), which is not a code implanted, or set of rules, but a Person. This is the life of the still, small voice's constant broadcast to the inner man—easily heard unless one lets the devil keep anger and commotion stirred up, leading to unnecessary talk and busyness as escapes. The world thinks solutions come from more analysis. Just when the Holy Spirit puts His finger on a point, the pull comes toward another distraction.

However, we wait on God while dying to initial impulses, knowing that Christ at our center is not tit-for-tat, proving our rightness in everything. When we know His rightness, impulses to self-defense are allowed to go unexpressed. Much more gets overlooked that formerly provoked wrathful responses. This might sound like an excuse to let others get away with things, but it is really the call to peace by Christ our keeper. Despite the barrage of impulses, anger does not go anywhere destructive but is left in the unexpressed zone that feels bad but is not sin.

When James says "the anger of man," he means the lie of independent self—anger that seems right to express but would be provoked by hell. If this anger is unleashed without the restraining check of the Spirit, the result is every work of the flesh, which James calls "filthiness" (1:21). This filthiness is worn as a false garment when not knowing that a Christian is not filthy at the core but only wearing filthy garments while still in unbelief. By tapping into the life of Christ, to whom every believer is grafted, one can throw off that filthy garment any time and walk in the Spirit since filthy garments are not any Christian's identity. Recognition of that living union brings forth life.

Mirror Mirror on the Wall

No one can see who he is by looking directly at himself. Everyone needs a mirror, which mirror is the Spirit of God, a mirror that can only reflect liberty. Knowing this, you marvel. Conviction of sin turns out to be grief over the blindness and bondage once considered freedom, but which now are recognized as satanic darkness and lies.

The new birth is by the word "implanted" (James 1:21), meaning union with Christ. This is what the mirror shows, namely the new man who operates supernaturally. This man did not create himself, nor does he maintain or keep himself. All comes from God. The implanted word (Christ by His Spirit)) quickens the inner man and easily leads to fruitful doing, even when contrary thoughts and feelings protest. Pain on a soul/body level does not mean that hearing does not move easily into doing, for life becomes spontaneous.

However, if hearing (which is really the same as receiving) does not move into doing, forgetfulness ensues, and a man forgets who he is, drifting into the noise of the outer world (Heb. 2:1). Yet he is who he is if he has been brought forth by God. Only the mirror can project the image of the new man, who harmonizes hearing and doing. In the new man, all comes from being, and faith knows that the mirror is the mind of God given to tell us what we can know in no other way.

Now we see the miracle man, the new creation. Why do more people not look into this mirror? It is costly and the end of flesh level living, but it is the satisfying way, and the way of contentment. Others will notice the change in what we say and do. There will be harmony of word and deed. When the severity of outer pressures comes, which it surely will, the man of the new birth does not swap the mirror of the Spirit for the images cast at him from privation, abundance, opposition, or flattery. None of this tells him who he is or what to do. He remembers the mirror.

The Royal Law of Liberty

Because of the Fall, we were born showing partiality. We couldn't help it since we were slaves to sin, and so everything was about self-for-self. Power and riches ruled the day, and the needy stayed needy, even getting needier as those of the world exploited them. In the modern Western world, we are used to democracy and the rights of man, but where democracy is not an extension of the Spirit, it eventually becomes the selfish tool of a world destined to yet another satanic use of an idealistic theory.

In the world of James' day, there were no food stamps, welfare, employment programs, social insurance, and other helps to those in distress. If no one in the church helped an orphan or a widow, those without means remained helpless since most women were not wage earners. Things look better today, but misuse of power and a spiritually destitute public could eventually topple the progress of social reform and end what started well.

James says that the rich dragged people into court and exploited them. Today we see the opposite—huge settlements favoring the victim. The poor have more voice, but without Christ, social justice will eventually fail because its roots are merely political. Man seeks freedom, but freedom is only in Christ, despite idealistic political theories.

James does not call money and influence sin, but if the path to them is not self-for-others, what good are they? The result will be more politics and rule-oriented religion without Christ. Then the prophets will have to cry out again for salvation in the blood and body of Christ alone.

True faith does not fall prey to becoming a religion of rules, morals, and ethics. Religion, as James puts it, cannot keep God's law, so it invents flesh-friendly forms needing no miracle to observe. Therefore, James brings up the royal law of liberty, where every person is a vessel, and all good comes from Christ in you.

February 16

No More Comparison with Others

The equalizer among people is that everyone has broken the law. Aspiring to live by the law means that one must keep it all of the time. Since no one has, God's love rescued us in Christ, not leaving us in the darkness of self-for-self misery that feeds on measuring one's self and then comparing the results with others. Each Christian is complete in Christ (Col.2:10), and all the complete parts make up the same body, with Christ as head. The picture then is of one person—Christ.

Since Christ's body is many members, no member is tasked with more than the particular commission that God assigns. No one carries everyone's burdens. Such worry can lead to obsession and paralysis, even going back to law. Jesus walked about in life meeting the needs of the people He encountered—the person in front of Him. It is one obvious person standing there that the Spirit wants to help, and in that moment, faith operates.

James is strong on this and scorns religion that makes rules, compares people, and acts preferentially. Christ is not preferential, so His body by definition is not preferential. However, religion sets up rules about who is not doing enough. Then the atmosphere turns to guilt and more resolutions. The tipoff on religion is the increase in trying, with less and less to show for it because love's spark and spontaneity are quenched, as the joy of Christ helping others gets replaced with comparison.

No wonder James brings up Abraham. Abraham was an ordinary man who became extraordinary by hearing God's voice and pressing through to do the next thing that God required, no matter what it was. That was the proof of his faith. To have faith means quickening results from that faith. The witness of the Spirit comes up under faith with confirmation not requiring comparison with others but enjoying fellowship with others.

Teachers

James advocates thinning out the ranks of teaching aspirants. This sounds a bit chilly and selective, but he says that we all "stumble" or "offend" (3:2). He illustrates with horses: who wants to ride a horse that always stumbles? Teaching sounds lofty, but it means being like a faithful horse. It's not so much about being admired as it is helping others. James then mentions a ship's rudder, which is small but guides direction.

Error with the tongue leads to misdirection—back towards the hell from which we have been delivered. Yet no one can control the tongue, so what hope is there? To be a Christian is to have been brought forth by the will of God and the word of God (1:18). This word is "implanted" (1:21). The idea that James expresses is the same as "Christ in you" as Paul puts it, or Peter saying that we have been made "partakers of the divine nature" (2 Pet. 1:4). John calls it having the "anointing" (1 Jn. 2:20). The apostles all declare that no one can say and do rightly on his own but can only live the Christian life by the Spirit. All flows from the Spirit; we just make ourselves the horse and ship of the Spirit so that we can point the way for others.

Teaching also means settling into the fact that trials are normal, along with recognition not to throw matches on hay in the midst of daily irritations. Constant friendship with the Cross counts trials as joy and avoids reckless provocations. Leadership gets developed by learning to divide spirit truth from constant pulls to falsely engage on a lesser level, which then only stirs turmoil until a calm hand takes the bridle or rudder. Then we have the often uneventful journey, but it is reliable and turns out to be a hidden world of rich fulfillment. The world thrives on unnecessary drama, whereas believers find rest in letting unnecessary conflict go.

February 18

Taming the Tongue

James addresses Christians with tongues "set on fire by hell"—full of "deadly poison" (3:6-8). On the surface, the tongue appears to express of itself both good and evil, but this is false. Nothing can ever be reliable that seeks to be its own good and evil. Such thinking comes from the tree by which Adam fell and is the obsessive mind arguing about good and evil instead of drawing from God's life. Therefore, it is always arguing and never enjoys the rest that comes from simply looking to God for His discernment of good and evil. Rest comes from dependency on the Spirit, not efforts at knowledge derived by wanting to be one's own discernment.

God knows good and evil: He knows that He *is* the good, for He *is* love—the only source of love. This love is self-for-others; what passes for love in the world is self-attachment and evil. To live out of union with Christ means life flowing from the Spirit—not trying to originate one's own good or evil, which is impossible and is Satan's lie. This lie leads to lack of discernment, which then leads to double-mindedness, followed by instability. Confusion and bitterness mix with the sweet water of who we are (James 3:11). The mix does not work, for we are to manifest only one thing and are at center only one thing. The answer is in the fountain's source. God says, "Do not add anything of you to what is only of Me." Satan did that, and he still is the same deceiver who tries to turn teacups into tea.

Everyone lives from an operator, which is why James talks about two opposite wisdoms—one from below and one from above. Everyone always expresses one or the other. Since our identity is the sweet water, there is no point to letting bitter water in, which is "earthly, sensual, and devilish" (3:15). It is from hell. The wisdom from above is lovely and defenseless looking, yet healing and easy to walk in. Hold to your identity, and the tongue will follow.

Ending Quarrels

"What is the source of quarrels and conflicts among you?" James asks. The lost world must live with these as a given, but not believers. The lost have neither Christ living in them nor the Spirit's fruit. What can the world do then but war? However, for Christians to war in the same way implies head knowledge, not faith—living like "mere men" where the lie of needy-self dominates. Discernment is lacking between flesh and Spirit (1 Cor. 3:3). No matter what is obtained on an outer level, obsession rules, not contentment. Asking God to meet needs and accepting what He provides has not taken root, so covetousness dominates, leading to quarrels, which James calls "friendship with the world," making one an "enemy of God."

This is severe talk to Christians, but even with such warnings, God does not make Himself an enemy to His fleshly children but yearns for them to know who they are (James 4:5). He longs for His carnal children to weary of their fleshly ways so that union with His Spirit may flourish and bear the beautiful fruit of wisdom, which is "pure, then peaceable, gentle, open to reason, full of mercy and good fruits" (James 3:17). God wishes for His own nature to be satisfying and need-fulfilling for those who belong to Him. To prompt His carnal children, "He gives more grace" (James 4:6).

God never goes back under law in order to correct His erring children: He can only offer more grace because that is all that He is by His chosen nature. Therefore, when James says "submit" and "draw near to God" (4:7-8) he does not mean a list of "do good" resolutions. The devil opposes grace as the means of correction, but he is a legalistic coward who runs off in rage when a seeker trades form for reality. Then quarrels are stopped by one party not quarreling but responding from Christ's very own mind. This takes the Cross and is hard, but the resurrection experience is worth it.

What Does It Mean to Be Human?

Wolves masquerading as sheep will either say that the answer is to get past being human or to accept the fact of being merely human. Neither works or is the truth. John himself heard, saw, and touched "the word of life" (1 Jn.) and wrote in his Gospel: "the Word became flesh and dwelt among us." He does not explain how it happened; he says that it happened, and he was there when it did.

This is not a boast, as if one needs to have walked with the human Jesus. John writes as a historical witness and reporter to warn against those advocating that Christ was not fully human, an error asserting that to be human implies a mix of good and evil. Humans cannot be saved if to be human means being a mix of good and evil. Salvation would then mean translation out of the realm of being human, implying that God does not save humans but saves them from being human. Spirit would be good, but being human not so.

Since we are human and know it, however, sin cannot be understood unless it is seen as an invader into our humanity, an invader that can be cleansed away. This is the reason for Christ's blood. Otherwise, sin will become accepted as inevitable and justified by saying, "I'm only human." Once sin is accepted, the next thing is a works program to decrease sin while increasing good works. Soon, humans will be in full swing with self-management, redefining good and evil, and not needing a savior.

However, knowing God means walking in the light as "He is in the light" (1 Jn. 1:7). Light is the one we walk in, not something we are, for "God is light" (1 Jn. 1:5). Only Jesus never left the light, so the first order of business is to admit that we did leave the light and needed to be cleansed by Christ's blood and placed, still fully human, into the light so that what formerly was impossible to do, is now done by being in the light and the light in us.

Confession

I noticed in my year at seminary that when a professor invited questions, students often asked about 1 John 1:9. That seemed curious. We asked because no matter how often we confessed sin, the sin consciousness never went away. Relief did not come. Part of that came from confessing what is really temptation, or what are merely thoughts and feelings in the soul/body realm that the undiscerning believer interprets to mean, "This is who I am."

John means intent to sin and sins actually committed. God convicts of sin in the safe keeping of the Holy Spirit, without a condemning sin consciousness. Otherwise, there will be wallowing in the guilt and the torment of, "How could I have done that?" when actually there is no self apart from God's keeping that could have done differently. Apart from the Spirit, any sin might occur.

Confession opens the heart to receive God's forgiveness but does not cause forgiveness. Forgiveness is already in God who is "faithful and just." Faith simply agrees with God's eternal constant in Christ—not based on our groveling. Do not linger as if forgiveness is not true, and do not add penance or even sincerity to what Jesus did. Where the Holy Spirit convicts of sin, see the blood covering it. That is the last word. Clean means clean. Therefore, no matter what accusations and threats come from the devil (often through others still under the law), the point is standing on Christ's finished work, not taking feelings of doubt and uncertainty.

No one need be a prisoner trapped in a relentless chain of guilt and torment based on past sins. Others may think it too easy to get off so mercifully, but those who protest may not have seen how efficacious the Lamb's blood is and how total His keeping now is. Christ, the word made flesh, atoned for our sins so that we may walk in the light, abide, and no longer sin.

Judging

Everyone, Christian or non-Christian, is sensitive to judgment and hates being on the receiving end. Though it might feel stimulating for a while to dish it out, the harshness will eventually extinguish one's spark. James says not to "speak evil against a brother" and yet his letter is severe (4:11). His tone, however, is not against people themselves but their toleration of evil. Clearly, James has a beautiful, clear picture of people made by God for the purpose of His indwelling, so his indictment of sin and unbelief is never to reflect on people themselves but only upon the devil's misuse of the human self through the deception that the human is independent. The devil hides this because he does not want to expose himself where he might be discovered as the problem and not the human self.

While this deception persists, the one judging does so as if people operate by law and not by Christ's Spirit in them. This asks the human to do what only God can do and shifts the focus away from faith, putting the one judging in the position of being God, whereas there is only one God and judge. Judging carried out as if people are independent leads to self-righteousness, with sins that follow, whereas the grace of God in us never wishes anything but healing and restoration for others. Pride and partiality, therefore, fall away, and oneness in the Spirit manifests.

Hurt and anger give way to forbearance and endurance in seeing who that other person is. Fear and suspicion are defeated. When irritated with other Christians, the focus on their blind spots is a dead-end if at the expense of who they are, for love covers a multitude of sins, and when others do not know who they are, there may be a multitude to cover. It is better to be on the covering side than to fall back into judging by law, taking on the devil's accusing spirit. Love wins many battles in which it looks foolish, but the foolishness of the Cross is our defense at all times.

February 23

Temporal and Eternal

We make plans, and then the unexpected often occurs because our lives are not our own, and we are not in control. God created us to plan and do exploits, yet James says, "What is your life? For you are a mist" (4:14). We give our all, knowing that our time on earth is given by grace, and meant for whatever God's commission to us is. Faith takes hold of the invisible and its sure rewards, making the little time available count toward an eternal weight of glory.

James implies that it is not hard to know the right thing to do next because life is a continual scenario of being for others, one person at a time. The single eye makes this simple, and God's will easy to discover. Only the separated viewpoint and veil of *my* anything makes God's will seem remote and difficult to know. Jesus says, "My sheep hear my voice (John 10:27)."

James mentions slavery to money and things, whereby people become objects. Money itself is not evil; it is a gift of God. But when obsession with the present world eclipses the eternal, evil enters. Especially heartbreaking is not paying people a fair wage, not paying them in a timely way, or using their services and not paying them at all. The root is self-for-self and demonic. The Bible constantly warns severely against running people into the ground or even endangering their lives for the sake of earthly gain.

This is the devil's nature, and thankfully no one has to remain the devil's instrument. The idea that one is trapped with no escape is false. At all times, God is completely accessible with the gifts of repentance and transformation. The Gospels show us that there are those like Matthew and Zacchaeus who in their hearts hoped that they could break loose from their abuses and live the life of love. Underneath the appearances, there are many who are waiting for Jesus to come along—as us.

February 24

The Fruit Will Appear

James advocates fairness for all as a hedge against the same old religion driven by greed and insensitivity. The prophets in the Bible have always said the same thing about this, and it holds true for both perpetrators and victims. The person being unfair, and the person on the receiving end, can both drown in bitterness unless there is a healing answer. Those in power who are misusing others may have been misused themselves and not responded with grace, so there is need for a faith that works when we are misused by others, so that we may enter into the grace of the Lord and not become perpetrators ourselves.

This is why James says, "Be patient…until the coming of the Lord" (5:7). That sounds so futuristic that it lacks present action. After all, isn't Christ in you about living in the now? Yes, and living in the now means assurance that present suffering is not the last chapter of the story. Think of how many movies we have watched where the hero rights everything at the end. It is worth the wait; it is worth the patience and endurance under trial. God is a God of long-suffering, and He initiates His sons into the same.

When I began to see patience in my life, I knew it was not me because I had tried my whole life up to that point without being able to hold on through trials. Despair would always set in. So when patience arrived, I knew it was the Spirit, and I was willing to simply receive and wait. Many mornings drinking my coffee and reading God's word, tears would come wrenching and flying from my eyes suddenly and unexpectedly. Some word from the Scripture, quickened by God's Spirit, brought that on as patience had her perfect work.

We are used to sitting through movies, and we are a movie being shot on location right now. We are the characters in the greatest story ever told. The fruit will appear.

Anointing

John writes, "My little children" to those learning to get up and walk fully cleansed when they have sinned (1 John 2:1). Jesus Christ is our advocate with the Father when sin occurs, but how wonderful it is as well to enter the young man stage where sin does not have to occur. In a child's mind, sin looks unavoidable—too big and persistent to resist: and flesh looks too weak and unable to hold out against temptation. True, flesh cannot, but the young man rises up in faith to overcome the evil one by what John calls the "anointing." He says, "the word of God abides in you." Abide conveys the idea of where a person lives. It means home. The Spirit of God has made you the home of deity, so help now comes from within. Two become one, so sins stop.

If this does not happen, one would ask why? What if a medical student studies medicine and claims to have absorbed it but cannot treat illness? That would make no sense. As my old mentor Norman Grubb said, "What you take, takes you." Thus to take the anointing of God and the word abiding in you means this: you cannot help but manifest the life of God, which is light and love—with darkness passing away, and day ever more shining.

Deceivers, however, introduce false ideas of grace and teach that since we are not under the law, there is no law, which is why John says, "sin is lawlessness" (3:4)—the same thought as Romans 7, where Paul affirms that the law is "holy and good," and that it is error to minimize law or throw it out. That is a false way of dealing with sin. The true way is to let the law be all that it is and let efforts to keep it prove vain so that the seeker realizes the need for deliverance by Jesus Christ living in us by His Spirit—the anointing as John calls it. This is the tree of life.

February 26

Children, Fathers, and Young Men

The sequence of children, fathers, and young men in 1 John Chapter 2 is not chronological. Children are naturally coupled with parents, while young men have been learning to handle life's pressures without constant supervision. Fathers raise the children and provide a source of counsel when needed for the young men.

John addresses each level twice. John first tells the little children, "your sins are forgiven," but in his second mention, he calls them children instead of little children, adding, "you know the Father." This is because the children have grown a little and driven their stake of faith that God is always faithful to forgive. Thus, they know the Father's nature, even though they have not endured testing yet like the young men. But they have the basis now of knowing God's nature, having entered into the warm trust of His love, and His constancy in not casting them off because of their sins. They know that His delight is in them as children and that they are truly His beloved family.

John addresses the fathers the same way both times: "you know Him who is from the beginning." This does not mean static lack of growth. The Cross is always the same Cross, the Godhead is ever constant, but the fascination with God never fades. Think of the role of fathers: they help raise children, give guidance to young men, and fellowship with other fathers.

The word to the young men is, "you have overcome the evil one." This means having dealt with titanic opposites and learned the meaning of yes or no, not muddling them together. John forces a stand, not making a place to say, "But we always have failures and never really overcome." Only by faith does experience manifest. If a person plans for failure, failure will never drop away. The occasion of failure, therefore, is not meant to water down one's will to overcome, but to turn it to faith that stands against appearances until the witness comes.

February 27

More on Young Men and Fathers

John says to young men, "you are strong, and the word of God abides in you, and you have overcome the evil one" (1 John 2). Who believes that? Most Christians would consider themselves too defective and too presumptuous to say something of that order. They make a supposedly humble case of always being in a process that really has no chance until the magic wand is waved over them at death.

But what if you discovered that only God is strong, and you hung out in His house all the time, and He in yours? You would take the One who *is* the word, and He would take you. In fact, He invited you to this—called you even before you knew of Him. You would learn the secret whereby the One you take to keep you, does keep you. This means safety from the evil one, for though the enemy always attacks, the enemy cannot gain power in the members of the one walking by faith in the keeping. John calls this abiding.

The evil one doesn't necessarily start out with direct solicitation to huge sins. The ploy could be to get something slightly off track first. In the garden, why did Eve answer the serpent as if she, Eve, was qualified to answer on her own? When we abide, two answer the enemy, not one alone. She answered as one alone.

Because of the Fall, we are born needing the road back to two joined as one. The Cross provides that. What mercy it is! Some grow to be fathers, and then we learn through them of our completeness, recognizing when supposed need is not really need but evil solicitation suggesting that we are not whole. We learn to hear for ourselves from God, not proceeding in anything without that. Now God is first, and fathers a distant second, yet with more reverence and respect than ever since they pointed the way to the Father, and God still often addresses His sons through other sons. The young men now are well on their way to being fathers too.

Antichrist

John says, "it is the last hour" (1 Jn. 2:18). No other hour is coming; this is it, even though Christianity has stretched out over 2000 years since Christ, which seems improbably long. History is in its last hour. Not surprisingly, John's readers knew about history's ultimate villain and blasphemer: it is antichrist. The danger is not just one person: "many antichrists have come." As believers multiply, so do antichrists, making a demarcation between those who believe Jesus Christ as God's only solution and those who oppose Him. History repeatedly shows this demarcation, and Paul told the Ephesians that wolves would come in, and they always do wherever faith and fellowship in Christ is pure. Some say, "Jesus was a good man, but there are other ways to God."

To flesh ears it sounds exclusive and judgmental to say that Jesus Christ is the one atonement for sins. After all, look at all the humanitarians and sincere people who do not believe that. How can they be lost? It is not our job to hand out verdicts, but it is our job to assert that denial of Christ is antichrist. That is merely discernment. John says the test is sustained fellowship among those who preach Jesus Christ as the only way to the Father: "No one who denies the Son has the Father."

This will be unpalatable after a while to those who think that other religions hold equal truth and salvation. If they cannot water down the Gospel, they will finally leave because they have no appetite for Jesus Christ as who He really is. The defense against these wolves is keeping to the Gospel. It is hard to see anybody leave. We want so much for people to stay, and we yearn for them in Christ. Surely a compromise is possible so that we can all be at one table. However, the cost is too great if it means a revision of what we once held as the Gospel.

The Gospel Has not Changed

John says, "Let what you heard in the beginning abide in you" (1 John 2:24). The emphasis is not on trying to change others; it is on holding to what the anointing taught in the beginning. This is why John said earlier, "He is the expiation for our sins, and not for ours only but also for the sins of the whole world" (2:2).

What could be plainer? Christ's blood is not just God's way for one part of the world but for the entire world. If anything is secure about a biblical view of the nations, it is that the promise to Abraham encompassed all the nations, and biblical eschatology repeatedly affirms the same. The God of the Bible will rule the nations, and every tongue will confess that Jesus Christ is Lord.

The "anointing" teaches John's readers the very things he is saying, for "you all know"; so his letter is not to scare them into introspection about themselves but to shore up their awareness of antichrist's strategy to erode the fellowship. Note that John is not talking about church splits over other points of doctrine or gray-area, behavioral issues. The one thing in view is the centrality of Christ's blood as the only way of salvation offered by God to the world.

John urges us to abide so that no one will "shrink from Him in shame at His coming." The inference is that giving in to deceivers is people-pleasing—shrinking from Christ, leading then to the unrighteous living that deceivers practice and seek to justify. This multiplies shame because the one who does not abide falls back into the life that he or she escaped from through Christ. However, John, like the writer of Hebrews, sees his children as those who *do* know and who will not succumb to the subtle deception seeking a foothold among them. His tone is not fearful but a reminder to remain in the joy already present in Christ and growing in them by the anointing.

Outer to Inner Gravitation

1 John Chapter 3 can be a confusing chapter apart from the context of what John has already said. On the surface, Chapter 3 can sound as if to commit a sin makes one belong to the devil as master, or as if a Christian cannot commit a sin. Neither of those options makes any sense. However, John never uses the possibility or actuality of sins committed as a reason for anxious introspection over one's salvation. How beautiful to say, "Beloved, we are God's children now."

John then says, "we know that when He appears we shall be like Him." Somehow we are not like Him now, even though John later says, "as He is so are we in this world" (4:17), so the idea in 3:2 is about outer form, not inner being. Mortal bodies still carry around the light of Christ, but we do not look like the glorious beings we are because Christ is living in our bodies of dust that wear hard and fall apart as the years go by. What we long for is the new body, which Paul also tells us: "Here indeed we groan, and long to put on our heavenly dwelling" (2 Cor. 5:2).

The major point for getting through our outer decay is inner life, saying the believer is to "purify himself as He is pure." Purity means unmixed, so the idea of purifying does not imply self-works or self-improvement—an impossibility—but rather faith that learns to resolve its doubts without foolish visits into Romans 7 living. John calls it abiding, which means staying put. We stay put in who we are.

John says, "No one who abides in Him sins." This is the parallel to Paul's Galatian statement, "Walk in the Spirit, and you will not carry out the desire of the flesh" (5:17). When facing temptation to sin, success comes from walking in the Spirit. The magnet of the Spirit draws the children in, and they learn not to fight the drawing. They are kept, and sin drops away—both sins and the sin consciousness.

He Who Commits Sin

John says, "He who commits sin is of the devil" (1 Jn 3:8). This does not mean that every time a Christian sins, he is of the devil; one doesn't flip-flop between belonging to Christ and belonging to the devil, as if a person is a slave of one master one day and of another master the next. Ownership is definite, and a sin in a Christian does not shift ownership to the devil, just as a good work in a non-Christian does not shift ownership from the devil to Christ. We are slaves of one master only.

As a youthful Christian, I wanted God, but also the flesh if that would work. Not wanting to be a lost person, I simply wanted to be carnal, but go to heaven without having to consider, "What is love? What is best for another person?" If the carnal mindset had any chance of working, depression would not be the big business that it is, and we could get on with life as saved animals, awaiting our great grazing pastures in the pearly beyond. God, however, intends us to overcome the evil one and take our place as lord over creation like God created Adam to do. Therefore, He uses depression to drive us out of the lie and into who we are.

Why then does John say that those who commit sin are of the devil? He affirms that unbelievers belong to the devil and are of the devil. Cain illustrates this in his envy and hostility toward his brother Abel about the need for blood atonement for sins. Abel saw that we have no righteousness of our own, and so he needed a blood sacrifice to worship God and be made right with Him. Cain, however, based self-worth on what he himself accomplished with his hands, and so he presented the fruits of his own labors, which could not be accepted, for such would be to say, "Despite the Fall of my father Adam, I present my works to justify myself." This is the dividing line between belonging to Christ or to the enemy.

Why John Mentions Cain

When Cain saw that God accepted Abel's sacrifice but not his, the devil surged up in Cain, leading Cain to murder Abel. Cain acted as the slave of the devil. Apart from a new birth like Abel's, Cain had no control over where the devil would take him. What began with hurt, angry feelings became unapologetic hatred and murder. John uses Cain as an example to his beloved children but not for their fearful introspection as if they still belong to the devil.

John's point is that the unsaved person is not an independent and self-operating person who can reform: "Cain was of the evil one." Only the new birth with its anointing freed us from the same master. We have all had the same master, and our only chance at life was to receive a new master, Jesus Christ, who lives His life in His children.

This is why carnality in Christians is dangerous. It is flirtation with a murderer who will stop at nothing to destroy anything and anybody no matter how harmless and enticing the seduction appears at first. To toy with carnality is playing with matches. The Christian who wishes to be carnally minded thinks, "I will only go so far and will not get out of control." This is dangerous because giving one's self to a supposed lesser sin, opens the door to flesh level control by the devil, and though he does not own us anymore, he always operates the same way. Little enticements lead to bigger ones, and even murder becomes possible to Christians not walking in the keeping.

Such a Christian still belongs to his owner, Jesus Christ, but he has wandered into darkness and death, and the consequences can be dire. John is saying, "When you play with sin, you do not know how far it will take you. Do you really want to take a chance with the devil?" Any sin is possible, yet life can be so simple by walking in what John calls the anointing. Life is still excruciating, but the kept one remains safe.

Thought, Word, Deed

Words without deeds indicate lack of completeness because completeness includes thought, word, and deed. This does not include fluctuating soul thoughts which do not reflect intent, but rather the spirit-level thought underneath reason and emotion. God created us to discern the difference between soul thoughts and spirit intent.

Satan aims condemnation at out our spirit level, and so John says, "whenever our hearts condemn us, God is greater than our hearts, and He knows everything" (1 John 3:20). God knows our emotions and thoughts and sees beneath them to His intent in us, and by the Spirit we do likewise, not taking the condemnation. Thus, we can proceed from thought, to word, to deed in the confidence of the Spirit and give no credence to the constant barrage of thoughts and feelings that have nothing to do with who we are, and we certainly do not go back under law in an effort to manage the attacks as if God does not mean for Satan to tempt us. But we do not take condemnation for that.

This includes what others say about us. What does the Holy Spirit tell you about what they say? A person finally must know inwardly from the Spirit and begin to ask God Himself, especially about needs in others and what to do for them on a body level. Body level action is intercession, and much false guilt can be misleading when need provokes fear and uncertainty about how to help. We feel inadequate and perhaps unwilling. Condemnation looms; however, no one has to take that dart. Simply say, "I don't take it!"

Trust that God has not made an error in facing us off with a situation of need in others that looks overwhelming. God knows what He wants to do by you in that situation, and guidance will be clear. The world always offers a material answer for a spiritual problem, so your deed may or may not include what the other person hopes for, but it will be the perfect deed of love for that moment. Nothing needed will be withheld, regardless of how things look.

Sin Is of the Devil

John says, "The one who practices sin is of the devil" (1 John 3:8). He means those who belong to the devil: sin is their home base; therefore, occasional or even frequent good works do not change that. The issue is always home base, and we only have one. Home base is not a nature that we have, either good or evil, but the one we belong to.

Who Am I? by Norman Grubb has a chapter named "Have We Two Natures?" One phrase that has stuck in my mind for years is his "centre and circumference" (72). Norman says, "The centre is the set of our lives, and circumference is what may temporarily influence us." He goes on to say, "So now a slave of Satan can go and do a few good and religious things for a time, but that doesn't change his basic slavery. So equally a slave of Jesus can be tempted to exercise his human freedom in the ways of the flesh and does so, but back he comes to whom he belongs."

I can't say it better than that, and I think Norman perfectly captures John's intent. When John talks about those who "commit sin," he means those who still belong to sin and can never rise out of it, despite good works, because they have not yet taken Christ as their savior. They still see their works as their own, which is pride.

Anyone can live in the assurance of being a child of God. Even a disobedient child knows who his father is, and a Christian caught in sin will return home. Things can look messy and take a while, but the Father does not abandon His children, and they will find their way home again and again. Eventually they settle into home life as their abiding life, especially when they see that sin is not an independent human who does evil. For the lost, sin is the devil operating his enslaved children. For the saved, sin is the devil temporarily misusing one of God's children who does not yet walk in God's keeping by the Spirit.

No Need to Fear

John separates the spirit world from the matter world (1 Jn. 4). Without that, people appear independent, like mere human selves with opinions and the worship of reason. Discernment tests the spirits to live competently in a world where everything derives from one of two spirits —the spirit of truth or the spirit of error. Where fear exists about how to distinguish the Spirit of God from the spirit of antichrist, John assures us that the anointing makes this clear for those born of God. The anointing gives the witness that the eternal Christ came and manifested Himself in human form, as fully a man in every way.

Failure to confess this is the spirit of antichrist in false prophets, who speak from the spirit of error operating in them, based on arguments rooted in sensual self-interest at all costs. This could make the world seem terrifying, as if believers are overmatched by demonic power, but John assures even little children that they are "of God, and have overcome them." He does not say that they will overcome but that they have overcome, "for He who is in you is greater than he who is in the world." Therefore, it is not super spiritual, nor is it for superheroes to defeat the forces of darkness. Even a child in Christ can recognize deception regarding who Christ is.

Certainly feelings of fear can crop up for anyone, since to live in the world means desire to subsist and cohabit, not wishing to make enemies or stir up conflict. However, the devil never rests, and so the devil's agents constantly bring trying circumstances against the children of God. This is no mistake, for God has assigned the devil as the tempter and accuser only in this age of perfecting the saints unto faith. John calls the enemy "he who is in the world" (1 Jn. 4:4). However, there is no need to fear evil more than trusting God, for John's whole appeal is that we have the anointing to guide us and swallow up fear.

His Love Is Perfected in Us

John says, "we also ought to love one another" (1 John 4:11). This can sound like legalism, but it is no different from saying, "A plane ought to fly." If it is a plane, it ought to fly. That's what it's designed for. By love, John does not mean human love or human charitable works, but love that comes from God Himself. This love is of the Cross.

To this, John adds, "No man has ever seen God." God's love was manifested in the form of His Son, Jesus Christ. That was God's chosen means of showing His love. Now that Christ has ascended, we have the historical record of that, and love is presently expressed to the world in the form of Christ's body—those in whom He abides.

Only a few saw God's Son, Jesus Christ, while He was alive on earth. However, Jesus Christ is on the earth in multiplied form. We are the love, meaning we who believe, and "His love is perfected in us." Perfecting sounds like a process, for it is true that we did not see all this at once: we experienced the shocks of coming to the end of seeing ourselves separated from Christ. However, perfecting also means to bring to completion, and John's point is to remove the gap that still makes provision for a separated self not expressing Christ.

Perfecting means that Christ's love would be incomplete if He alone as a human expressed the love of God. The children of Christ are as Christ. They are His love, really and truly in a human form in this world, and that is why the exhortation to love is so important. It is not just the love, but also who the love is.

Yet what about the *ifs* and *oughts* in John's letter? One day when Norman Grubb was visiting my mother-in-law, Mimi, in the 1980s, I asked him, "Why does John use the words *if* and *ought* in his epistle? Without hesitation, Norman replied, "So that you can take them out!" That is where faith comes in—the switch from outer eyes to inner eyes.

Love Overcomes Fear

Knowing comes by the Spirit; we cannot know a thing merely of ourselves. It takes the witness of the Spirit to confirm a thing, and that is exactly what the Spirit does. We may experience a gap between a faith stand and knowing the Spirit's witness, but that is God's business.

Thus John says again, "God is love"—and God's love is "perfected with us" (1 John 4:16-17). When he mentions perfecting, he adds that it gives us confidence for the "day of judgment." Perfecting means that we see God's love as perfect by us in every situation. Now you see why that takes faith; who feels that way? John makes the great affirmation, "as He is, so are we in this world." Like Son, like sons, for the Son Himself is in the sons.

The main enemy is fear. At first it is a challenge to believe that we are safe in God's love. We relate to God and get secured in knowing His nature and learning from His Spirit. Then there is that brother to relate to, which can be stressful. Fear wants to make us think that we cannot do it. Fear says that sooner or later we will cave in and not love, but hate. Trailing behind fear comes dread.

This is great testing, though unwelcome in immature days. John says, "perfect love casts out fear." The word *perfect* carries the idea of completed—a person being what he is made to be. The perfect watch is the one that tells time correctly. It perfectly does what the watchmaker made it to do.

Yet we can look at our brother, look at ourselves, and think, "It can't be done. It can't last." So we look to the One who can, the One in us who *is* love. Feelings and thoughts tempt us to sink, but faith believes love. Even when settled about one challenging person, here comes another. How great! If the other person ignores me, hurts me, or doesn't meet my needs, love goes on for that person by faith.

Love and Discipline

"Whoever believes that Jesus is the Christ is born of God" (1 Jn. 5:1). A new family is procreated, with God as the parent, and we as His children; and we know how parents are about their children. A parent may be upset with a child that needs disciplining, but let an outsider attack the child as worthless, and the parent will rise up!

As children of God, we are stuck with each other and even told to love one another: "whoever loves the Father loves the child born of Him" (5:1). Thankfully this is not based on whether others are right or wrong, or our emotions, but on God's nature in us. Sometimes it is our place to offer correction; much of the time it is not.

How can one know? Each Christian has the same built-in capacity with the new birth to hear God and obey His personalized directive, whether it comes directly from the Spirit, or through exhortation from others. Either way, it has to be quickened by the Spirit in the hearer.

Much stress arises from conflicting views, so we have to know God's voice: "My sheep hear my voice" (John 10:27). It is not hard, just costly. Discipline requires discernment as a way of life since we do not live by law. When others need discipline, we may not be in authority to offer it but can only watch and pray—perhaps not even watch. Why watch what is not our business? The world does not know this, and so its ways are constant gossip, meddling, and turmoil—full of blame and accusation from the enemy.

However, John tells us, "Whoever is born of God overcomes the world." We are not obligated to the chaotic, endless passions that rip the world or our carnal brethren apart. Faith operates from the quiet stillness and certainty beneath surface turmoil. John says that no one can overcome the world except by believing "that Jesus is the Son of God" (5). Therefore, when you see people doing the impossible—overcoming the world—you can know that it is the faith of Jesus.

The Three Witnesses: Part 1

John identifies three witnesses: "the Spirit, the water, and the blood" (1 Jn. 5:8). Water means purification, as evidenced by the red heifer in Numbers Chapter 19, where the water of purification was for cleansing after contact with corpses. This correlates to Hebrews 10:22, where our bodies are "washed with pure water" now. Water also means living water, as when Jesus offered living water to the Samaritan woman (Jn 4).

However, the water in 1 John 5 means baptism. Think about how many people assume that baptism has saving powers, yet many people get baptized who do not believe. Baptism saves no one, just like a wedding ring is not a marriage. This puts earthly, baptismal water in perspective compared to true baptism—that of the Spirit in the living water of the new birth. John the Baptist baptized in order to bring repentance and prepare for the one who would baptize with the Holy Spirit.

When John baptized Jesus, the Holy Spirit bore witness from the Father about God's only Son. This is the real interest in mentioning earthly water—the coming of the Spirit to Jesus, and then to us in rivers of living water. Jesus' baptism was not about Jesus needing to repent except as being made sin on our behalf (2 Cor. 5:21) so that we could die and be reborn in the watery womb of the "mother" from "above" who is "free" (Gal. 4:26).

This is evidenced also in Moses, a type of Christ. After his birth, his mother hid him, and then put him in a little basket like an ark floating close to the river bank. Moses was as dead unless the water became a birthing womb from above, which the rescue by Pharaoh's daughter proved to be, who returned Moses to his mother. Baptism, therefore, is going from death to life—becoming a newly born son of God out from the living waters of freedom's watery womb.

March 11

The Three Witnesses: Part 2

The account of Jesus with Nicodemus reveals water as the womb for the new birth. After Nicodemus puzzles about the necessity of being born anew, Jesus says, "unless one is born of water and the Spirit, he cannot enter the kingdom of God" (John 3:5). Nicodemus has focused only on earthly, ritualistic water. Jesus, however, speaks of living water and a heavenly womb. One must be born again from the "mother above" as Paul calls her in Galatians 4:26—born from the womb of living waters. This is a supernatural birth producing a new creation (2 Cor. 5:17).

No wonder John's epistle mentions three witnesses— "the Spirit, the water, and the blood." The new birth is so radical that it must be differentiated from earthly images of water under the Old Covenant and according to the natural world and its rituals. Water must be living water and not dead water.

The blood is the third witness and is the blood of Jesus for the expiation of our sins. The new birth requires the blood of Jesus to wash away our sins. None of the three witnesses can be left out. They are all supernatural witnesses—not earthly water, human reason, and animal sacrifices.

The point is that one either has divine life or not. Christianity is not self-improvement but the life of Christ in human forms. Eternal life "is in his Son" (1 John 5:11). Therefore, the meaning of Christianity is this: "He who has the Son has life; he who has not the Son of God has not life."

I remember a conversation with a lady on an airplane who took offense at the idea that Jesus is the only way. I told her that I did not come up with this but that Jesus Himself says it, and He is the one I believe. John has labored in his letter to say the same—that life is a person—God's only Son—who came into the world also fully human, to save us by His blood and His Spirit through a new birth.

The Sin unto Death

John mentions the sin unto death (1 Jn. 5:16). The pattern in John's epistle is that people always move in one direction or another—either more into light, or more into darkness. John explains darkness in three ways. The first is not admitting personal sin. The second is not coming to faith about who Jesus is and remaining in that. The third is not learning to abide.

John lines up with Paul's statement, "if indeed you continue" in Colossians 1:23. Peter says it this way: "The dog turns back to its own vomit" (2 Pet. 2:22). Hebrews Chapters 6 and 10 convey the same idea where we read of those once enlightened "who have tasted the heavenly gift, and have become partakers of the Holy Spirit" (6:4) and those who "sin deliberately after receiving knowledge of the truth" (10:26). But John had affirmed his readers, so were they to introspect with dread and torment over whether they were really God's children? Of course not.

John is writing about the same people that he has written about all along in this epistle—those who do not see the need for Christ to save them. They never seek a remedy apart from their own works (really the spirit of error in them). Yet we experience the dilemma of the church, in which not all who start in the faith remain in the faith. Some overtly or non-overtly choose antichrist, which may not be obvious. In fact, moving toward a non-Christian world view may start subtly and grow subtly. This is the sin unto death if persisted in.

John says, "I do not say that one is to pray for that." The reason is simple. We know that death is supposed to be our wages until we come to Christ (Romans 6:23). It can be no other way. Therefore, John says not to pray for different wages for those who refuse the one and only remedy for sin. It is pointless to pray for the wages of sin to change.

Anyone Born of God Does not Sin

John says, "no one who is born of God sins (1 John 5:18). We know by now that John doesn't mean commit a sin. His point is that God is a magnet pulling in His children so that they find sin dropping away as they discover the highly energized orb of union with Christ, centered in rest and keeping. Increasingly consumed with God and His love interests, the children of God cannot help but discover how God expresses Himself as them, and they do not try to be like Christ but find instead that His love abides within, consuming them as surely as fire burns fuel. However, in this fire, we are not consumed but glorified. The burning fuel looks like the fire, but it is fire in its union with fuel.

John adds, "He who was born of God keeps him," meaning that Jesus keeps us. He keeps us as His children, and He keeps us from sin. In the carnal Christian, God acts as a gentleman and determines that we see how unsatisfying the works of the flesh are, works which lead eventually to the wretched man experience of Romans 7. God means this to separate out fleshly wants from our real desire of union with Christ.

Christ's ways eventually win, and they do, not by trying, but by trying and wearing out with trying. Trying is still the mark of self, whereas faith is the invisible ease of knowing God's keeping despite the excruciating aspects of life in a world full of groaning and mortality.

Our keeper is Jesus, who "was born of God," meaning that He is the only begotten Son, and that by His death, burial, and resurrection, He became the "first-born from the dead," as Paul says in Colossians 1:18. Because of sin, we could not be born from the dead, but Christ could, and since we were crucified with Christ, we also died in Him and were raised in Him. Because Christ was born of God as a human, and we in Him, He keeps those born in Him.

Safe from Evil

"The evil one" does not "touch" us (1 John 5:18). It feels like the evil one touches us, but the evil one cannot touch the inner man, only the outer man that is perishing anyway. Jesus said, "the ruler of this world is coming. He has no power over me" (John 14:30). Since Jesus is the one keeping us, the ruler of this world has no power over us either. Becoming convinced of this is the young man stage that John described earlier: "I am writing to you young men, because you have overcome the evil one" (2:13). God already knows about us the identity that we through revelation come to know, and God knows how to bring us to know.

A very unpleasant sifting process takes place to accomplish this, and no one is exempt. Jesus told Peter that the devil would sift Peter, but Jesus also told Peter that He had prayed for Peter's faith not to fail (Luke 22:31). What could be more assuring?

John tells the result of such sifting: "We know that we are of God, and the whole world is in the power of the evil one." That includes something we like to hear and something we don't. On the one hand, it is good to know we are of God. One indication is our obvious contrast to the world. The part that causes suffering is living in the lost world.

It might even look like there are two powers, one power being God, and the other an evil rival. Yet God reigns supreme, and the devil is only a created being running out of time in his short influence over the world. God would have removed him by now except that God means the devil's works for a good purpose. The devil is evil, but God means evil for good, as Joseph said to his brothers (Gen. 50:20). The devil is God's convenient agent, and since for now we are in a Satan-soaked world by God's intent, Satan has a right to come against us within the prescribed boundaries set by God. However, the evil one does not touch us.

From Sinner to Saint

Conviction of sin is the blow to pride as the law shows us we are wrong, which must happen before we can be right. Who wants to say, "I have sinned," or "It is sin in me." It takes Spirit conviction for those confessions, and such confessions open the door to faith, like Abraham had, followed by faith reckoned as righteousness. Faith itself, however, is not righteousness, for faith receives Christ's righteousness in the same way that swallowing receives food.

In 1994, Louis Tucker explained to me in his living room how we are righteous. He likes to say to groups, "On a scale of 1 to 10, how righteous do you think you are? Write it down on a slip of paper." Of course, when it is time for disclosures, modest and humble sounding answers come forth. Louis will then say, "Every Christian is a 10!" What a shock, but he backs this up with the scriptures in Romans that say we have the righteousness of Christ. Christ is a 10, and if He is our righteousness, we are a 10 as well.

This means letting go of the trick of differentiating righteousness as positional but not conditional. As great as it is to know that by position I am a 10, the need also is to appropriate righteousness into my condition. What do I care about a position that I can't know as my condition? It looks good on paper but leaves us still wretched to ourselves.

To believe the word of God means receiving it so as to manifest it by faith. The word of God *is* God; it is His *living* word. God always works by mixing Himself with people, and that is powerful and transforming. It is the mixed life that I care about, not the life of God other than in my experience. There is no point in living bread sitting on a pantry shelf in me but not living as me. Faith receives, digests, and goes forth refreshed. The self, no longer the vessel of sin, is the actual vessel of Christ.

Putting It All Back onto God

All except Christ have sinned whether under the law or not. Fast asleep and out of touch, one must wake up, and God uses conscience and the law to do that. Apart from waking up, a person lives merely as an animal with a better brain—not the life God planned for a ruling son. Therefore, He undertook to wake up anyone listening. This means Spirit conviction of sin that the self has no righteousness of its own. Then comes acceptance of God's righteousness by faith: He is the only righteousness a person has. It is not a *property* called righteousness, but the only righteous *person* in the universe, namely God. Therefore, righteousness can only be *received*, not self-produced. We do not try to manufacture any good on our own or from ourselves. Christ is our righteousness.

However, Paul knows that humanity tends to glorify the idea of elite people striving to attain sainthood—relegating common humanity to a life of meaning well but not being too holy. "I'm only human; I'm not perfect" becomes the standard for acceptance. Just be kind enough to apply this self-measure to your neighbor too. "All have sinned" turns into "All have made mistakes, and hopefully mine aren't as bad as those of criminals. God understands." This does not fit the dire tone of Romans 1-3.

Sainthood, therefore, is not the property of the spiritually elite but is the promise to every born-again person. Paul needs an everyman for a test case, and Genesis affords one, namely Abraham, who was not a religious person: he is not in a church, reading scriptures, performing rites, or studying over a code to follow the rules. He is an ordinary man who heard the voice of God and followed it wherever that voice led, regardless of the consequences. When he did lie or act self protectively, he did not even make resolutions or do compensatory acts but simply returned to God's promise with new conviction in his faith. He put all of his problems and hopes back onto God.

March 17

God's Promises Never Fail

Abraham was justified by believing God's impossible sounding promise that he would sire a son who would make him the father of many nations. This was not easy to believe with a barren wife. Years dragged on, and his and Sarah's bodies withered beyond expectation of the promise being fulfilled. Still, we do not see Abraham resort to religion, codes, and performance to be worthy of the promise. He did let Sarah cajole him into a Plan B that divested God's promise of its miracle element, and Plan B was a flesh plan. Abraham and Sarah did believe God's promise: they just thought maybe they were not doing their part.

God did not want them to do their part other than just to continue aging until absurdity provided the occasion for a miracle—one fit for laughter, not of unbelief, but God's humor, and resurrection bringing life out of death. Abraham believed *before* he was circumcised. Yes, he was a filthy, uncircumcised male when he believed and was reckoned righteous. Abraham is the common man, the non-religious man, the uncircumcised man; but none of this matters, because he is the believing man. He takes the promise of God into himself, finally all the way into himself, never wavering. He never lets go of the promise. To receive the word of God is to receive God; and to receive God is to receive all that God is.

Abraham's faith reached miracle level: "he believed, even God, who quickeneth the dead, and calleth those things which be not as though they were" (Rom. 4:17). He believed in resurrection life—life that comes out of death. No wonder Jesus said that Abraham believed the Gospel. Abraham learned the practice of looking at what is not, but seeing what is, when the invisible is getting ready to manifest its reality. Despite time and outer decay, God's promises never fail.

Seeing Through

As a young man in my 30s, Norman Grubb seemed larger than life, as if he had been born Norman Grubb, man of faith. One day I looked at his World War 1 photo in his autobiography *Once Caught No Escape*, and there stood a regular looking young man. For the first time I thought, "He's like everyone else." The way is open to all. I could see him as being like Abraham in the sense of not becoming a man of faith by works but by receiving.

Norman was a regular guy with a typewriter who answered letters, and some of his letters concerned conflicts among the brethren. I was still one to major on negatives, whereas, he used them to see through, to probe for what God was doing. He may not have known what God was doing, but he knew God was doing something, and that was the point.

He knew it would always be life out of death in an impossible situation. One letter he sent me quoted Romans 4:17: "'calling the things that be not as though they are' (because they really are)." The part that Norman added in parentheses floored me. I realized that real to Norman meant the unseen. Yet, he did see—by faith. Manifestation eventually follows; it has to.

Norman of course was rooted in Paul's letters, and Paul directs us to the ultimate life out of death, Christ in us. As proof, Paul loves to go back to Abraham as our father of faith. Just as Isaac was resurrection life out of a dead womb, Christ is righteousness out of a dead human. We don't make Him happen; He makes us happen.

First we learn that for ourselves. God's promise to us becomes more to us than every contrary appearance that time and resistance from others throw at us. We are guaranteed the manifestation—just not in a certain way and time at first. No matter, we are now timeless. I thought Norman wore rose-colored glasses in seeing through. Later, I wanted a pair for myself.

Fruits of Justification

Romans 5 declares our justification. What God does, God maintains, so we are not off-and-on with justification. Our place is simply faith, which anyone can have because faith means receiving. What we received is Christ Himself and His righteousness. Looking at Him, therefore, is our peace, whereas, looking at self never brings peace. Looking at Him leads to seeing Christ's complete work and its completeness in us. We see ourselves through His eyes.

God did not start war with us. We were the rebels and started the war, forfeiting peace. We could never, however, strip the peace from God's heart. He has the Cross forever in His heart through His fixed choice to be self-for-others; therefore, He can only be a God of peace, no matter what grief and agony we subject Him to, and Paul tells us of the longsuffering of God (Rom. 9:22).

Now, through Christ, we see that resistance to Him is foolish and self-destructive. It only keeps a person enslaved to sin and Satan. Thankfully, through the Cross of Christ, there is deliverance, which Paul increasingly clarifies throughout the great treatise of Romans Chapters 5-8. Therefore we say, "I am no longer God's enemy but His friend." You might be tempted to think that you do not deserve friendship with God, but that is not for you to say. Life is getting used to grace.

Paul says that we stand in this grace, not shrinking or retreating in fear. There is a secure standing despite perishing bodies and a world full of the sorrows. This includes suffering, since peace does not mean disappearing into the landscape of a trouble-free life. Troubles of body and soul still afflict us, but a new you—Spirit energized—trusts God's keeping and purpose in suffering. Endurance becomes precious, and waiting becomes a privilege, while assured of the certain manifestation in God's time and way, always perfect.

Settling into Faith

Perseverance implies waiting with endurance. This is faith's muscle, and God gives us a constant workout, like with Abraham. Paul affirms this in Romans 5 for our comfort so that we will not think that we have lost God's best through delay and the impossibility of what things look like when the miracle hasn't manifested yet outwardly.

Endurance leads to "proven character," which is proven faith (Rom. 5). We do not improve as selves, but the self settles into faith as a way of life, which means receiving words from God and mixing with them by faith. Manifestation eludes us, often for quite some time. With Abraham, the promise of a son appeared to conflict with Sarah's barren condition, along with their bodies wearing down over time to a feeble state, with no strength to procreate. However, God intended all along for the birth of Isaac to be impossible to human efforts.

While we are waiting, we hope. The word hope is not wishful uncertainty like, "I hope it rains soon." Hope sees fully in the Spirit 100 per cent of the manifestation that is on the way that makes us look like fools in the meantime. We hope for what we do not see outwardly yet. That is normal, God-level living. What gets us through is God's love poured out in our hearts through the Holy Spirit (Rom. 5:5). This is our supreme gift, the Spirit of God and God's love poured out in us.

Christ did not die because any of us were worthy but because of His nature (Rom. 5). Our justification is not based on either our rebellion or on our good works. Works have no place in grace. This is God's love to us, and then as us by partaking of His nature, now resident in us (2 Pet. 1:4). We have been saved from the wrath of God into the love of God, the wrath having been our former complicity with the enemy against God's love. But the old you has died, and God trains the new you not to be in a hurry. We walk in perfect timing.

God's Fixed Nature

We have been saved from the wrath of God (Rom. 5:9), which is not the same as the ill will of sin and Satan. Unlike Satan's wrath, God's wrath does not churn and seethe in hatred but is simply the fire behind His light. Consider the sun. When rightly related to it, we experience light and blessing, goodness and warmth, with results we like. When wrongly related to it, we get burned. Similarly, God is ever constant, and in our properly created orbit of cohabiting with Him, we enjoy eternal bliss. Out of orbit, we experience a condition never intended for us. Hebrews says, "Jesus Christ is the same, yesterday, and today, and forever" (13:8).

God's power comes from evil being something that He eternally said no to. This means that in God, evil is a swallowed-up possibility that never can manifest. It is the "not God" aspect of God. Freedom to choose in a creature (including Satan) equally mandates that who we are draws its power from who we choose not to be, so when the Bible speaks of the wrath of God, it means failure on man's part to reconcile to the only manifest aspect of God for all eternity—His light and grace.

Since we are creatures and not the eternal God, we cannot choose who we are as if we ourselves are the nature of good or evil. As vessels, we choose the nature that we desire to contain—either Satan, who tries to be God and thus experiences eternally God's wrath and tries to get others to enter into the same damnation—or Christ, who is eternally the Lamb slain.

This puts all the more emphasis on reconciliation with God (2 Cor. 5:20). God is already reconciled to us. His plan to reconcile Himself to us unfolded in history because history in a fallen world operates by time, but in eternity, there never was a time when God was not entirely love and sacrifice. He can be no other because He has eternally chosen to be no other.

It's All in the Roots

Beginning with Romans 5:12, Paul takes up the root of sin versus the root of righteousness. Everything proceeds from its root. My first training with this came in my 20s when I wore out a paperback copy of Watchman Nee's *The Normal Christian Life*. The glue in the binding got brittle, pages separated and fell out, and it took tape, and finally also a rubber band to hold the book together. This represented what we all experience when drawn by the Spirit. We sense availability, we intensely desire, we don't let go, and finally, the jewels of another's life get worn on our everyday garb.

I learned that when Adam sinned, everyone born from Adam sinned. The whole race sinned and fell at the same time in the same deed. It doesn't seem fair that a baby born in 1949, namely me, should be born already having sinned. Watchman told me, convincingly, that this is exactly what Paul means in Romans 5.

Where is Eve in this? She fell first. However, our lineage comes from our father, and so we partake of Adam in all that he was and did. My mother-in-law, Mimi, always lit up at Romans 5:12. Dan Stone liked to say, "Romans 1-4 talks about sins, plural; Romans 5-7 talks about sin, singular." I noticed the correlation with what I had previously learned: unless the producer is eliminated, the products will continue.

Without this insight, we will just go on as if we are only forgiven sinners. This is great, but as Dan would say, it leaves us with no answer for the present. Since the future isn't here yet, one at best can only hurry up to get the present into the past so it can be forgiven. God solved the problem at the root so that we do not have to live like this. He crucified us with Christ so that sin lost its container. In the resurrection, Christ fills the container. The self is ever the same, a container, but the occupant is new! You don't have to share your body anymore with the old master.

How Adam's Fall Affected the Race

Romans 5 gets to the producer level regarding sin. It looks at sin on a deeper level than the individual acts of Adam's descendants and takes sin back to a root. When Adam fell, sin entered into him, and death as well. Everyone born of Adam dies because of Adam. The proof is this: God assigned death as the penalty for only one specific sin—eating from the forbidden tree. No other sin by any other person carried that sentence. No other code of law and penalties existed until God gave the law to Moses, so there was a big gap between Adam and Moses during which everyone died. This means that they died for only one reason, Adam's sin, which everyone sinned when Adam fell.

To illustrate this, I line ten people up along a wall, the first being Adam. Only Adam violated a law carrying the sentence of death, so he dies. However, no new law gets introduced between Adam and person number ten, yet they all die. The reason can only be Adam. By him, sin came in, along with death, and condemnation.

Our problem was being born into the first Adam. We were one with what he did. However, God changed our outcomes through Christ "much more" than what sin did. There is no comparison when we look at what we gain by getting birthed into the Last Adam. As devastating as the losses were by being born into Adam the first, incredibly more glorious and not to be compared, are the benefits of being born into Adam the last. These benefits include righteousness, life, and no condemnation.

In our blinded, lost state, we do not think that we need a new birth. The resistance comes from Mr. Sin, the enemy, hiding in us with his lie that humans are independent. Thus, God has to awaken us by the law, which exposes sin and Satan's hold on us and paves the way for repentance from thinking that we can be self-operating selves.

Law Prepares Us for Union

What can one expect from the law? Law exposes sin. That fact contradicts man's blind optimism of thinking that God gave the law for us to keep. Nay, God never ever thought that we could or would keep the law. We're the ones who thought we could climb our way up to righteousness by law keeping. God eternally knew that He meant the law only as a tool to expose our inability to keep the law. In God's mind, the point is always the tree of life—union with Christ the person, not a code attempting to be like Him.

God knew that we had to drown first in our own futility of trying to do the impossible before we would be open to His real purpose. Only when we see that independent striving is the mark of sin and Satan will we run to Life instead of trying to be Life on our own. From Paul's thoughts across his letters, we see that Satan and sin owned us before we were saved, and they continue manipulating even God's children until they see that God caused us to die to sin in Christ.

The law was given that "the trespass might increase" (Rom. 5:20). That sounds awful. God knew, though, that the sin was already there, just not evident to us, and so as Watchman Nee puts it, God gave the law as a broom to stir up the dirt (lie) already there. The broom doesn't create the dirt; it gets it airborne and visible to the ones who need to see it.

Then we are ready for how God put the producer of sin out of us so that we can live freely—dead to sin; for the scripture says that believers are dead to sin. Romans Chapter 6 makes sense when we throw out time and space. Then, by the Spirit, it is clear that we died in Christ, were buried in Christ, and rose as new creatures in Christ. We died to sin being our master, and we are alive in our new master, Jesus Christ.

Sin's Dominion Is Over

I remember in college sitting on the steps of a beautiful, old campus building. While reading Romans 6 and Galatians 2:20, I did not see at all how I could be crucified with Christ, since He lived 2000 years ago. It is comical how at an institution of higher learning, one might totally miss higher knowledge. In higher knowledge, a person is not just an independent person. Therefore, it is not correct to say, "I'm just little old time-bound me." Paul has shown us in Romans 5 that when Adam sinned, we sinned because we were in Adam when he sinned. Likewise, Paul will now show that since a Christian is in Christ, we died when Christ died.

First Paul clears up a possible misunderstanding that some had after his statement that the law came to make transgressions abound. That could sound like it is time to have a sin circus, a revelry of rebellion. No, Paul is not sounding the trumpet for that; rather, he says that we are *not* to continue in sin. The reason is not so much that sin is evil, though it is, but that we died to sin.

That strikes consternation and disbelief when a person is still sin conscious under the law and thinks, "I have two natures." To say, "I am dead to sin" sounds like sin is now an impossibility, which cannot be correct. I certainly knew that I found it easy to sin. Also, I felt like sinning all the time and knew I was constantly tempted to sin, so I reasoned that I could not really be dead to sin. However, Romans 6:2 says that a Christian is dead to sin. Against all appearances, Romans 6 sweeps aside everything except the fact that when Jesus hung on the Cross, God unzipped Him, put us into Jesus, and zipped Him back up.

Therefore, nothing has ever happened to Jesus since that did not happen to us, despite the appearance of time. Our spirits are resurrected in Christ, kept by Him, and free on every occasion not to sin. Sin's dominion is over.

Switching Masters

In Romans 6, Paul does not identify sin as a person like he does in Ephesians 2 or in 2 Timothy 2, or as Jesus does in John 8. I have pondered that many times, but then Paul tells the Romans later in this chapter that he is limited in how he can address them because they see things so much from a merely human perspective. That is the thing about Paul; he will adapt to his audience if needed and not worry that he is not filling in every detail. Therefore, to argue Paul's theology from only one passage or one letter misses his wisdom in giving the needed word for an audience of the moment.

Clearly, though, Paul writes of sin in Romans 6 with powerful force, not simply as deeds that we commit from our own lusts, but as an enslaving entity with brute force that the Romans would be familiar with as violent conquerors. Their emperors and generals took whole populations captive and subjected them to whatever whim they desired. The analogy to sin's mastery is easy: sin is the master of every unbeliever, and the slave does exactly as the master says.

Romans 6:23 puts it well by naming death as the wages of sin. The wages of sin get summed up in one word, death. What a terrible irony to use the word wages, for the wages are no wages at all, but more bondage to the one who thinks in terms of what he independently does (supposedly) and what he deserves for what he did (so he thinks).

So there it is. We were slaves of sin in our former condition, which Paul calls here the old man or the old self. What does God propose for the old man? He knows that no reform is possible and that the old man must die, so God unzipped Jesus on the Cross and put us into Him, then zipped Him back up. The result is that sin is no longer our master. We have a new master, namely righteousness— and guess who that is.

Old Consciousness to New Consciousness

In Romans 6, Paul uses the term baptism to describe the fact of being put into Christ's death, burial, and resurrection. Death in Him takes us out of the first Adam because of sin, and ends us up in the last Adam. Sin is no longer master. Righteousness is. To say that I am baptized into Christ implies that my master is a person. Therefore, I'm a new man with a new master. Notice that slavery does not disappear. We simply gain the best of all masters, the Lord Himself. What a master; He served us by dying for us and as us. By accepting His slavery, we even become His friends, as He told His disciples.

Friendship operates by the obedience of faith, in which we live with our members presented to Him as instruments of righteousness. The leap to faith is simple, regardless of conflicting feelings or thoughts. Paul does not even bother to comment that one might not feel like presenting his members. He does not even make that an obstacle but simply says that this is what a new man does. Nothing is gained by fussing and bothering over how one feels as if there might be a different plan.

Paul did say in Romans 6 that his readers were bound up in their human way of looking at things, and so they were slow to see that being human is not an impediment to living out a life where righteousness reigns in one's members instead of sin, and Paul adds that sin never did anything for anyone anyway.

We died to sin and do not have to serve it. This includes the consciousness of sin. Why should I live with the consciousness of sin as if I am always tainted? The devil thrashes around in the outer man on a temptation level, but by faith my members obey my master. Instead of a sin consciousness, I live in the consciousness of the new man who with ease expresses Christ without fear. That is the life of a slave, who is a friend, and a son.

Deliverance

Deliverance is the answer for chronic, unconquered sin. This is the sin that whips a person until the cry comes forth, "Who will deliver me?"—uttered with such force and certainty that the answer carries equal force and certainty. One sin becomes the sum of all sins. For Paul, it was covetousness. He doesn't say what he coveted, which is wise because coveting is the point: therefore, no one can say, "Paul was beset with such and such, but I'm not tempted in that direction."

Something a man wants but cannot have bores the deepest, most persistent hole in him. He knows that he cannot have it, yet he lusts for it and cannot stop. This makes him still a slave of that forbidden thing, and his craving drives him crazy. He tries every way to withstand temptation but always fails, leading him finally to say, "Wretched man that I am!" As long as he thinks he has power or should have power to rise above it, he will fall again. Not until he discovers the keeping of the Lord will peace come in his members.

The doorway through is the discovery of powerlessness. A human has everything but power. Power is what we do not have over sin, or ourselves for that matter. When insight comes, the shock is that God did not create us to be power, or to have power, but to contain power.

Paul tells us how he came to see this—making sin the problem, not the human. An intruder (Satan) has maintained control in the man who loves God. The intruder does this by hiding the fact that self-effort is Satan's nature and seduction whereby the enemy keeps the focus on flesh, though deliverance is by the Spirit. Flesh left to itself will always serve sin, even when the mind serves the law of God.

How does one then line his body up with his spirit? Stop believing that flesh is an old nature in a Christian. Soul and body must follow the spirit, and the spirit is in union with Christ.

The Two Nature Theory

Romans 7 does not teach that Christians have two natures, nor does it teach that a human even has a nature. It teaches that a human is a vessel to contain a nature, and that the human is not either of the natures—sin or righteousness. A human simply expresses one or the other and is the home of one or the other, depending on whether the person has been saved. We have already seen from Romans 5 and 6 that we started out slaves of sin because of Adam's fall.

Now we come to the agony of the reader who relates to Paul's biography where with his mind he serves the law of God, but he finds sin in his members. He has suffered because he loves God but cannot figure out how to serve Him. Covetousness keeps him tied up, and nothing he tries will deliver him from it.

Paul affirms that the culprit cannot be the law, for the law is holy and good. Then comes the revelation that the culprit is not Paul himself, but sin. Sin is not Paul; sin is not you or I. Sin is a person—the enemy, the slave master who was in the garden and stole us from God and from ourselves. This is great news. To be a self is not to be defective. The old man only expressed sin because of his union with sin—the combination of which is the "old man."

To deliver us from sin, the old man is crucified in Christ—baptized into Christ's death as Paul puts it. This severs our union with the sin nature—the enemy—and causes us in death to be an empty vessel. The old nature is out! The old man died. This is final.

Christians in the main don't know this. Therefore, even though they have received Christ Himself, who is the new nature, they try to serve God with their flesh, which keeps sin operative, though Christ indwells them. Freedom comes when one sees that Christ *is* the new nature, and the heat is off of us.

Who Will Deliver Me?

We don't change until we have to. Despite repeated failure, one thinks, "What if another rally will yield success?" But what if it won't? That means we are defeated. In Romans 7, Paul came to the point with his wretchedness that he called it a principle: he did the opposite of his intent. When he wanted to do good, out came evil. He knew that the law was not evil, and that his human self was not evil—both huge revelations; but he still was locked in sin's endless repetition in how he tried to overcome it.

He could have thought, "I have an old nature," and many interpret Romans 7 like that. However, Paul has already twice said, "it is no more I that do it, but sin that dwells in me" (7:17, 20). Something is operating in Paul. It's not Paul himself, but sin in Paul, and so the remedy is its removal from Paul. He cannot drive it out himself, so he finally says, "Who will deliver me?" This is beautiful music because he no longer will try to do what he has affirmed as a fixed principle that he cannot do.

He knows what will not work and will not try it again. Therefore, he reaches out. Immediately deliverance is there in Christ by the Spirit. What could be better? Paul has discovered that God does not condemn humans for not being able to do what only God can do. Do you get it? Why would God condemn you for not doing what only God can do?

God never thought that humans could or should keep the law. We were the ones who thought that. He gave the law to convince us that we cannot keep it, so that we would then ask, like Paul, "Who will deliver me?" As soon as we walk in the Spirit (the deliverer), the Spirit brings quickening faith, and we do not give in to sin's lie because the sinless one is alive and well in us, keeping us. The lie cries out as always, and flesh feels impossibly contrary, but Spirit triumphs every time. It's miraculous.

The Miracle of Life

To know that I can never humanly do good or avoid evil is important, but life is actually the Spirit of God, and so Paul says, "the mind set on the Spirit is life and peace" (Rom. 8). This is the miracle life, where we do not live as we formerly did since we are carried along in the Spirit of God, living a supernatural life.

How well does this work? It works all the time if you want it to. If you do not wish to be kept all the time, you can have your slice of sin, but if you are done with that and see where that road always leads, the endless righteous life is yours to enjoy every moment. Yes, you can still sin. God bless you. You can still operate by the works of the flesh if carnality holds a fascination for you. Every craving imaginable is always there to convince you that you really want it.

Not only that, the devil will never say, "Oh, well now you're delivered, so I will go take a nap." His job is to make you think that you are your cravings and that sooner or later you will give into them, so why try to hold out. It is true that your bodies and emotions never stop begging for you to yield to their urges. However, this does not mean that the devil has you or that you have an old nature. God's word is the truth—that the devil has lost his control over you and that your spirit joined to Christ discerns not to live by emotions and bodily desires.

It is the best of news that we are not condemned for what the devil tempts us to, or for flesh level cravings. However, it is the best of news as well that we do not have to give in to either. Laws will not keep us, and to know that is to stop adding more layers of law out of a fear driven consciousness. Love ends fear, for love lives by keeping, by which God is our pleasure.

Life in the Body for Others

Paul coins two important terms in Romans 8:8-9: "in the flesh" and "in the Spirit." The former designates a non-Christian—a person in whom the Spirit does not dwell; the latter means someone who has received Christ and is now the Holy Spirit's (1 Cor. 6:19). Elsewhere, Paul says that the Satanic spirit indwells the non-Christian (Eph. 2:2).

His point in Romans is that for believers, temptations relate to the tension between flesh and Spirit. Jesus experienced the same thing when Satan tempted Him on every level we are tempted on. Temptation is part of being human in a fallen world, and the tension of eternal life in a body that is dead because of sin (Rom. 8:10). To walk in faith and thanksgiving while experiencing the same afflictions as others demonstrates that joy is known on the spirit level, not on the soul-body level.

Romans 8 parallels 2 Corinthians 4 where Paul chronicles many of his sufferings to make the point that we bear about the dying of the Lord Jesus in our bodies in order that they might express the life of Jesus for others. Without death and resurrection in us, the life of Christ cannot go forth to others. In one sense, Jesus can never die again, "Knowing that Christ being raised from the dead dieth no more" (Rom. 6:9); but in another sense, as the body of Christ, the church expresses the ongoing death of Christ for others until the day of our bodily resurrection.

The death of Jesus through His church does not mean further atonement for sin. The whole of the atonement for sin was completed in the one-time shedding of Christ's perfect blood. However, Christ's dying through His church continues God's expression of love as we sacrifice self-level comfort and flesh comfort so that the Spirit might be formed in others. Christ indeed lives in bodies dead because of sin, but not bodies designated to *continue* to sin. Christ laying His life down in our forms points the way to Christ being formed in others.

What Does Paul Mean by Vile Body?

The body is "dead because of sin" (Rom. 8:10). However, Paul does not call the body sinful; elsewhere he calls it "our earthly house of this tabernacle" and says, "in this we groan, earnestly desiring to be clothed upon with our house which is from heaven" (2 Cor. 5:1-2).

Speaking of the future resurrection he says that God "shall change our vile body, that it may be fashioned like unto His glorious body" (Phil. 3:21). The word *vile* does not imply something to despise, for the NAS translates *vile body* (KJV) as *the body of our humble estate*. Today we often think of *vile* as morally debased or filthy; but King James English from the 1600's draws on an old meaning for *vile* seldom used today: "of little value or account."

The "body of our humble estate" or "vile body," therefore, describes our present earthly bodies as perishable and not comparable in glory to the future, spiritual body of the resurrection. Speaking of the present body, Paul says, "It is sown in dishonor; it is raised in glory: it is sown in weakness; it is raised in power: it is sown a natural body; it is raised a spiritual body" (1 Cor. 15:43-44). The humble state and vile aspect of the present body does not make it unimportant; it makes it transitory—passing away—and not the investment for the future.

Since our present bodies are the Holy Spirit's temple, we nurture them with care—treating them as fitting instruments for God's grace to flow out to the world. As we maintain our cars and our houses, we all the more maintain our bodies and do not submit them to Satan's self-indulgent and destructive practices. But we expect our bodies to eventually perish, except for the generation translated at Christ's bodily return.

In the mean time we live from the eternal life already indwelling us in our spirits where, joined to His spirit as one, we enjoy our assurance that the real "I" never dies.

Adoption

Our high calling now means that we "through the Spirit do mortify the deeds of the body" or we "are putting to death the deeds of the body" (Rom. 8:13). Obviously we do not attempt to shut down all functions of the body and try to make the body not exist (the taste not, touch not mentality of Col. 2:21). We do, however, say "No" to urgings of the body that do not harmonize with the leading of the Holy Spirit. Our command center is the Spirit, not the body. Therefore, Paul says, "For as many as are led by the Spirit of God, they are the sons of God" (Rom. 8:14).

Satan likes to create doubt about our son-ship and throw fear at us to trouble our assurance. He sends waves of condemnation concerning every thought and feeling, trying to convince us that our flesh impulses mean that flesh dominates us rather than Spirit. Paul, however, comforts us by affirming our adoption by the Spirit. The fact that we cry "Abba Father" witnesses to our adoption. Adoption does not imply the modern Western concept of taking into one's family a child not born of the adopting family. The new birth is being born "of God" (John 1:13). That *is* being in the family by birth.

The usual translation as *adoption* is an effort to translate the Greek *huiothesia*, which lexicographers interpret as a compound made up from two words, one for son, and one for placement. The idea is son-placement. The context of Romans 8 is a mature son of God—an heir—who knows his place in God's family to restore man's dominion lost in the Fall. We gain confidence when the Spirit witnesses to our spirits that we are God's children and therefore His heirs as well (Rom. 8:16).

Satan's lie is that our bodies still belong to darkness, but the Holy Spirit affirms that the lusts of temptation are not sin but a place of death as springboards to practice faith.

We're Going to Suffer
So Why not Make the Most of It

As soon as Paul mentions son-ship, suffering comes up. Everybody suffers since earth is not paradise but full of misery from death and disease. However, a son interprets suffering as a means of glorification in being for others. Having been delivered from the real suffering—Satan's enslavement—we live in hope, which is a form of faith. Hope means seeing in Spirit what will manifest on a body level later. Apart from hope, there could only be futility, thinking that nothing will ever be transformed.

Scripture says there *will* come a time of transformation when earth and heaven will mirror the new creation already going on vibrantly in the sons. Christ lives in them, and their suffering bears fruit, no matter how much waiting and endurance they experience before seeing the manifesttation of what they interceded for.

The world is in bondage, and the lost live in futility of inner needs that feel overwhelming to them and to us, especially since their hurts are deeper and more painful than what they lack outwardly. Inner pain is always worse than physical lack because life is inner, and peace only comes through Christ's peace in us. Therefore, God gives us people to believe for, even before we know how to intercede.

We do not even know how to pray, but "the Spirit helps us in our weakness" and "intercedes for us with sighs too deep for words" (Rom. 8:26). If we tried to mentally analyze the needs around us and calculate how to pray, we would be swamped and discouraged. God knows this, so He tells us that it is perfectly acceptable to be weak, for He sighs in us in ways too deep for words, and His Spirit says the prayers in us. Sometimes we only know that God is working everything for the good for those who love the Lord. We do not have to understand, just believe. Understanding may or may not come, but hope is the faith that sees fruit before it appears.

Freedom Is a Person

When we believe and others do not, there is agony. Thus, Romans 9 is a difficult Chapter because reason attempts to affirm the doctrine of election and still account for freedom. This is exhausting and can only be exhausting since reason is not spirit. Freedom is not a quality apart from God that He gives us whereby we make choices; rather, freedom is the foundation of God's being, out of which God operates, beginning in the free sea of nothingness and proceeding to His eternal choice to be for others, which is why there is a Cross in the heart of God.

Therefore, when God gives us freedom, He cannot give it apart from Himself. All He can give is Himself, making even freedom a process in God alone, into which we enter and in which we decide whether to unite with the Cross in His heart or to shrink back from it. Shrinking back would mean entering into misused freedom, which in God is only a potential because of His eternal choice to be the Lamb slain.

Paul has just affirmed in Romans 8 that nothing can separate us from the love of God, but now Paul is willing to be accursed and cut off from Christ for the sake of his countrymen, the Israelites. This is his voluntary depth of love and not a legalistic constraint, and Paul does not think this up himself; it is the completeness of his son-ship to say this. As a son, he embraces what Jesus embraced in going to the Cross. Paul is willing for Christ to do in him, Paul, as Christ Himself did for us.

Paul is not saying that Christ did not complete everything required for our salvation, for nothing can add to the blood and body of Christ that saved us, and no other can accomplish that for us. Paul mirrors Colossians where he says that the one who knows Christ living within, also desires to be used up in intercession to offer Christ's finished work to others because sons can only do what the Son in them does.

God Uses Every Negative

God completes what He begins in a son. Jesus, Himself, is the firstborn son, the Last Adam. Therefore, united to Christ, the justified sons follow His same path to glorification through suffering. This is not only for themselves, any more than Christ's glorification was only for Himself. We are eternally for others because that is love. How can the sons be other than Christ's life being lived in them?

Yet love is not always understood by others. Sons can expect opposition—adversaries accusing and condemning them. These opponents have not overcome the accuser of the brethren, who hates freedom and constantly tempts sons to see freedom as too dangerous. However, faith knows that the purpose of freedom is to express Christ in union—based on containing Him, not imitating Him. How wonderful liberty is. It is not for the purpose of fleshly advantage over others, even our enemies. Rather, opposites stir tension by which sons refuse going back under law as if they are independent selves. The tension prompts the Spirit of grace all the more to believe for others.

Accusers suggest that tribulations prove God's lack of favor, and that faith is foolish and useless. The comfort is scripture's word that nothing anywhere, any place, or of any kind, can separate sons from the fixed and constant love of God in Christ Jesus. Romans 8 quotes Psalm 44, where the Psalmist cries out that God's people were being killed like sheep but not because of sin. Job also is a reminder that terrible things happen to everyone.

Our keeping as sons is that in everything, "we are more than conquerors." This is surely not on a feeling level. We feel what we feel, but spirit runs deeper. The conquering place is by faith alone when nothing appears that way and when faith appears ridiculous. When Paul gave his testimony to King Agrippa in Acts, the king thought that Paul had lost his mind. In one sense he had, but he had received another mind—the mind of Christ.

Supernatural Birthing

Readers might think Paul's passion for the Gentiles sprang from disillusionment with the Jews, yet Paul tells us how deep his love in Christ is for the Jews. It is not lessened, no matter how much he is called to the Gentiles. Not many Jews at that time received the Gospel—only a remnant. However, this did not mean that the Gospel failed. The Gospel is even more a success for moving from outer identity to inner. Paul has already said, "He is a Jew who is one inwardly" (Rom. 2:29). Fleshly, external identity is not one's identity. Christ is our identity.

Works, good or evil, have nothing to do with God's choice of a person. We see this in God's word to Sarah where the promise had nothing to do with natural birthing. It was about supernatural birthing when the natural level fails. A son of God is a son by miraculous Spirit conception and not external, natural means.

The fleshly mind protests: if our good or bad actions are not the determining weights on the scales of justice, how can life make sense? Isn't the universe capricious and random? No, because the new birth must be one that is not dependent on anything about the human but only on God's mercy. Why God created those He knew would reject Him is His business, and Paul says that God did this in order to birth sons—those who are offspring only by His mercy. He called the Jews by mercy, and He now also calls the Gentiles by mercy.

Paul writes Romans 9 as a passionate apologetic for his ministry to the Gentiles. He tells us about Sarah and Isaac, then Rebecca and Jacob, in order to make a point: the GENTILES! He shows that God *all along* intended to open the door to those not apparently called. He did this with the patriarchs, who had no precedent for being called. Then He used a barren woman, and later a promise about a son who was not the natural first-born. The whole framework for birthing is supernatural and by faith.

God Calls Real People Who Will Believe

Under the Mosaic covenant, the Jews were called, and the Gentiles were not called. Paul affirms this in Ephesians Chapters 3 and 4, saying it was a hidden mystery that the Gentiles would be invited into the family of faith as the elect. Yet in Romans 9, Paul uses Old Testament promises to show that scripture always revealed to the eye of faith that all nations would be invited into the elect family.

This does not now exclude the Jewish nation. It means that the non-Jewish nations *are* included because Christ fully forms Himself in anyone who receives Him—pressing that person on to know that fruit-bearing son-ship is the point. The Bible does not recognize partial versions of salvation in which a believer settles merely for going to heaven. God is after sons to operate the Father's business of restoration and dominion in the world.

God calls real people (anyone who will believe) to know Him as His friends and heirs. He does this according to faith, and in Paul's day, God opened up this calling to anyone in the whole world who would like to be included by miraculous birthing in the Spirit into the body of Christ. Naturally, Paul thought a lot about Jews and Gentiles. We might not think so much about them, but because of the Fall, everyone seeks elite status over others in some way until Christ in our hearts melts away that evil unbelief.

The Bible shows that God cares for all of creation. When He talked to Jonah at the end of the book of Jonah, He even mentioned "much cattle" (4:11). The idea that God only concerns Himself with the well-being of a remnant misses the agony of God over everything and everyone that He has created, whether they believe or not.

Love cannot harden itself. It must suffer, and God cannot avoid suffering Himself and does not even choose to avoid it. He reaches out to save all who will believe. God knew all along that the Old Covenant was meant to prepare us for "whosoever will."

I Lost My Religion but Found Christ

Romans Chapter 10 is an open door to the world. Paul has agonized over his countrymen but stood fast on God's call to the Gentiles despite resistance. To a Jew, there existed only two types of people: Jews and non-Jews. Today it seems strange that for a Jew, the world was "us or them" depending on whether one's flesh traced back to the line of Abraham, Isaac, and Jacob. However, the issue is not archaic because there is always an in-crowd to a mind that thinks in an in-crowd way. Only a miracle can break that.

The issue is always law, even when it comes to tolerance. What good does it do to tolerate or celebrate varieties of people if the emphasis is still on trying to keep God's laws as independent selves? The tension is so great that one will either discover the miracle of how we are kept—producing the Spirit's fruit—or else one will reinterpret God's word as just another religion of human virtues to work on, which is really misguided "zeal for God" and "not enlightened" (Rom. 10:2).

Apart from the Spirit, nothing changes inwardly: religion merely takes an idealistic form in which one measures righteousness according to the self and not according to a standard that only God is, and which only God can produce in a person. If the Christian life does not take a miracle, it is not the Christian life but just another reconfiguration of the same old plot—effort to look good while remaining the same inwardly.

Getting to the end of self-righteousness is painful, not only to the one going through it, but to those walking in the Spirit looking on, whose intercession is for those still clinging to the hope of keeping God's laws themselves, or clinging to hope in laws of their own making. All of the law is fulfilled in Christ. Law is not needed to bring flesh into compliance because Christ lives His compliance in our members.

April 10

God's Way Is not That Complicated

Paul wished the Jews to see that what they thought required laws for a resolution, finds its completion in Christ. All law is fulfilled in Christ because Christ is the nature of love and goodness behind the law. To have Christ is to never need law to keep flesh from sin. A person hangs onto law because of pride that wants things to be complicated. Moses said, therefore, that no one needs to go up to heaven or over the sea to get God's answer for needs (Deut: 30:11-14). The answer has always been near—"on the lips and in the heart"—needing only faith for activation.

The devil's lie is that the answer is far away, which keeps a person in the consciousness of need and lack. God is always near, which is true even for those who only see the glory of God revealed in nature. However, the urgency of the Gospel is no way decreased by this. How can anyone be satisfied short of knowing a living savior? Fullness is the point. Yet how they can call on one "in whom they have not believed? And how are they to believe in him of whom they have never heard? And how are they to hear without a preacher? And how can men preach unless they are sent?" (Rom. 10:14-15).

Leaving people to only the light of nature is not an option, just like God did not leave the Jews to only the Mosaic Law. God wants full disclosure to all the nations. The whole Jewish, prophetic tradition pointed to Christ, which Jesus saw, and now we see it by the Holy Spirit. Fruit may not have come yet in numbers among the Jews, but their ingathering is promised because God's election cannot fail. Abraham and Sarah did not give up on God's promise because of the long wait, and Paul, like the prophets, did not give up on the Jews. I always remember a line from Norman Grubb's book *The Law of Faith*: "Faith's only sin is giving up."

Miracles Are Our Desire

If people whom you thought would believe do not, God has others you did not expect who will. It is a mystery, but those we think most likely to jump at who they are may not be the ones who hear and believe. Romans 11 has the same plot: God used the unbelief of the Jews to reach out to those "who did not seek me." His family of sons now includes any who believe.

How thankful I am to be included in that family despite the disturbing number of those whose adversities still seem to them just their own and not God's calling cards. The card says, "Incorporate yourself by faith into Christ's death as you, and risen life as you."

There was a time when I was among those who had not believed, and others could dismiss me as too hardened and having had too many chances already. In 1994, living in a halfway house where so few recovered and so many took their checks and spent them on useless items within a few days, the house parent said to me, "Don't get your hopes up for recovering. One in a hundred really recovers."

I said, "I'll be that one!"—not meaning to be arrogant or to wish that others not believe. The door is open to all. I had simply come to the place in life where I did not live by percentages but by faith. "If anyone can believe, then I can and do believe"—that is the message of Romans 10. No matter what others do, or what their background has been, this is the day of opportunity for the Gospel's full offer is to any struggling soul. Anyone may believe and live an abundant life.

My old mentor, Norman Grubb, seemed impractical to me. He would tell people in impossible situations, "I'll stand with you in faith for that person." I thought that he should be giving behavioral strategies, but Norman knew how controlling that could be. Faith, you see, relies on God's miracles. Those are our desire.

Salvation and One's Sense of Time

Acts is a thrilling book, and the birth of the church is sensational. "And the Lord added to their number day by day those who were being saved" (2:46). What a concept it is, "being saved." It is Satan's lie that everybody is saved already as if Christ lives in everybody. What a foolish notion. The Spirit of God created humanity and is omnipresent, and God is as close as breath to all of His creation. However, man fell in Adam and is in the slavery of sin and Satan. Because of that, one must desire salvation and find it in one who can deliver from sin. It is a refreshing thing to be saved: "He has delivered us from the dominion of darkness and transferred us to the kingdom of His beloved Son" (Col. 1:13).

Jesus Christ is coming soon: "And behold, I am coming soon" (Rev. 22:7). The more you know eternity in your spirit where you are joined to Christ, the more timeless your consciousness becomes. Life is short and fleeting. Even sinners know that. Having already come in the hearts of the redeemed, Christ makes time a minor point as eternity speaks to us in our spirits. Those who see time as long eons that disprove God are only applying their knowledge in a prideful, finite way. They try to reason from time and the flesh—coming up with increasingly impressive distances and calendar measurements, none of which matters to God who lives outside of all this, and the adopted sons in Christ live outside of it as well.

When the external is finally shaken and then removed, and the new world appears out of Spirit, those in the kingdom will agree that everything went by incredibly fast. "Soon" will mean what it says except to those who chose time and the temporal world as their consciousness. To them, even one moment will be excruciating beyond compare. For those who believe, time died on the Cross in the body of Christ when we died in Him, and eternity rose in us with His resurrection.

April 13

Israel Will Repent

One of history's great sorrows is Israel's national rejection of its messiah, Jesus Christ. How could a nation so gifted of the Lord reject the only prophet that ultimately matters? No pathos runs deeper than this: "He came unto His own, and His own received Him not" (John 1:11). Accordingly, many commentators focus on Paul's declaration that "He is not a Jew, which is one outwardly but he is a Jew which is one inwardly" (Rom. 2:28-29). They see this as a reason to discard Israel as an elect nation of faith, especially since the Cross broke down "the middle wall of partition" between Jew and Gentile, namely the law, so that the two are one now (Eph. 2:14). Paul wrote that "there is neither Jew nor Gentile" (Gal. 3:28).

So why does Israel matter as a nation? It is because *our* intercessions today for impossible looking people are no different in principle than Paul's intercession for Israel. Intercession's completion is not based on whether others deserve restoration, or the time elapsed, or whether reason says it is likely. Paul could not let go of God's blessings to Israel and cast them off with finality. In his grief over his unbelieving countrymen, he said he would suffer separation from Christ to see them saved—not meaning every Jew or every generation of Jews, though God is "not willing that any should perish" (2 Pet. 3:9).

The question is, "Did God begin a work in Abraham, Isaac, and Jacob that He intends to complete through His elect nation?" Will Israel at some point nationally accept Jesus as messiah? Paul's agony for Israel may seem remote to us today. Some think that Israel nationally forfeited any future domain because of her rejection of Jesus as messiah. But that stance is difficult to reconcile with Paul's intercession for his people because an intercessor always sees the completion of his calling—even if it means seeing by faith from afar, as Abraham saw the heavenly city from afar. Israel's day of repentance will come.

Promotion

Paul's intercession goes back to Genesis and God's promise: "The elder shall serve the younger." This was before the twins, Esau and Jacob, were born—before they had done anything good or bad. Apart from works, God reversed the tradition of the first born male receiving the birthright. God foreknew Jacob as the faith man, so He elected Jacob, not Esau: "For whom He foreknew, He also predestined" (Rom. 8:29).

Jacob's choices honored the promises God made to his father Isaac and grandfather Abraham. Jacob was consumed with these promises and how they could come true since Esau was the elder. Jacob obtained the birthright for a pot of stew, to Esau's shame. Rebekah later conceived the daring plot to secure Isaac's blessing for Jacob. We can debate the conniving of mother and son, but Jacob operated at root out of faith and his passion for God. This is true even if one does concede some working of the flesh, for Jacob had his mind set on God's business of blessing the world through a nation out of the patriarchs' loins.

God intended to create a nation of faith the same way. Paul quotes from Hosea about the Gentiles: "I will call those who were not My people, My people" (Rom. 9:25). God gave the Gentiles the gift of righteousness, which they received by faith, whereas the hardworking, deserve-a-promotion Jews, except for a remnant, failed to receive the gift of righteousness because of their self-effort delusion.

The application remains today in the religious world. Consider the regular churchgoer who has not committed gross outer sins and who seeks respect and influence, yet the Spirit's anointing is not there. Now consider the flagrant sinner rejected by the self-righteous crowd that says, "I would never do that." He seeks Christ's righteousness by faith and receives it, plus the Spirit. Someone has just been promoted to the top who does not deserve it.

What Is It That We Imitate?

No one perseveres by mental assent alone. Doctrine is rich and deep, but it takes the power of the Holy Spirit to work conviction and truth into one's spirit, where union with God through Christ is real. Until then, those who teach us seem like special human beings instead of ordinary people with extraordinary faith. To see others that way is really to make of them something other than their faith, and to remain in the imprisoning lie that life is what we do rather than what God does in us.

I so much wanted to honor my teachers and imitate them, but had it wrong. Consequently, they would eventually disappoint me because I eventually disappointed myself repeatedly. The way of imitation is not what we thought. At seminary, I said to a friend and fellow student, "I don't want to imitate these professors." My friend wisely replied, "God wants us to imitate their faith." This took the pressure off of the professors, and off of me, but I wasn't ready to see it all the way yet.

Imitation is not on a works level; instead, it means to have faith, and to wait on the Spirit's quickening rather than live by reason and argument on a human level to prove things. That is why biblical morality is almost extinct today; it is impossible to live it, so it must therefore be outdated. The biblical view is that impossibility is the indication that such a life can only come about supernaturally, not by me, but by Christ in me. This is radical because it leaves no part of the human as the source: spirit, soul, or body.

Paul says in 1 Thessalonians, "you turned to God from idols to serve a living and true God" (1:9). It is idolatry to see man as merely a sensual being living a material existence. It is idolatry to say, "I'm just human; I can't help what I do." It is wiser to say, "I have been living the lie that I am only human." Satan gets exposed, and the whole human steps into life as Christ's only form of—you.

Giving Thanks for Others

However people affect us, it is always good to give thanks for them. It puts our view onto God and not the person only. Just as we do best when we look away from ourselves unto God, we see others better when we look away from them unto God. The Spirit is a mirror in which we see people—ourselves and others. It is indirect seeing, rather than only looking at the human and trying to sort things out.

Giving thanks to God for others may be a simple thanks, or the Spirit may add words to say. Giving thanks is like tuning into a radio station: once there, no telling what words we might hear. Even if the words are few, the Holy Spirit is a bond of unity with God in which others are seen instead of their seeming to be just independent selves—or worse, agents of the devil.

This takes us to the top, even if the results do not show up now in external change. The first change is our seeing. This is quite different from the world, where helping people is at the human level, and principles rule, along with exaltation of what people do from their own wishes so as to be perceived as good.

One teaches by the way he or she lives, so if we live by the Spirit, the Spirit is what we teach. No wonder teachers learn from students in the mutuality of the Spirit's fellowship. Love is a fruit of the Spirit, and Paul called upon the Thessalonians not only to love, but to labor in love, and to hold steadfast in their supernatural, new life. God matures us so that we persevere in God's love even when attacked by the devil's worst. The devil will not always be such a convenient agent, but he is for now.

Someday Christ will return to conclude history and manifestly rule the world. The days of faith will be over as we know them at present. For now, however, we live constantly contested, and to realize that is to move ahead with greater ease.

By God's Mercies

Romans 12 brings exhortations. They are serious but not dark and foreboding since Paul expresses them "by the mercies of God." Not seeing life by what we think is owed, releases us. Supposedly the world lives by scales of justice, but how can those scales be properly assessed when self-interest is at center. The old man, not born again, is quick to know when wronged but blind when inflicting wrong.

Even when justified in wanting others' sins punished, it is self-centered not to seek the offender's justification as well. No wonder the angels sang to the shepherds at Christ's birth that the messiah would bring peace and good will into the hearts of men.

Therefore, we present ourselves. The word *present* in Romans 12 is the same word used in Romans 6 where Paul says to present ourselves as "those alive from the dead" and our members as "instruments of righteousness." He is not talking about presenting an old self but rather a resurrection self. This means seeing who we really are, new beings born of God.

In Romans 12, the appeal includes seeing our bodies as living sacrifices unto God. This is voluntary acceptance of adversity as part of being for others. Such is a redemptive role in the lives of those around us, no longer asking, "Why am I going through this?" as if everything is intended just to teach us another lesson. Now the point is, "This is God's plan to expend me for others." This is renewing our minds, walking in the Spirit's mind, which is not self-help appeals to human reason. Life becomes supernatural transformation by the Spirit of God, where the believer goes along not resisting. This carries the one receiving into the passion of the Spirit expressed as us.

At the same time, we discover sanity—a sound mind. Life is supernatural while being ever more practical. Our gifts and callings are clear—no guesswork needed, because God's will is simple and simply known.

Burning Coals of the Seraphim

Romans 12 is full of passion in its low-key looking exhortation. It only looks low-key because it is not contrived. In my early years, I knew I did not know the naturally supernatural, so when I spoke, I used a lot of notes and grinded them out. One day when first launching out as a Bible teacher under Norman Grubb's tutelage in 1981, it was my turn to give a lesson at summer camp in Hixton, Wisconsin. It was always hard to teach with Norman sitting there.

I was 31 years old, and he was a renowned 86. After my talk, I heard him say in a low voice to someone, "Where's the fire?" It stung. It hurt, but he was right. What can one do? Norman often said not to try to get the witness of the Spirit but to just say in faith that one has it. Stand on faith like a nail driven in and don't pull at it.

The witness did not come soon after. I put Norman to sleep at times. Yet Romans 12:11 reads: "Never flag in zeal, be aglow with the Spirit." Fear not, what you take will take you. Don't give up on fire; keep on by faith. Fire is there in the midst of opposite appearances, in which negatives invite faith. Keep helping others, even when they do not appear responsive or appreciative, for love can only be love. Its quality is the will to see others birthed, and faith sees them there already. Rest in where the script will end, not where it appears midway.

Some we help will be enemies. God's way is to "heap burning coals upon his head" (12:20). This does not mean destructive coals, but rather holy coals, like Isaiah experienced when one of the seraphim took a burning coal from the altar and cleansed him, turning him into an intercessor (Isa.6). We want for others the same cleansing experience that we needed and experienced. This is intercession. Ours is to continue in faith; the Spirit comes with the witness in God's timing.

Questions about Government

Questions about government arise since cultures operate by politics. History is governmental forms giving way to other forms, according to new theories and military strategies. However, government does not transform others, since external law cannot bring internal peace. Paul always declares internal, new birth first—pointing to Christ in us to manifest qualities impossible without the Spirit. Simply put, Christ is our government. Christ has humbled Himself, however, for a season to let the world try its way, knowing that worldly peace is short-lived, and history will always revert to greed and war.

Nonetheless, positions of authority are instituted by God. We may not like them or agree with them, but favor comes by seeing them as instituted by God and accountable to Him. Therefore, we respect leadership positions and pay our taxes. Obviously citizens are not obliged to carry out works of the flesh if such are demanded, and disapproval of the government is never to be a cloak for wrong doing. Notice too that Paul makes no pitch to get involved or not get involved with the government. He prefers righteous people in charge instead of unrighteous people, but he does not argue to get involved, assuming that as the Gospel takes root in more people, culture is transformed.

Romans 13 is not a mandate, therefore, for trying to change the government or not trying to change the government. The Gospel is simply the Gospel, and this implies God's sovereignty. When we know that God is the only power, we see through evil decisions in government and continue to declare that God is in control. His government will manifest at the climax of history as the Bible foretells, and the devil will find himself without any property. As always, the Bible tells us that evil is temporary and that we already live in the heavenly government within our hearts, and the heavenly government guides us. Our walk will be counter to the world, but this is nothing new or unexpected.

Nurse and Mother

Paul avoided five things: error, uncleaness, guile, flattery, and greed (1 Thess. 2). Paul did not teach error but correctly interpreted the scriptures by the Holy Spirit, showing that Jesus was the messiah foretold by the prophets. Further, Paul and his coworkers did not practice uncleaness, also translated as *impurity*. Let's be real here and read between the lines. Here are three men out on the road working—away from home, wives, and children. Travel could seem an escape from a boring grind at home, which could lead to seeking excitement and escape from dreary routines. Yet the apostles had no mixed motives (the word impurity implies a mixture that should not be).

Then too, they are guileless, which is also translated *deceit*. "What you see is what you get," meaning no trickery. They are not bored, and therefore not meddling and manipulating others like a drama or soap opera, in which gossip always feeds off of discontentedness with the simplicity and beauty of truth. Guile also involves flattery. To win allegiance, flattery uses manipulation to build someone up, seeking to trigger the narcissism to which people are tempted. Grandiosity knocks on the door as the flatterer puffs someone up to get a return. Then greed flares up, and the flattered one becomes more likely to jump at hasty schemes instead of living life's daily grind by faith in the sober mind of the Spirit.

The apostles disavow such schemes as repulsive. Instead, they are like "a nurse taking care of her children." They are like mothers who love their children and sacrifice for them. The apostles assume a feminine and maternal role, saying, "you had become very dear to us" and they meant it. The new man is androgynous in his spirit because opposites are united instead of at war. The masculine and feminine are not at war in God's being, so neither are they at war in us since Christ's sacrifice ended the gender strife caused by the Fall.

When Your Children Are Attacked for Their Faith

It is a dire thing that those who resist Christ not only injure themselves but also interfere with others wanting to hear. This evokes some Paul's strongest language (1 Thess. 2). He explains that those who hate and resist others being saved only increase the wrath within themselves as they continue to resist. Just as faith moves from glory to glory, wrath spirals increasingly into darkness, giving the devil more power, as the unbeliever's will yields to further hardening. The language is frightful: "But wrath has come upon them to the uttermost."

God does not soften this: He wills that wrath do its job as the convenient agent to wake people up to desire escape before it is too late. Wrath experienced internally is a calling card toward grace and eternal life in Christ. For believers, the Gospel now sounds its warm notes of affection. This is felt in Paul's desire to visit the Thessalonians again—"to see your face." The apostles have felt "bereft" of the Thessalonians. This is intimate and real.

The reason that no visit had yet occurred was "Satan thwarted us." Satan does not have equal power with God; God is in control and means us to recognize the enemy and then know that we have overcome in faith. The devil's interference with the Thessalonians fit God's purpose of solidifying them when they were attacked, so as to trust God for themselves while others cheered from a distance.

As a parent, Paul wanted to be present and rescue his children—to run to them when they were attacked. Yet parents get weaned just like children do, so that the children will learn to stand and walk on their own—and go on to teach others the same. Sometimes from a distance, all we can do is sing and pour out hope, joy, exaltation, and glory in standing with others in their faith when we cannot be physically present with them.

Heavenly Glue

Paul's theology and fervent love are intertwined. His ardor could be uncomfortable to someone recovering from clinging attachments, but God's love knows no such merely human dependencies. It is an all-out flame from Christ Himself, which makes it self-for-others, not me-centered. The question is always, "What is best for that other person?" This means "death works in us, but life in you" (2 Cor. 4:12).

This is the safe ground for all-out passion of expression (1 Thess. 3). For example, Paul had to know how the Thessalonians were doing under persecution in his absence. Did this mean that he did not trust God? How do we see Paul's fear that the Thessalonians might have slipped? What, fear in Paul? This was not fear from unbelief but fear that quickened Spirit action—in this case writing the Thessalonians during the time of their trials to see to see how they were holding up. Their temptations and trials activated Paul to send Timothy to see "if the tempter had tempted you and that our labor would be in vain." God can keep a mentor away from the scene of action, so that the mentor is even pressed, so that the only thing to do is to stand and believe for the precious ones elsewhere under attack.

Paul knew that the tempter had been tempting; that is what the tempter does. Paul wanted to know if they had recognized temptation as temptation and were using it as an opportunity for faith. The Thessalonians had in fact stood fast, so Paul celebrated their "faith and love." This was the first order of concern—that they stay true to God. Then secondarily, Paul says, "you always remember us kindly and long to see us" (3:6). They were united in Spirit.

Though we might seem overly concerned with how others are doing and how they view us, the point is Spirit concern, not soul attachment. When the connection is in the Spirit, the bond is deep with others who walk in the Spirit. We are connected with heavenly glue; therefore, Paul says, "We live, if you stand fast in the Lord." That says it.

Salvation

The Holy Spirit is our witness that Jesus Christ is Lord and rose from the dead and is coming again to rule the world forever. The only block to seeing this is Satan, who authors materialistic and random world views, claiming that man can evolve slowly into the consciousness of the God already within him. Such false views claim a union consciousness that does not need Christ's death and resurrection as the payment for sin.

The devil's false version of oneness with God plays upon the fact that God is love. Sin is discounted or redefined in such a way that the Cross is never necessary. Any higher power will do, and the supposed freedom to choose one's own higher power does nothing more than deify the self that needs to be saved in the first place.

To be a Christian means that the Holy Spirit has authored a new life in a believer, one that could never come about by any means but the Spirit, whose nature is to manifest the Cross in our daily living. Otherwise, we would revert back to living like unbelievers, who just know escapism as their way to deal with life's everyday grind. Only a soap opera of constant gossip and intrigue satisfies the craving of those still on a flesh level. The anathema to them is remaining celibate or getting married. If they get married, the anathema is staying married, working a job, and not meddling in other people's business.

An ordinary life of faithfulness is boring to someone motivated by lust and the fickle changes of emotions and physical craving. Even if the flesh avoids outer sins that would wreck marriages and jobs, secret sins take over. The point is that the heart has not changed. Its first love is a self that looks good and shuns suffering.

In contrast, a Christian loves someone else more than self, namely Christ, and then one's neighbor as Christ leads. Christ does not help us—He is our life, and need-consciousness disappears.

Three Vital Things to Everyday Living

Before the age of free sex, young people knew that maturity would mean settling down to marriage, a job, and giving up the party life. That was a sobering decision. Actually, it takes the Holy Spirit to make it work, or else life hums its way toward boredom. No wonder the world's appetite for entertainment means constant stimulation of God-given appetites toward lust and perversion.

Thus Paul tells the Thessalonians three vital things to everyday living: intelligently picking a spouse (if one is called to marry), faithfully working to meet one's needs, and staying out of the gossip and meddling loop (1 Thess. 4). What the Holy Spirit begets in a person is sexual purity, fidelity, practical work habits, and miraculous lack of interest in tabloid quality conversation.

Many claim great revelations about God and consciousness of the divine, but without the Holy Spirit, the only life possible is feeding on what any fallen human can indulge in without needing a savior and the miraculous keeping of the Holy Spirit. The Bible mocks this and warns that God is "an avenger in all these things" (1 Thess. 4:6). We need not condemn those stuck in the old life or take vengeance. In the present age, God is keeping the door open to salvation from the old life.

The answer to the old life is a new life, by miraculous conviction and power of the Holy Spirit. To the Spirit minded man, the deepest and most fascinating topics are purity, industry, and minding one's own business. But they are costly to know because they cannot be known by emotion or human reason (soul). Neither can bodily appetites know the deep things.

The devil keeps the lost person and carnal believer trapped in the lie that soul and body can find truth, whereas they can only be the outer clothing of the Spirit man. They are the instruments to express Spirit life, not an end in themselves.

When History Drags On

It is nothing new to feel baffled by eschatology. This does not mean, however, indifference to it. Eschatology became central with the promise to Adam and Eve that the seed of the woman would "bruise the serpent's head." The prophets sought to understand about the messiah's coming, and believers do understand why Jesus came.

Looking to the future and seeking to understand the next great manifestation means seeing that history is not separate from a plan and a creator. History is not random or chaotic; rather, it is a clearly arranged plan executed by a God who is in control and who sees history as the chain of redemption leading from man's Fall all the way back to his glorified body in the new heavens and on the new earth.

Most of life is struggle to survive, making future things seem remote, whereas discovering who we are and how to live today is paramount. That is true, but it is also grounded in our security of eternal life. Some in this body may live past 100, but what then? The mortal body finally goes to the grave. That is the ugly end of the old body except for those alive at the return of Jesus in His glorified body when the last trumpet sounds. In the meantime, Christians want to know victory in present trials, and this includes eternal life in Christ even now during this grim and short life here as we stand on Christ's keeping of us.

The Thessalonians also wanted to know about those who did not make it alive until the last trumpet. Paul tells them that death means being "asleep" (1 Thess. 4:13). If someone only falls asleep, then that person will wake up! This is the present comfort when history by appearances drags on. To be "absent from the body" is to be "at home with the Lord" (2 Cor. 5:8). Jesus says, "he who lives and believes in Me will never die" (John 11:26). My mother-in-law, Mimi, loved to say, "We have died the only death that matters" (Rom. 6).

When the Trumpet Calls

One generation of believers will be alive at the coming of the Lord. However, those "asleep" will rise first (1 Thess. 5). Those still alive will hardly complain that the dearly departed rose first. Now, for the first time since Adam's Fall, believers will no longer be in the world but not of it. God will take every remnant of the old body into the heavenly dimension, where it will be "raised in glory" as a "spiritual body" to express your spirit, (1 Cor. 15:43-44)—which has already been "in the heavenly places in Christ Jesus" from the moment you were saved (Eph. 2:6).

The tone of the final bodily event is a mighty blast—a "cry of command" and "the trumpet of God." It will be a worldwide phenomenon. For those who do not think that Christ will physically come back, this Chapter must seem juvenile. In Acts, the apostles saw Jesus ascending, and heard that He would return the same way. He came incarnate; He will return incarnate but in His glorified body.

In the interim, believers live by Galatians 2:20 in the Spirit. We are thought fools for that, and equally so for believing that we will rise bodily with the returning Christ in His glorified body. The first meeting will be in the clouds, which signals new spiritual powers for the body, like those that Adam lost and forgot.

A timetable for all of this seems in order, and charts proliferate, but it is sad when believers try to chart the external but do not know how to walk in the Spirit. We are called to see the finish line by faith and to run the race supernaturally now in the Spirit, even while in these mortal bodies. When we look up at the clouds, we know that we are going up into them some day. For now, however, the call is to be fruitful in intercessory callings as the Lord leads, and we are to set our minds on the job at hand of seeing Christ formed in others in the present disturbing world.

April 27

From Eschatology to Identity

Paul does not give the Thessalonians a timetable for the Day of the Lord, saying that they do not need one (1 Thess. 5). This was a young church. Would it develop a more filled-in eschatology chart later? The answer is not given to that, but Paul says that they know "the day of the Lord will come like a thief in the night." Expect the day of the Lord at a time when the world thinks peace has been attained. Then suddenly, like birth travail, destruction will come—but not for the saints. This sounds like the days of Noah—there is a crazy guy hollering flood, but nothing ever happens.

Paul stops there to affirm that the Thessalonians are not living unaware, so as to be surprised by a thief. No, they, and Christians of all ages, keep their focus on evangelization and discipleship in order to build up the family of God, for God is a family man, raising a vast family of sons to manage His universe. These sons get raised in hard times, not good ones, and the fallen world is always a hard time.

Therefore, Paul moves from eschatology to identity teaching. The Day of the Lord is only a fear to those who are not awake to repel the thief. We are awake and not asleep—"sons of light and sons of the day." Light is always the escape, for "God is light" (1 John 1:5).

The sleep metaphor changes from those who have died, to those still alive who live soberly in the light. Paul highlights the armor of God that he expands in Ephesians 6. First mentioned is the breastplate, since attacks come at the heart. The breastplate is "faith and love": faith is to believe, and love overcomes fear (1 Thess. 5:8). Next is the helmet of salvation—believing God's word against appearances.

Rather than not mention the enemy because it would be too frightful, Paul proclaims the armor protecting from the enemy and then exhorts them to live in the completeness of their sanctification, not in wrath consciousness (5:9, 23).

From Revelation to Fellowship

The heart informs the head, as it should, since life is not intellectual, but intellect informed by revelation. The helmet of salvation is "the hope of salvation," not meaning, "I hope it rains today," as if doubt exists, but rather faith that 100 percent patiently expects manifestation of what the inner eye already sees as done (1 Thess. 5:8). Hope is a form of knowing—produced by Christ "who died for us," reminding us that Christ did indeed live as a human, died, and rose to produce His consciousness in us by the Spirit (5:10). He "loved me and gave Himself for me,"—His blood for sins, His life the life lived in us.

This is our encouragement and fellowship, expressing the same, one risen Lord as branches of the same tree. In fellowship with God, we create Spirit flow together. Fellowship began within the Godhead, then quickened among us the sons. Formerly, as members of the devil's world system, no one was to be trusted because self-promotion was assumed, causing suspicion and fleshly comparison. The world is filled with grumbling and complaining about everything. Stimulation from talking about others and their faults is a constant way to drum up energy and create intrigue. Life is a soap opera and a miserable one.

In the Spirit, every son can enjoy completion and fruit bearing in harmony. There is a new attitude. Now, when problems arise, they occasion a new script that begins with rejoicing by faith. Trials and temptations do not feel or look any better, but supernatural gratitude looks at God to say, "What's up Lord?" Rather than being negatively obsessed and defeated in tribulation, a Christian possesses supernatural power to express prayers of faith. Accordingly, we do not "quench the Spirit" (1 Thess. 5:19), implying that the Spirit is ever-present and ever-ready. I often say, "Walking in the Spirit is easy, just excruciating at times." Focus on the ease, the story in the making.

Can You Outrun God?

Faith and rejoicing often seem too hard to do. The devil likes to remain hidden and introduce the thought, "I should have more faith. I should be rejoicing." Thus, a saint might slip into "That's me" and take condemnation—trying to have faith and rejoice, while moving further from both. Stop! How do God's commands always get met? First, let the negative be the negative. It will be anyway.

Then, watch God bring His chosen words or actions out of the nothing and into being, knowing that He is doing just that, while we experience the lag of not enjoying the manifestation just yet. This is the territory of faith's will to inactivity, which is not evil passivity, but means that we wait on the Spirit's doing of what we have already learned is impossible for us to do.

Fran Giles once said to God, "Lord, I don't want to run ahead of You." He replied, "How fast can you run?" We have been studying 1 Thessalonians, and Paul has talked about eschatology, which could leave hearers frantic to run take cover until the world ends. However, he follows up with teaching about our complete sanctification now in negative situations while constantly calling Spirit life into being. This is the deep drive of prophecy—not *what* we do, but *who* it is in us that does it.

The central point is always on an identity level of who Jesus is, then who we are, then how that plays out in us and out to the world. By following teaching on eschatology with teaching on who we are, Paul gives the secret of living a heavenly life in a hellish world. We live by faith and rejoicing. This includes specific words of faith for others that the Spirit brings up in us. Christ, as us, keeps the door open for others to awaken to Christ's salvation.

This is costly because the change comes in us first. Others do not change to suit us; therefore, God takes us through the Cross repeatedly as sacrificial lambs for others to be released.

Now Safe Sons

When two unite, they attach. God attaches through Christ, and a man attaches by receiving. On God's side, the means is the Cross; on the human side, the point is just receiving. Then, two in union receive from each other. God receives our weakness, and we receive God's strength—a match made in heaven. We "hold fast to what is good" (1 Thess. 5:21).

Holding fast implies the function of the human—faith. It is good to exercise faith and be on the receiving end of God's nature, which is the fountain of all manifestations. Peter details these (2 Pet. 1), and Paul catalogues the fruit of the Spirit (Gal. 5). But how easy and refreshing it is to simply say, "Hold fast to what is good," and know that readers will understand that the good is God Himself.

Similar brevity is expressed in the verse, "abstain from every form of evil" (1 Thess. 5:22). The foremost evil is to depart from one's first love, a warning from the ascended Christ to the Ephesian church, which had remained clear on moral evil but had lost its first love (Rev. 2). The first sign is a slight cooling off, which then leads to more focus on law and less on God Himself.

Coldness unchecked can grow when trials hit. God's ways are challenging, and when suffering comes, the devil says, "So you serve a God who lets that happen?" Life is laden with trials, but God is our peace in the midst. My mother-in-law, Mimi, always said to others, no matter what the problem, "God's got you!" It sounded impossible, but extremity demands the impossible—God's everyday fare.

After the Fall, Adam and Eve hid, and people have been hiding ever since. But God pursued His fallen sons to bring them out of bondage with a plan to rescue the whole person—spirit, soul, and body—which is sanctification (1 Thess. 5:23). The whole person is made clean through Christ and restored to taking dominion as a safe son.

The Miracle Life Amid Trials

Life is full of disturbances. The naïve spend their time trying to avoid them or resist them, yet God means disturbances to try our faith and then to invite us to believe for others. "How does this affect me?" leads to, "What are you up to God?" It is natural to feel the impact of trials, and not sinful, but the natural gives way to the super-natural—looking away from self to God. God mirrors back the image of ourselves taking up the Cross for someone, which changes what we want for others.

Initial negative thoughts and feelings about others may not change immediately. This is because the move to faith, and the Spirit's insights, can occur while the negative is at its worst. God is on the Spirit level, so of course He pulls us to stay on that level while the devil is attacking with the aim of inducing choices based on lies, self-for-self, mere emotion, and three-dimensional reason.

Suffering, therefore, is never random. By it, the believer is grounded, and then becomes purposeful for others. It is a lie that suffering is ever random or meaningless. Suffering feels that way, but suffering makes one "worthy of the kingdom of God" (2 Thess. 1:5). When one suffers, God always shines light on a target at which to aim. Focusing on that target feeds our new consciousness, once that consciousness is birthed; and such focus always swallows up obsession about what is painful and an apparent threat to our rest.

In the willingness to say or do nothing, while standing in the misery, knowing that the rescue is there, the rescue will appear as a miracle time and time again. This is not an airy ideal, but a way of life lived supernaturally in the face of all that makes one feel foolish. Anger for justice clamors loudly; however, wrath and vengeance are never the point, only the Cross, which keeps doors open to others, while waiting and enduring as an intercession. Only Christ in us will go that far.

God's Sovereignty

Freedom eventually results in a fixed choice about who Jesus Christ is. It is shocking that God's sovereign plan includes the fixed choice by a number of people to refuse the "gospel of our Lord Jesus" (2 Thess. 1:8). The time will arrive when God will "repay" the rebels with "eternal destruction and exclusion from the presence of the Lord" (1:9). This does not mean that God did not give His all in utmost love to prevent such from happening.

Since Christ is our life, we as Christians love God's enemies and pray for their salvation, wanting their best and leaving to God the Day of Judgment. Those who refuse the gospel exclude themselves from God's presence. It is hard to imagine why anyone would do that, but freedom is freedom, and that is the mystery—that some love darkness.

Our place is to live in the Holy Spirit's meekness and gentleness, seeing others as who they are in Christ or as who they can be if they believe. God takes care of the rest. I must not refuse the gospel because others refuse it, or because of my own ideas about justice. Those ideas turn out to be Satan's ideas, not my own: those ideas are the enemy in disguise as a supposed fair and independent third party who becomes the judge.

God is in control and will achieve every aim of His plan for a new world with a redeemed family made up of those who took Him at His word. They do not say, "God would not really let someone choose against Him and suffer eternal consequences." That is a fearful place of presumption. What they do believe is that God's word is clear and faithful in its warnings—and intended for the well-being of all.

Sons are those who believe and are willing for the Holy Spirit to keep them through terrible times and opposition. This refines faith into gold and equips them to stand against all evil at all times and to reign with Christ in His kingdom.

Fast Forwarding at Times to the End

Rather than discount the intense end times awareness of the early church, it is more accurate to see that the prophets of old and the apostles experienced out-of-time seeing. It only appears like they were wrong about the end being imminent. People bound only in time are wrong. It is not just the early church that has these intense moments of seeing Christ's consummation in history; anyone who is living eternal life is bound to have them periodically.

After the apostles left Thessalonica, believers there got confused about whether the day of the Lord had arrived; thus Paul wrote a second letter to review and further clarify things. A world-wide rebellion will take place that signals the end of the Gospel missionary era, ripening the world for the catastrophic ending that the Bible predicts.

Not only will the rebellion be world-wide, Satan will find his ultimate anti-type to Christ. Just as all of God's love is revealed and summed up in Jesus Christ, Satan's hatred is summed up in the ultimate narcissistic man who will claim that he is God, once divine restraint is removed. This will be the final proclamation of man's independence from God and assertion of himself as God, and will manifest with "pretended signs and wonders" (2 Thess. 2:9).

God's keeping throughout history is implied by mention of the restrainer. Satan's power is so delusional that no one would ever be able to come to the Lord and be saved were it not for God's restraint upon the devil. But when the time comes that refusal of Christ world-wide is unbending, God will give the lost world what it wants, and Satan's delusion will be an intoxication of evil that will parallel the days of Noah.

However, just as Noah had an ark, we do too. God comforts us as we live our daily lives and harvest fruit now. Paul's words after these prophecies are full of comfort, grace, and admonition to avoid sensationalism and idleness. God will take care of the rest (2 Thess. 3).

Evil Cannot Win

Law is simply the way a thing works, and God's nature is self-giving love. Therefore, God's laws are really descriptions of how love works. Even under Mosaic law, love was underneath as the intent, though the people were not ready to see that yet, and therefore law acted as a "tutor" to bring people to Christ (Gal. 3:24). Lawlessness, however, attempts to abolish the law, not fulfill it, but Jesus said that the law does get fulfilled. Lawlessness is not an option, but signals rebellion against God's order. God is God, and man is the creature designed to contain and express God through faith.

Lawlessness denies this, exalting man as God to deny the need for Christ and His Cross. Lawlessness posits a false version of grace, in which it is assumed that a person can invent his own code and God will endorse it. Someday history will reach its peak of lawlessness, and the "man of lawlessness" will appear. Then "the Lord Jesus will slay him with the breath of His mouth and destroy him by His appearing and coming" (2 Thess. 2). Thankfully, when the Day of the Lord comes, there will be "our assembling to meet Him," which means that the Day of the Lord is not an event assigned to believers but to unbelievers.

This does not mean that Christians do not suffer; history is full of martyrs and persecution, but at a certain point, the biblical focus turns to final judgment of the unbelieving world, and therefore Christians are not part of that since they have passed from wrath to life. This came about by being born into Christ by God's Spirit, with Jesus as Lord. As tragic as the world's final rebellion is, as always, the saints keep their eyes on the glory of their savior and His destiny for them as God's heirs for eternity.

Never let it be said that evil wins in any way or diminishes the joy of the saints. Suffering, including daily dying, becomes occasion for praising the Lord for His keeping of us.

Stand Firm in Glory

"God chose you from the beginning to be saved" (2 Thess. 2:13). This is important to know in an evil world. Are we of that world anymore? No. Naturally, a temptation is this: "Am I really God's child, and will I hold up under stress?" Paul's answer is yes: the same God who chose Paul's readers to be saved by faith and kept by the Spirit is still doing the keeping no matter how hard the times.

When swamped by demands, it is tempting to think, "Should I be doing more? Am I giving God good reasons for His choice of me?" Don't try to look at your track record and subtly mesh it with God's reason for choosing a person. God's choice was "from the beginning," meaning that it had nothing to do with works, but simply "sanctification by the Spirit and belief in the truth" (2:13). God does the choosing and saving of those He foreknows will believe. This is the plan that He put His stamp of approval on.

There is no new Gospel that pops up when times are hard. It is the enemy who would like to switch things back to works with evil pressure to start keeping score and discounting the Cross as God's only reckoning. The Cross makes perfect sense to believers because they see it with Christ's indwelling mind, and therefore, they do not give in to an angry world at large bent on self-improvement as the mark of a good person. Non-validation of mere human works and independent goodness apart from Christ's atonement and the Holy Spirit, insults the world's pride and brings on persecution.

Paul knew this well: he had been one of the persecutors. His turnabout was to "obtain the glory of our Lord Jesus Christ" (14). He saw that Christ is the sacrifice bringing man back into the presence of the One above the ark in the most holy place. The end in view is the restoration of God's glory in man. This reverses the Fall. No wonder Paul says, "stand firm."

The Eternal Gospel

Paul was no self-appointed man. He did not awaken one day thinking, "What do I want to become? I think I will be an apostle." God called him to it, starting with his dramatic conversion to see that Jesus Christ rose from the dead and is God, and He dwells in those who believe (Acts 9). This is the cornerstone of the Christian faith. Later, Paul wrote the Galatians letter to a group of churches in the region named Galatia, which today is central Turkey.

In it, the role of Christ is clear; He came because of our sins. There was no other way. If humans could improve themselves, Christ could have stayed in heaven, waiting for us to improve enough for us to cross over to where He is. However, the issue is not just individual sins but the corporate effect, which Paul calls the "present evil age," so there is no help from the world (Gal. 1:3). This means that the Tower of Babel can never be attempted again with success. The earth is drowning in evil, and everyone needs a savior from sins. One must be "rescued" and "delivered."

It is sad when someone gets delivered, lights up in the Spirit, and then falls back in fear. This "astonished" Paul. So great had been the Galatians' joy that Paul could not imagine them reverting to law and the inevitable flesh works that reappear when trying to keep the law. Paul calls it "deserting," meaning turning away from a person, namely Christ (1:6). Suddenly, the Gospel is no longer the Gospel.

Yet, the Gospel is fixed and not subject to change by man or angel. It is eternal, unchanging, and never based on any idea that departs from everyone needing a savior and needing Christ's keeping life within by His Spirit. Any shift from those is founded upon a lie from Satan. Galatians is fierce on this point, unbending. This is the Holy Spirit's severity to keep clear how we are saved, which means being rescued and delivered from sins into Christ's blood and body.

Not According to Man

Paul hated Christianity and tried to wipe it out until struck down by God on the road to Damascus. Then he softened, and his violence against Christ turned into acceptance of Christ as the messiah. No more would Paul be a slave of his own ambition for success among peers. Only Jesus Christ mattered to him now. Instead of trying to be a better Paul in order to please God, he knew that Christ had been revealed in him. No longer would Paul be the one living, but Christ by the Spirit. Whereas Paul formerly could not make a move without conferring with others, he now could accept direct orders from God.

This was so radical that Paul rarely associated with the eleven apostles who walked with Jesus. He learned not to fret over that and to get on with God's commission for him. No doubt he was interested in what others thought, but he was not allowed to get into the loop or worry about that. This took faith. He had it. Eventually he was led to Jerusalem for fifteen days. This was after three quiet years in Arabia. Then fourteen more years after that, the Lord sent him to Jerusalem again. Think of it; the Lord made him spend all that time away from Jerusalem where his whole career had been rooted as a young Jewish leader.

Surprising to Paul, God's plan for him was to the Gentiles. Paul still loved his countrymen though, because he went straight to the synagogue in towns where he traveled. Then, to the horror of the Jews who did not see Christ by the Spirit, he went to the Gentiles and told them too that Jesus was the messiah, using Old Covenant scriptures to prove it. This brought him persecution from the Jews everywhere he traveled.

So much for diplomacy; the Gospel is the point, no matter what others think. Christ came to earth from heaven, became a human, died for our sins, rose again, ascended to heaven, and then came back to live in those who believe. It's quick, it's sharp, it's simple.

It's not What Kind of Vessel, Just That It Is a Vessel

Galatians 1 is tart, and Galatians 2 is just as tart, but it brings out the sweetest of the sweets. Paul has been on his mission to the Gentiles. That might sound ho-hum to us now; who cares about Jews versus Gentiles? However, the lessons run deep because the point is a timeless one about the in-crowd and those stuck on the outside looking in.

This is not an indictment of God for making the Old Covenant exclusive to the Jews; they were His pilot project to prove what any test group would do trying to keep the law. God already knew and spoke through prophets that in Christ the nations would come under the same grace as the test group. The point of the Mosaic group was to show that all have sinned and need a savior. This got perverted into a self-righteous, legalistic view of truth.

The Mosaic Law was designed to produce a nation of people who identified themselves as "chief of sinners"— not seeing themselves better than those not in the test group. This would lead them to Christ, and they would then know God's answer in Christ for all nations. Elitism dies hard, however. Only the Cross cuts us down to nothing in order to see all humans as vessels to contain Christ, not as independent selves to imitate Him. A new test case brought this to the surface when Paul came to Jerusalem with the uncircumcised Gentile, Titus. No one forced circumcision upon Titus, not that he would have accepted it.

Fellowship went well until news came that men sent by James were coming from Jerusalem to Antioch where Peter and Paul were fellowshipping freely with a group of Jewish and non-Jewish Christians. Peter separated from the Gentile Christians, which gave us the setting for Galatians 2:20, which is Paul's proclamation that our identity is solely Christ joined to whatever vessel invites Him in. Christ is the same life and righteousness in any human.

The New Creation You

The reasons people do not accept each other are not simply differences in food, clothes, culture, etc. The point is to see others with Christ's eyes. Therefore, the Bible is not a book of positive thinking or trying to like people's differences, but rather a book about Christ in us—Christ our savior, and then Christ the savior offered to others. We witness to the revelation that God gave the law to prove everyone a transgressor and to make Christ the point. God offers everyone the gift to say, "I am crucified with Christ" because everyone's "old man" (Rom. 6) has to die, so that anyone who believes can be born a "new creation" (2 Cor. 5:17).

The playing field is level for all: Jews, non-Jews, and all distinctions like gender, social standing, and economic class. God sees all believers the same—as vessels now dead to sin and alive to containing Him. Soul and body differences, then, are varied expressions of Christ in supernatural living, for he who is a Christian does not live life; it is Christ who lives it. We might say, "There is only one Christian in the universe, Christ Himself." But He does not like being the only expression of Himself, and so He lives in a variety of soul and body appearances, in which we do live, but wait, it is not we, but He.

This sounds like impossible logic except to the one desperate enough to take it. It is not I, but Christ; yet there is a life I am living in the flesh, yet lived by the faith of Christ—my faith grafted into Christ's faith. His faith takes over as mine. Odd as it sounds, I am most originally me, when I know I am really not I but He. Then I see it as also possible for the person that I was once least likely to accept. What else would bond the most unlikely people together but Christ living in them? This is how you become the real you. When you look to Christ, He mirrors back the new creation man: yours, and anyone who believes.

The Antidote to Foolishness

My mother warned me never to call anyone a fool since Jesus said that a person is in danger of hell for that (Matt. 5:22). The context is a hardened state of anger that no longer sees the image of God in humanity. This is exactly what the devil thinks of humans: "They are fools," which is entirely different from God's view of humans as wonderful vessels to contain Christ. To God, sin is the problem, not the human self. Obviously then, for Paul to say, "O foolish Galatians," he means sin, and sure enough the Galatians had been "bewitched" (Gal. 3).

"Bewitched" connotes witchcraft, which in the Bible is never a good thing. It means an evil spell that turns a person from God to selfish indulgence and rebellion. True, *The Wizard of Oz* has good and bad witches, but the good witches are more like angels in the form of women. In Galatians, Paul plainly means that Satan attempts to deceive people by masquerading in false religion which specializes in seeing litigation as a way to righteousness.

Those practicing witchcraft do not even look or sound like witches except to those who discern in the Spirit. The deception is that the allure looks good, not evil. Trying to keep the law sounds noble and upright. Is that not what a self-respecting person ought to do? But if law can be the answer, why was Christ "publicly portrayed as crucified"? If people can be good, they do not need a savior, and Christ was crucified for nothing. In fact, His crucifixion becomes foolish since His teaching alone would be the point— aiming others to live more from morals and philanthropy.

But just as the spirit of evil is at work through deception, the Holy Spirit is at work in those coming to know who they are in Christ. Christ indwells them by His Spirit, which replaced the enemy's hidden residence in them in their lost condition. Through the Cross, the spirit of error has been expelled, and the Holy Spirit continually speaks of Christ's completed work of cleansing and restoration.

The Promise to Abraham versus Law

Righteousness is very simple and for anyone. Everyone's chance to believe under the New Covenant was hidden in plain sight in God's promise to Abraham. It is all by faith, which everyone has the capacity for because to be human is to be a vessel. The point is receiving. How could Abraham become a father of many nations unless the people of those nations could become sons?

This does not take place by law, for law cannot justify anyone. Those under law are under a curse—exactly what the human race is under apart from grace. To make an A in "Righteousness 101," a student must achieve 100 on all tests. Vessels do not make 100; in fact, they do not score at all. They only *think* they do when still deceived. It is Satan's lie that an independent human self exists that can produce righteousness, for righteousness has never been of human doing. Even when lost people do good works, it is the Lord in them (not in a saving way, however), and their sin is pride if they do not recognize that.

However, God did not leave us under deception's curse because Christ became the curse by being hung on a tree, which was a curse. He took the curse and gave His Spirit in return, which was always the promise. The Galatians, though, had let deceivers confuse them with the false assertion that the Mosaic Covenant was still in force. Galatians 3 reaffirms that the Mosaic Covenant came 430 years after the promise to Abraham and that the Mosaic Covenant was only a temporary "tutor" to expose sin and prepare the world for Christ (Gal. 3:24).

The tutor was given to point out sin, not prevent it, because only faith in Christ's keeping prevents sin. Christ is our righteousness, and it is He who fulfills the promise to Abraham to have offspring that no legal system can procreate. The Mosaic Covenant was applicable only for a season of tutoring and could never abolish the promise to Abraham now fulfilled in Christ.

Christ Is the Seed of Abraham

When God made the promise to Abraham's seed, the word "seed" was singular and really meant Christ Himself (Gal. 3:16). Thus, God made a promise to His Son by making it to Abraham, and no promise made from the Father to the Son can be abolished by a temporary covenant of law, which is only a tutor to point out sin, not prevent it.

God spoke the promise 430 years before the Mosaic Covenant. That promise is the point, irrespective of time. In the Spirit dimension, promises and faith have always been the end in view for bringing people into fellowship with God, regardless of the wait and endurance.

It is good to ask though, "Why was the law given?" In a blinded condition, the assumption is that God gave laws for man to become righteous and gain approval. No one doubts human ability to comply—until getting into the task. That is when alarm sets in for those honest not to bend the rules or lower the minimum passing score (100%). Plus, the rules are a reflection of God's nature.

As love for God increases, frustration and fear increase over not being a right person. His hooks are in the seeker, who must now press through to discover what this is all about. Then comes the shock. Instead of the law being an instrument for improving human behavior, the law suddenly becomes known for what it is—the means by which sin is brought out of its hidden, subconscious recesses and exposed for its controlling, unrelenting dominion over human flesh. The strongest will cannot break it, and no resolution brings one closer to success. The task is impossible.

Further, the law does not cause sin because sin is already present. The law is the mirror that shows it. When someone senses that and fights, what was already there hidden gets stirred up by efforts to resist it. Now, only deliverance will work. The seed, Christ, awakens us to His saving, keeping life in us.

Sons Born of One Seed

The law is not evil just because it stirs up sin. Law was "ordained by angels"—intermediaries then between God and man (Gal. 3:19). The intermediary now is Christ, who makes us one with Himself and His Father by a leap of faith when law has done its work. Angels brought the law to those who saw it optimistically and pledged to keep it, unaware that later it would prove too difficult and unappealing to self-interested self.

The need of an intermediary meant that man was separated from God. Sin and separation go together since sin is the choice to withdraw from God into a supposed state of independence. The problem gets complicated when wanting to close that gap of separation, and the striving human cannot do it. The striving human does not see yet that nothing will work from the human side because only God can remove the separation.

How does this relate to God's promise to the seed of Abraham, the seed being Christ Himself (Gal. 3:16)? Christ would birth a family of sons by first becoming a human being, who was also God, in order to save us, not by teaching that we should imitate Him, but by taking our old man into His body to crucify it and bury it, thus cutting us off from Satan and sin.

Christ did not come to teach man how to imitate concepts and become a son of God. He came as the sacrificed seed so that we could be born anew out of that seed. We are not the old man reformed through teaching and imitation (impossible). The new man is born by resurrection in Christ when Christ was resurrected. We become God's offspring by union with His death, burial, and resurrection. The old man is dead. As faith stands in the new man, the lie falls away. Christ appears—in you. There is the unveiling—in you.

May 14

We're the Sponge and not the Water

Being joined to Christ as one body removes separation and intermediaries since the end in view was oneness with God, which we were created for, and which disappeared at the Fall. The Fall was catastrophic and erased our memory of who we were and the purpose of being created. Creation is always the means of expression for God's glory, but sin brought darkness and the lie of independence.

The Fall called for an intermediary. "Now an intermediary implies more than one; but God is one" (Gal. 3:20). God is one within Himself, and His created beings are intended to be part of that one. However, an intermediary was needed until that got accomplished. When two parties become one, the job ends for the intermediary. Christ is the intermediary who reversed the Fall.

By faith we are one with Christ, partake of Him, and receive His righteousness as our own. We are the sponge and not the water. What is it that you feel though when a wet sponge touches you? The human never disappears! We get swallowed up in a greater glory that is presently hidden in the earthen vessel of a simple sponge. The lost world only sees sponges and their varied sizes, shapes, and colors—always comparing and warring among the sponges based on outer characteristics. But the saints make living water the point and glory in the water, and then marvel at the variety of sponges.

Sponges without water are only arrogant sponge comparers, whereas the saints enjoy not only the water but then also all the wonderful qualities of being a sponge. We die to being just a sponge because there is no point to a sponge if there is no water. Yet the sponge is vital because water needs an applicator, and the sponge works perfectly. It is the perfect sponge. Thus our humanity never disappears; it just takes on oneness with God thanks to Christ the intermediary. This is the good news of the Gospel and our completion, which we discover by faith.

Promise Fulfills Law

The Mosaic Law did not overturn the Abrahamic promise because God eternally had the promise in view, and the law could not overturn the promise but instead conditioned people for it. Just as a seed cannot grow without soil, God's promise needs hearts that grasp it, and this must come from desire produced in us by failure. This is where the law is our friend even though we cannot keep it. The law is holy but cannot produce righteousness in us because the law is not life but law (Rom. 7:12). Yet, because the law mirrors God's nature, it is holy. God Himself does not live by law but simply used it to describe His being for man, by types and foreshadowing, that led up to the manifestation of His only begotten son, Jesus Christ.

God's plan is that in our failure to keep the law, we would seek the life of the one who is the law. In order for God to get sons, all had to be consigned to sin, and that is what the law did in order to tear away Satan's deception that there can exist an independent self that is able to fulfill it. The rebellion against this truth is violent. No wonder the lost world loves scientific theories based only on materialism and random occurrence, viewing man as just an animal who lucked up enough to rule over the other animals. No wonder it is popular to seek the answers for all of man's problems in brain chemistry.

But if we live in a universe of accountability transcending the material, and which calls for submission to a creator, the picture is different: it is critical to know the meaning of the Fall and sin—our separation from God apart from the Cross. Until the Cross, the law kept us "confined" and "under restraint" because history awaited one who would forgive our sins and fulfill in us everything that the law cannot do, holy as it is (Gal. 3:23). Christ is not a model to imitate; He "is our life" (Col. 3:4).

Tutors and Custodians

"But before faith came, we were kept in custody under the law…the law has become our tutor" (3:23-24). Brett Burrowes pointed me to research showing that a tutor back then meant a servant who got the child in his charge to all of the child's lessons and appointments and oversaw the child's safety. The law does this; it gets us to every lesson in life that teaches us what we cannot do, so that we are ready for the real teacher—Christ in us.

As to custodian, the idea is like saying, "So and so was taken into custody yesterday and arraigned at the jail." This is severe and by the letter of the law in justice, so there is nothing improper about the law taking all men into custody. The friendlier side is that God wants to show mercy and not only justice. Accordingly, the law must hold you bound and guilty until an inner transformation can make you a safe citizen to walk the streets of the kingdom.

The same is true when custodian implies parenting and guardianship of someone not transformed yet inwardly. Knowing one's self as a safe son requires a new birth, a supernatural birth, whereby God produces a son, even a family of sons, by His own nature being implanted.

Who are we? We are not just ourselves, but the union of Christ and the self. This is two as one, quite different from the world's endless categories for measurement in comparison with others. In the world, achievement is relative to one's peers: "I did this; I did that. Therefore, I have an identity." This identity needs authenticating by others who notice, and Satan is the author and producer of all that.

In Christ, identity is automatic—supernatural and imparted, and accountable only to one. God certainly speaks to us by others, but they do not constitute our identity. Further, nothing of the past identity remains because the resurrected self in Christ is not a repaired old self, but a new created self, authenticated by the Spirit.

The Sons of God

Our identity is simple: "for in Christ Jesus you are all sons of God by faith" (Gal. 3:26). How is this true? Union starts with Christ's death. No one jumps into Christ's body on His resurrected side without having first jumped into His body on the death side. I like to say that God unzipped Christ's body on the Cross, put us inside, and then zipped Christ back up. Therefore, everything He went through included us in Him. Thus we are sons of God through faith, and His identity is now ours. True, we are created beings, never the infinite God or the source of holiness; but we are now one with God through Christ in union whereby all that He is, we are, each and every son. Though differing in gifts, all gifts come from the same Spirit.

This fulfills God's promise to Abraham to be a father of many nations by faith. Paul has explained that the seed of Abraham is Christ Himself, linking us to Christ and making union with Him the point (Gal. 3:16). That link points *us* to faith like Abraham's: "faith was credited to Abraham as righteousness." He was reckoned righteous even when he was still uncircumcised (Rom. 4:9-10). A Christian, therefore, inherits the promise made to Abraham, but made also to Christ. No wonder when *we* believe, we too are then sons of God and offspring of Abraham's seed—Christ.

Being a son of God makes one an heir. A son is an heir, and the distinction is not between those born of the parent and those not born of the parent, for to be a Christian means to be born of the parent. The modern world's definition of adoption implies heirs not born of the adopting parents, but in the Bible, adoption *does* mean being born of God through Christ the seed and from the womb of "our mother" (Gal. 4:26). To be joined to Christ is a union so deep and complete that heaven does not question our sonship. Only the devil does.

From Elemental Spirits to the Holy Spirit

Satan likes to create doubt about our son-ship in order to stir up fear to trouble our assurance—sending waves of condemnation concerning every thought and feeling, trying to convince us that our flesh impulses mean that flesh dominates us rather than Spirit. That is what it means that we were under "the elemental spirits of the universe" (Gal. 4:3). This phrase has numerous translations, but the idea behind them is basically the same. The word *elements* suggests something basic—the external world of matter and the fight to survive based on how-to thinking. We could just call it flesh—trying to cope in the natural world of the five senses. How do we get food and clothes? How do we get property and set up a social grid? These are the basic questions, along with how to protect ourselves and stay healthy. All of this is elemental: psychology, sociology, politics, science, and religion to name a few.

God knew the human propensity in the Fall to set up self-managing systems, and so He initiated the system He wanted by giving the law until the elemental things wear out and depress the heirs so much that they are ready for faith and adoption as sons. Then "God sent forth His Son, born of a woman, born under the law, so that we might receive adoption as sons" (Gal. 4:4).

Galatians affirms our adoption by the Spirit; our cry of "Abba Father" witnesses to that. Adoption in the Bible is not the weak, modern concept of taking into one's family a child not born of the adopting family. For one thing, we *are* born "of God" (John 1:13). We have the Spirit for the very reason that we *are* sons. Thus, we no longer interpret the world by all the external elements from the days when Satan hid behind purely materialistic and intellectual world views.

The Spirit speaks to the inner man, causing us to know truth and the personhood of God. We see Him through the external world even when others see only the world.

We Are Known by God

We were never free in our lost life like we thought. "You were in bondage to beings that by nature are no gods" (Gal. 4:8). It is easy to posit that "elemental spirits" in verse 3 and "beings" in verse 8 suggest demons, but Paul does not come out and say that like he does in chapters two and six of Ephesians. The *Oxford Annotated RSV* notes say a better translation would be "rudimentary notions of the world," and some translations take the approach of notions or principles, while others make the idea sound like beings. So what *is* going on?

The Galatians had been pagans, mostly polytheists. Monotheism was not the norm. Therefore, Paul reminds them that they used to worship gods that do not even exist, fabricated beings, with worship rules and rituals for these supposed deities, who are not really gods after all. Therefore, Paul does not take occasion in Galatians to explain that evil spirits are real and that Satan and demons are behind polytheistic worship because his point is to focus on their bondage to fantasies with rigid rules. For the deities to be proved nonexistent implies that the system of worship associated with them amounts to nothing.

Yet the pagan systems had common ground with the Jewish system, in that both were systems. No matter what religion is in view, whether the Old Covenant given by God or the false and pagan systems, the common denominator for perpetuating the lie is the efforts of the worshipper to placate God or the perceived god by independent self-effort.

This is the lie, and it originates with Satan. Reality is coming to know God, and Paul adds, "or rather to be known by God." We are not tiny, inconsequential specks in an impersonal universe. God is warm and personal—approachable and freeing us from every fear. Our religion is Christ Himself.

May 20

Imitate Faith, not Behavior

The Galatians had reveled in the joyous freedom of knowing God and being known by Him, but something chilled their experience of God. They fell back under the law that Christ had fulfilled and made unnecessary by sending the Spirit. The hook used to deceive was simple. Pagan forms of their former religion had rituals and calendars, as did the Mosaic Law—something other than dying and rising in Christ in order to experience eternal life.

True, the Galatians were not going back to a pagan deity, but they were getting pulled back into a system of doctrine and rituals, and the deceivers even had the appeal of saying that the one and only God, the true God, gave that system, which in fact God did give, but He gave it that sin might run rampant (Rom. 5:20).

Misunderstanding the purpose of the law is how controlling groups get started. A leader who lives by the Spirit lives out a legacy of faith that later, under legalists, gets "bewitched" into a system of compliance. Joy evaporates. This is the deception that the devil always uses, putting the burden back on the believer in a way other than looking away from self to Christ. The focus subtly becomes, "How am I doing?" instead of a new birth, with its energizing and guidance by the Spirit of God. No system can match that.

Paul wants us to become as he was. We start by thinking this means external imitation, mimicking behavior. Behavior, however, comes from within, which is the secret. No matter how much a person tries to bend behavior in conformity to a standard or to an admired person's life, all will eventually revert to what, or who rather, is inside.

The desperate ones know who is inside—Christ. And they know how He operates in us—by the Spirit. You cannot guess how He will be by you, but by looking unto the Spirit, a man sees it and walks in the miracle that is beyond flesh possibility.

The Real Fire

Paul says, "become as I am" (Gal. 4:12). The "I am" echoes Moses at the burning bush when God tells Moses the divine name. The "I am" also goes back to Jesus saying, "Before Abraham was, I am." Experts in the law wanted to kill Jesus for making Himself equal with God.

Paul of course is not making himself God or equal to God, yet he is doing something radical. He is saying that he has Christ formed in him and thus is the human expression of Christ by virtue of union with Christ. Union implies two joined, and so when Christ is formed in a person, that person becomes the expression of the greater part of the union.

The greater part of the union condescends to take on expression as the weaker form. Fire and iron provide the perfect example, because to dip an iron tool into fire gives the iron new manifestation. The iron glows with fire that is not its own but is now its manifest property by virtue of union with fire. To be a Christian is union with Holy Spirit fire even though our outer earthly form does not appear as it will in eternity.

Our present, weak humanity hides the radiance, but there is a quickening to the body even in this life because of the inner radiance that never fades. The Galatians had seen this. Paul had an illness when he visited, but despite his ill body and lack of glorious appearance, they caught who he was—and consequently who they were as well, and who every Christian really is.

Their joy had been unspeakable, and they would have plucked out their eyes and given them to Paul, thinking such to be poor payment for what he had transmitted to them. They had even received him as an angel—wait, more than that—as Christ Jesus. They had seen that God's purpose is to incarnate Himself in a family of sons.

The Galatians are enticed back to the supposed safety of independence, so Paul calls them back to the real fire.

The Point is not Natural but Supernatural

The Galatians were afraid that they had gone too far with liberty, but they had not gone far enough, because the real point is to know the human self as a container existing only to be filled with Christ. When one sees this, Christ is formed in that person. Constitutionally, there is no change, but there is transformation by the Spirit. The knowing of union permeates until it is seen as the normal state.

It is not the normal state to think of one's self as independent. That is Satan's consciousness of trying to keep standards to imitate perfection and arrive at self-operating holiness. The biblical norm is to see what God showed Moses at the burning bush, that humanity is His lowly, humble bush, and that He the Lord is the glory who creates the mystery of union with God through Christ.

No wonder Paul was disturbed over the Galatians, who had traded oneness with the Spirit of God for works and self-glory. Nothing snuffs the light and kills the fire faster than that. Watching this happen led Paul to review Abraham with them. Abraham was waiting for the son that God promised years earlier, but it was not happening.

Then Sarah all but throws Hagar into his arms to sire a son that will fulfill the promise, and Abraham goes, "Uh...er...well...that must be the plan." It is all entirely natural, and that is the problem. God never intended the miracle to be, after so much elapsed time, that Abraham and Sarah would concoct the scheme that Hagar should be the new wife and the promised womb for Abraham's seed—the seed that would bless the world and make the angels sing. Simply put, Ishmael was "born according to the flesh."

However, when God wants to signify what the new creation means, the new birth cannot happen except by divine insemination and birthing from a *heavenly* womb, making the supernatural the point, no matter how long it takes or how strange it looks.

Ishmael and Isaac

Ishmael was born according to the flesh (Gal. 4:23). But so is everyone born of Adam. Thus, Hagar representing birth into slavery is simply an illustration of what Romans 5:12 says about everyone except Jesus. Every baby is born of Adam except Jesus, who was miraculously conceived. For everyone else, procreation goes along normally: man meets woman, they mate, and they bear a child together.

Isaac was a type of Christ's birth and the birth of those born again. Though born of Adam, Isaac was a supernaturally produced baby. This set him apart from Ishmael, who was born the normal fleshly way without miraculous intervention. Ismael, however, is not reason to discriminate since the whole world from the Fall has been of Ishmael, representing Adam's slavery to sin, and ours therefore. The only exit out of sin's bondage is the new birth by becoming a son of God through Christ.

Isaac represented son-ship impossible apart from divine birthing to deliver us from Adam's Fall. It had to be a shock for Jews to read Galatians and find that Paul compared them to Hagar and Ishmael: "Now Hagar is Mount Sinai in Arabia, and she corresponds to the present Jerusalem; she is in slavery with her children" (Gal. 4:25). That is as blunt, offensive, and far from the Jewish mindset as a statement could be. However, it is also the same thing intended when preachers insist that many church-attending people are not really born again but just religious.

The whole, external church system can only be an external womb for the external worshipper who does not worship in spirit and in truth. Sanctuaries, programs, and curriculums are fine, but they are not the womb for the new birth—just as the hospital building cannot heal the sick. Externals can only point to the womb for the new birth— the same womb that quickened barren Sarah, and the womb that bears the sons of God through Christ the seed.

The Divine Womb

To be born again, we need a mother. Yes, that's right, we need a mother, and it should be no mystery that if there is an eternal Father and His only begotten Son, there should be a mother as well. She is the Jerusalem above, and Paul quotes Isaiah 54 to show the lament of the divine mother who cannot bear Her miraculous children apart from the seed, which Paul has said is Christ Himself.

So the divine womb has been in lament until the promised day of the fully revealed and activated seed, Christ, who could cause Her womb to bear, producing then a city of created sons to populate the New Jerusalem.

No wonder we had to be crucified in Christ, buried in Him, and raised in Him to be who we are. Resurrection is the miracle of the new birth, apart from which a man remains in the lie of being only a mere man—still lost, still a slave of flesh and law, and still a son of the devil.

No wonder Abraham had to cast out the slave son. Again, this looks like discrimination against Ishmael, but remember that Paul has just said that the Old Covenant Jew who did not move to faith was Ishmael, with further implication that anyone who is lost is Ishmael. Anyone who is not born from above is Ishmael.

Only in the final disillusionment with self, does anyone drop religion and move to a new birth. The whole world, every single person, is invited to do just that. Will everyone accept? No, but all are invited, so there is no discrimination; yet the mystery of freedom is that only those who receive Jesus Christ for who He says that He is— creator, lord, and savior—can be born again.

It is no surprise to cast out the slave son then. We cast out the old man when we become the new man. This means agreeing that the old man was crucified in Christ and died. That is casting him out. Our union with Christ is the new man.

Freedom False and True

See who the new man is and get on with him, which is to say our union with the ascended Christ who now lives in His people on the earth. These are the sons and the rulers that God is forging for the real new age, not the phony new age we have seen the last fifty years. That is a false version of the new age, a Cross-less one. The real new age is coming soon, and it is already here in hidden form. One day, when all is ready, the curtain will rise on the manifestation of the new age, and all remnants of the old will be the chaff, blown away and burned. We will not care because we are all about the new.

The genuine new age is rooted in freedom—not, however, the false political freedom that never frees because it is external and sees man as able to reform himself without Christ. That freedom cannot endure ill treatment without bitterness and vengeance, whereas true freedom comes with a cost—relinquishing bitterness and vengeance because they are not Christ, and therefore not the new man.

We were set free, to be free and to stay free. The implication is that freedom can be lost. That sounds odd. Does not freedom mean the free choice that everyone has all the time? It should, but think of addiction: people lose their freedom in many ways, not being able then to control themselves. That is why Paul says, "The good I would do I do not do" in Romans Chapter 7. Slaves of sin are not free.

So actually, we were not always free. When we did not know Christ, we were not free to do righteousness. When we do know Him, we are free not to sin. The reason is that we live by an inner controller, not us: "Christ has set you free" (5:1). A person sets me free—the only free person there is. To be free and live freely, a man must know this person and be united to Him—the only truly self-for-others person.

May 26

New Covenant Circumcision

Christians who do not understand Galatians 2 and Romans 6 might dismiss circumcision from being a spiritual issue, seeing it as only a health consideration. They think circumcision is superseded by the New Covenant and not spiritually relevant now.

To a Jew, however, circumcision remains a mandate: Abraham was circumcised, and the Law of Moses 430 years later preserved circumcision. The thought of not circumcising a male brings terrified feelings since under the Law, that male is cut off from Israel. This thought is so deeply implanted that only a new, radical thought can or should lead a Jew to ignore circumcision.

Paul gives us that radical understanding when he says that true circumcision is "the removal of the body of the flesh." He also says that Christians have "been buried with Him in baptism," signifying death (Col. 2:11-12). Being crucified with Christ is the New Covenant circumcision, as well as baptism. Apart from crucifixion with Christ, a person is cut off from the people of God.

It might seem odd that the death of the old man is New Covenant circumcision, but the connection to Abraham's circumcision means our inability to produce spiritual fruit by natural means. Abraham's flesh had to be cut off for Isaac to be born, but Abraham was spared the full implycation of circumcision because total circumcision would have meant mutilation (Gal. 5:12). This would have ended Abraham's conjugal life with Sarah.

Circumcision did make the point, though, that Isaac was to be a supernaturally produced child and a type of the new birth, not by Abraham's flesh or Sarah's barren womb, but by the Spirit's conception. Similarly, one becomes a Christian by death first, in being crucified with Christ. The old man dies, and in Christ, the new man is born. This is the key that unlocks circumcision and baptism once and for all.

Rituals and Salvation

The Galatians "were running well" until intruders influenced them back to rituals that had no meaning since being fulfilled in Christ (5:7). It was not that physical circumcision automatically meant going back to law; Paul circumcised Timothy in order to avoid unnecessary controversy (Acts 16: 3). However, Paul refused to make that concession when Titus, a Greek, accompanied him to Jerusalem (Gal. 2:3). The issue is not a ritual, but whether or not a ritual is considered essential to salvation.

Salvation is Christ plus nothing; that is our faith. No ritual or work can add to Christ's atonement. The tiniest concession to add something to Christ is the "little leaven" that "leavens the whole lump" (5:9). What enters the lump works its way through it all. Diluting the Cross by adding a ritual negates it, bringing a curse. It might not manifest immediately, but the seeds of turning one's focus back onto self are there. The Cross is a stumbling block, and it is meant to be, and meant to stand complete.

Paul's thought on practitioners who insisted on circumcision was that they did not understand the real idea behind circumcision as cutting off of the whole male genitalia and not just the nonessential skin. Who would opt for that? The idea was emasculation, and God was merciful in making only the foreskin the target in order to say to man, "Flesh life cannot produce Spirit life."

The thinking behind circumcision is alive and well today in other rituals born of the hope that the old man does not have to die and that modest cutting away of excesses or a programmed change of behavior will suffice. It is the idea that man's problem is only in mistakes needing fixing, and that a man can correct them. Yes, circumcision is alive today—the hope that man is good enough underneath and does not need the whole person to die and be resurrected in Christ.

Freedom: What It Is and What It Isn't

Freedom at root seems mystical because who really knows the mystery of choice and why? Facing the same situation, one person makes an upward choice in faith, and another makes a downward choice to despair. In Christ, God has unlocked the gates of bondage for us to be able to choose faith now, or else freedom would be forever lost to us in our darkness, with no escape possible. That is the deepest mystery of sin—that no one can escape it without God's hand having opened the possibility of salvation because of Christ's sacrifice.

This is why freedom does not work on a national or governmental level authored by man. That can only lead eventually into another Tower of Babel unless freedom is rooted in Christ. The documents of freedom are only as good as the person of freedom, and the only person who is free is Jesus Christ. When freedom is defined as the rights of man as intrinsic to man but not rooted in the image of God in man, freedom turns into selfish disaster. Democracy becomes the rule of "I have the right to do anything that I want. My life belongs to me." The focus turns into a wheel of self-centeredness and greed, and nothing is off-limits "as long as it doesn't hurt others." There indeed is the biggest fallacy of all.

Galatians tells us not to use freedom as "an opportunity for the flesh" (Gal. 5:13). Freedom is not permission for all thoughts and feelings to rush into manifestation. The person in bondage to impulse life is animalistic, wanting to fit in with fallen nature. Underneath the fallen version of human dignity and freedom is the deadly determination, "I will have my way no matter what."

However, true freedom is submission to Spirit control, even when every impulse and urge screams otherwise. This is love, which is self-for-others and sacrifices itself, which is really Christ in us doing that.

When It Feels Hard to Love

Love serves others, asking the question, "What is truly best for that other person?" Love also says, "If I must suffer to see it come about, I am willing, or, if necessary, willing to be made willing." God reveals that others are not different as human beings, just different in their God-made variety of human expression—created to be the expression of the one Spirit of God. Since all are vessels to contain and express God, in that sense all are the same, so now I love my neighbor as myself.

It matters not if you do not start by feeling like you love your neighbor as yourself. Living in a Satan-soaked world means constant temptation not to love your neighbor as yourself. This brings the will into play according to faith, and in the Spirit's freedom, you can walk in the Spirit even when flesh screams out in opposition.

Feelings and thoughts of opposition have been taken by many to imply an old nature, meaning that a Christian is still more beast than saint. This idea has done much harm to the church, leading people to take their eyes off of the one in them who is their life and put their eyes on flesh as if flesh is independent and therefore our identity. This is Satan's lie, diverting people from the truth that it is entirely normal for a Christian to go through the day with countless disturbing thoughts and feelings and yet say, "These are not me, and Lord, You *are* keeping me."

The truth is that any Christian can move on and not obsess over flesh-level reactions. Peace lies quietly underneath the constant bombardment of the enemy, and negatives get recognized for what they are—opportunities for faith. In every situation, you move forward by all of Christ in all of you. This sounds impossible because the self is too weak and failing for this. Ah, but Christ is the 100 percent keeper.

Easter and the Living Water

Not to recognize freedom in the Spirit to detach from evil inclinations is to lock one's self into an endless pattern of selfish behavior and attitudes. To miss real freedom is to "bite and devour one another" (Gal. 5:15). We are delivered from this. Christ is not remotely lodged in a Christian somewhere like a broom in a closet or a jewel in a safe. Christ is the everyday everything.

The Holy Spirit's job is to manifest Christ as you and send forth nonstop living water. Often, God uses common objects to illustrate a universal. One Easter morning I was watering the many new shrubs, an hour-long task. It seemed dreary, pulling the hose all around the house, then holding it over each thirsty shrub.

Standing and holding a hose was boring, but after half an hour, I started to notice and enjoy the pleasant sun overhead and the redbuds on the street. Unexpectedly, the hose seemed like part of me, with the steady, rhythmic flow of water catching me up in its mystery. It is the glimpse of water, running water, with its flowing and helpless availability, its outgoing function to bless others.

Suddenly, watering the shrubs was the resurrection of spring—the hose now an extension of a person: "Out of your belly shall flow rivers of living water" (John 7:38). How simple, how obvious. Norman Grubb often told the story of how at first this seemed impossible, so he told the Lord, "I'll settle for a muddy trickle." That was his start, and the rivers came.

Life is built upon opposites. First comes dryness: "I am dry and unable." Great! It is only a feeling, but if believed as truth, it turns into a lie and a false consciousness of need unfulfilled. However, faith agrees that the hose is on and the water is running. Every day is Easter's watering of dry ground. It is yours.

Spirit Trumps Flesh Insecurities

Simplicity in the Christian life is summed up by "walk in the Spirit" (Gal. 5:16). To walk in the Spirit is to express the nature of the Spirit, whose nature cannot be manufactured by any human and was never meant to be, since we are first and foremost the sponge and not the water.

God did not design life to mean dry sponges resisting toxic fluids. That would be self-effort, and will power eventually gives out. The way is by walking in the Spirit—the living water—and this is by faith, which always means taking what is available and desirable. Remain plunged into the Spirit, and nothing can invade you.

Faith is basically what I immerse myself in and take into myself. What a generous offer God made to give His Spirit by Christ's resurrection and ascension. He canceled out our debt and opened the gate of faith that we might be quickened by the Spirit to receive the Spirit, in which we may now walk freely, even when not comfortable to do so.

The opposite of walking in the Spirit is to leave one's members available for flesh-level use, which invites the enemy to retain the very power that the Cross canceled. Flesh is not just mere flesh, but always the expresser of an agent. Our human bodies are mortal for a season, but the Spirit quickens them to be instruments of righteousness, making the real tragedy not physical death, but letting sin have any dominion over the body. This can only happen by resisting the Spirit, which leads to the various sins catalogued in Galatians 5.

The sins listed there are the inevitable consequences of not walking in the Spirit. Apart from the Spirit, one can only default to satanic control, because self-control is the Spirit's fruit and not the false pride of supposed human discipline. Such pride is Satan's scheme for dealing with what the world calls "our insecurities." God calls us to look at His securities, namely His nature and promises. When feeling insecure, leap to His security.

June 1

A Little Discernment Goes a Long Way

Given the misery of breakdowns between people, no wonder the works of the flesh include drunkenness and carousing (Gal. 5:21). If you cannot get along, get drunk. If you cannot get along, have a party. No one is exempt from this; all have been in bondage to the works of the flesh. That is why we need a savior.

The Spirit is the rescue—but not offered as a luxury feature on an otherwise good appliance. Sometimes when I talk about the Spirit, people react like I am talking about dashboard options in a car, or yet more links on a web page. The Spirit is hardly that optional. Without the Spirit, flesh will prevail. It is as certain as death—in fact, death's preview of an eternity that you do not want.

Seeing flesh level living as over—what Paul calls "putting off the old man"—means arriving at certainty that flesh level living holds no hope for anything but the same consequences. On the way to this certainty, we all try to blend flesh and Spirit, which really turns out to be flesh since the two do not mix. We all try that. It is good to hit bottom and see Spirit life as the only life.

We feel like flesh most of the time, at least in the background. When we do not discern soul and spirit, flesh feels like it is in the foreground—like it is all that there is. Once we see Hebrews 4:12, all the bombardment can safely drop into the background as we walk in the knowing of another dimension—the Spirit.

Plainly, the Bible does not incriminate emotions and thoughts in and of themselves. Everything is determined by intent, so a lot goes on in the background that by faith never comes to fruition, and thank God for that, for we would all get locked up in an asylum. It does not matter that I feel like I am going crazy as long as I know that I am not; and I know that I am not because I know that I am kept. It is a fine line, but I do not mind walking it.

Fork in the Road

The fruit of the Spirit and the works of the flesh do not overlap, having nothing in common. Therefore, no one can be a citizen of both realms. The question is, "Where is your citizenship?" It only makes sense to believe and live where one's citizenship is. Therefore, to live a life bobbing back and forth from Spirit to flesh, when those are mutually exclusive and at war, ignores the fact of no gray area where warring parties can have tea and find common ground.

The only common ground is that we are human, and everyone suffers. How suffering is processed makes all the difference. When Adam fell, he did not want final separation from God but wanted his own way while still keeping a connection with God. This pattern is reenacted in rebellious children, who test out the dark side but never really let their parents go. If they do not harden themselves against the Cross, they will swing back and eventually see that the old man died in Christ, recognizing the works of the flesh to be a lie that they falsely gave power to before a steady walk in the Spirit by faith.

It can take a long time. Carnality has to prove its devastation convincingly enough for one to let it go. It is then recognized as false hope for relieving suffering, and God's way starts to look sweeter, more stable, and more delightful. We walk with God in our spirits now, having entered into rest by means of the new creation. And although we are mortal in body, there is a quickening in the body (Rom. 8), which is now "washed with pure water" (Heb. 10:22).

The answer is as simple as accepting the completeness of Christ's work, which makes us "partakers of the divine nature" (2 Pet. 1:4). We give up the false tree—wanting our own interpretation of things—and we eat of the tree of life. It never feels like the old man died, but this is where, as always, faith is the key. You are who God says you are, not anything else.

Reckoning on Joy

Joy can sound elusive, like happiness. The Bible does not fault happiness, but joy is the prize. Because of Adam's fall, happiness became our shallow pursuit—feeling good so that depression and despair hopefully never occur, or at least do not take hold. Positive thinking in a merely human way became the substitute for supernatural joy.

Joy is supernatural. It derives from the Holy Spirit and not from circumstances. James tells us to count it all joy when we fall into various trials and temptations, which sounds contradictory, but joy comes from reckoning it by faith. James, our psychiatrist apostle, says that negatives lead us to say, "God, what are You up to?" The one asking does not understand what God is up to but knows that God is up to something. Negatives are the necessary intercession on our part to bring Christ's life through us in specific ways to manifest God's love. Nothing goes to waste.

Counting a thing joy does not make it feel pleasurable. Agony and excruciating things occur, yet the Spirit quickens receptive faith into agreeing with God, "Yes, I choose to count this as all joy." Reckoning is a calculated step into the gift of more faith, and it likely happens through gritted teeth—or overwhelming feelings that appear impossible to cope with. Thoughts may run mad while the devil adds the incessant hammering of accusation and condemnation. Nonetheless, the capacity to reckon on joy is undefeatable.

This is because joy is not a human property. It is divine. My wife Tandy was in a Bible study discussing the fruit of the Spirit. People in it shared their efforts to imitate Jesus and thus show forth the Spirit's fruit. Perplexed, Tandy said, "But the fruit of the Spirit is the Spirit. You might as well try to be like an orange, but you are not an orange. An orange is an orange." They thought she was a little weird since they did not see yet that to manifest the Spirit's fruit, one walks in the Spirit, and the Spirit *is* the fruit, by faith, as you.

Peace That Passes Understanding

Thoughts about peace follow one of two tracks. One track works to obtain outer agreement, negotiating to get everyone in accord. The other track works from the inside, knowing that by faith peace is possible in a person's heart even when it is lacking in others around. This sounds like indifference to arriving at agreement, but consider the angels who told poor shepherds 2000 years ago about the origin of peace. It is the Prince of Peace, and only as He wins one heart at a time does peace multiply on the earth.

Peace is not coexistence and non-aggression with unresolved, seething hatred underneath. Eventually, pressure will expose held-in, unresolved beliefs and manifest a spirit level crisis. This does not mean that negative emotions or distressing thoughts have to win finally. Those come from soul/body and are tied to the temptation to believe that what one feels and reasons is what one is. The Spirit man knows that feelings of hatred are resolved, even at excruciating levels, by affirming peace within as the constant fruit of the Holy Spirit. Peace, therefore, is not absent because of constant negatives.

Peace is so otherworldly and such a gift of grace that it cannot be understood. In Philippians, Paul calls it the "peace that passes all understanding" (4:7). It defies human possibility for peace in one's heart, but there it is. How can that be? It is supernatural and not derived from the self but is the gift and manifestation of Jesus Christ by His Spirit. This is the same peace that Jesus promised to the disciples: "My peace I give unto you, not as the world gives" (John 14:27).

Peace is a miracle. Peace based on external circumstances will never arrive, for the Gospel is the simple truth of Christ living in vessels of clay in a world filled with strife. Believers do not pretend that the strife is not there, but neither are they bound by it. Union with Christ is always intimate and personal and in the moment.

Patience Means Waiting

The word *patience* can evoke the response, "Oh no," implying that things are not going the desired way. This causes negative emotions and thoughts, and probably waiting, with its lack of present gratification. It might mean the appearance of unmet needs, people acting in a way that we do not like, supplies not visibly at hand, or even mistreatment that shows no signs of abating. It also raises the question, "Why does God not do something about this?"

Waiting wakes a person up to not being in control. The world appears to be out of control, but God's sovereignty is not in question even when He honors freedom of choice and chaos is everywhere. God is still the architect of exactly the plan that He purposes and will complete, yet He must endure the contradiction of sin and the freedom of the creation to persist in sin.

For those no longer in the kingdom of sin, waiting means patience. To one still in the kingdom of sin, patience gets scrapped, and God's script is replaced with a self-devised one. The person enslaved by impatience (Satan's nature) moves into sin to speed things up. However, if one shuns sin, he accepts a God-engineered script beyond human capacities. For example, one common script is when God corners a person into marital woes. The easy, flesh answer would be divorce, adultery, or pornography. Anger rises up in justification: "What about my needs and rights?" God is more concerned in showing how the Cross cancelled the need consciousness behind flesh-level responses to those woes.

With need-consciousness, nothing ever satisfies since to put an external object in an internal place never works. What if life means living alone with only a Bible and the Holy Spirit, providing opportunity to believe that you are complete in Christ even in the worst of woes? This is miraculous contentment and from above, not of the earth.

June 6

Waiting and Enduring Are Normal in the Spirit

God has His way of getting the template of waiting and enduring stamped into our core, and they are the hallmarks of Christ in us, the hope of glory. Waiting can be merely annoying or it can be excruciating and protracted.

To embrace the pain and set one's eyes upon the Lord Jesus Christ makes the difference between falling back into anger and depression, or rising up into the light with praise and thanksgiving. God is not as concerned with the evil that is causing pain as He is with how we process the pain in faith.

Seeing with a single eye means that our bodies are full of light as Jesus said (Matt. 6:22). The single eye sees evil for what it is—evil; but rises above that and sees through evil to trust God's redemptive purpose. The details and intensity of the evil are not the real point. The point is that God will use the situation to manifest His love in a costly way.

Escaping the mire of time and circumstance takes a rescue by that which is beyond human. It must come from God. No wonder the Bible calls us vessels of the Spirit. He is the patient one, not we. The Spirit makes the patience of God real while we wait and endure—which is really He in us waiting and enduring. The process begins to disclose redemptive purposes of God that He manifests by intercessors who say, "I will go." The going may be where you already are and mean refusal to take less than victory on the spot of the floor where you are standing.

The devil appears to be in possession of that spot, and the assault of darkness feels insurmountable. Then comes the question, "Can you see this as a momentary light affliction that is working a greater glory?" Hold fast your word of faith while living one day at a time through the single eye. Waiting and enduring become daily friends, no longer resisted; and time and suffering fall into the background of God's perfect plan.

Kindness

Kindness is in how we treat people. The self-centered person does not notice others except as objects to use. For him, giving is calculated merely for gain. It is grievous when lack of kindness hardens into insensitivity that no longer thinks, "I know to be kind to that person but choose not to." It becomes blind to itself, barreling along unaware of its lack of concern for others.

Kindness means taking note of a neighbor. It could be in any situation (for unless a man is in solitude, he regularly has a neighbor at hand). The Spirit leads us to a need or occasion that kindness can notice. The point is, "Do you exist as a distinct human being on my map?" And—"Am I touched by the Holy Spirit over who you are, what you like, what you need?" Anything might work to show that you are someone—not just an extension of my own desires.

Kindness more easily shows up towards those we like or agree with or who are like us, but in any mix of two or more people, somewhere, conflict will stir. Suddenly, hurts or offences bring on the temptation to get out the legal books and make justice the sole recourse.

Kindness knows what justice is but often takes the weight of justice upon itself as an intercessor, seeing Christ swallow up hurt and emit kindness instead. It says, "That person can as easily be a son of God as I am." This diffuses a lot of would-be battles that drain energy and lay down unneeded lines of hostility. Excuses for coldness and apathy grow where kindness is meant to flourish.

Kindness most often starts in the next small gesture of interest in another person and in making that interest tangible in a show of respect. Agreement or disagreement is not even the issue. We may strongly disagree but can still ask God, "What is the highest and best for this person, and how do you want to be as me, Lord?" The still small voice is sure to respond.

Being Kind Anyway When We Feel Resistance

Kindness most often starts with small gestures. It is the will to show interest in another person in a tangible show of respect. Agreement or disagreement is not even the issue. We may strongly disagree. But we can still ask God, "What is the highest and best for this person, and how do You want to be as me, Lord?"

When we hear the answer, we often feel resistance. Fear not, soul reactions are not sin and not mandatory to follow. Neither are thoughts. What counts is intent, and we discern intent by the Spirit. Kindness, as with all the fruit of the Spirit, is impossible except to God. He alone by His Spirit is kindness. All human kindness is only borrowed kindness from the one fountain of it. Sooner or later, this becomes evident to those who find that God's demands go exceedingly beyond human ideas. That is when we tap into the supernatural, or fade like the rose at the end of summer.

Staying fresh and able to be kind takes immersion in God Himself, which is exactly what union with Christ is. He has made us His body, and as such, He is the life of the body, thus our life. He does not give a separate thing called life to us; He is our life. We just happen to be His manifestation of Himself on the earth as a family of sons that He enjoys and sired to run His universe as heirs.

Kindness is always known by faith. When every inner feeling and thought screams resistance against kindness, the one recourse is God, who works in us "both to will and to do of His good pleasure" (Phil. 2:13). That is the key—the supernatural life. That is where kindness is, in the Spirit, and therefore in us.

It is normal to not want to be kind to those who grate on us or are clearly undeserving. No condemnation is necessary however, since temptation is normal and not sin. Don't even try to be kind; just tell God, "Thank You that You are being kind in me."

The Atonement Is Essential

What about the good ideas and good works of those who repudiate Christ's atonement and choose instead to believe in a mysticism of all-ness, wherein there is a great spirit of oneness and goodness permeating the human race, and all that is needed is waking up and evolving into the universal spirit of goodness already latent in all people if they only knew it. Doesn't everyone feel good when performing a good deed or when expressing a noble sentiment toward others? Isn't wishing that all would be fed, and treated well, and included, an idea, which, if embraced and acted upon, would raise humanity to a height of goodness and bring in a golden age of oneness?

It will never happen this way because it cannot happen this way. No one can pull it off without the atonement. Eventually the one who tries will tip his or her hand with rage at being a created being held accountable to the inherent meaning of being created. The lust for independence from any authority whatsoever, except the will of the creature, will create chaos and darkness.

Christ will be crucified again. The rage of the legalists and the pride of the world's kingdoms will once again crucify Christ, not in His human form that He came in via the virgin birth 2000 years ago, but in the spirit of revolt against the need for Him to come as a savior. And since He has ascended, never to die again, the rage of the legalists and worldly powers will continue the battle against Christ's body, the church.

It may look at times like the deceiver is winning, but the accuser of the brethren knows that his time is short. His accusations cannot prevail, and he will find himself and his followers forever assigned to the place of their preference while the saints shine on in light and goodness forever, meaning union with their savior, Jesus Christ who died for them and gave His life for them. Lord, come soon!

The Cross Is Necessary

Good is an often used word. Something tastes or feels good, or gives a person a sense of belonging and community. People do good works to help others or to feel good about themselves. There is, however, a highly offensive use of the word good that angers people who do not believe that Christ's Cross alone is the sum of all goodness. If a person can be justified by doing acts of good for others, or at least by making the effort, then Christ's death is not necessary as the sole source of eternal salvation and becomes at most the noble martyrdom of a man who set an example for us to follow in doing good. However, the Bible says that unless Christ is a person's savior, that person is not capable of eternity with God. This is the truth.

That begins to divide the deep meaning of good from the superficial meaning. Deceivers use shallow versions for seduction of others into false hopes of acceptance by God. However, if only Christ is good, then human goodness must be Christ's alone or not goodness at all. Is this not what Paul says: "not having my own righteousness" (Phil. 3:9)? Crediting the self for good done on one's own is only short-term, superficial good in exchange for allegiance to long-term evil.

Lucifer wanted his own good, and look what happened. His desire to be his own good led to rebellion and his fall since the drive for independence cut him off from the only source of good—God Himself.

Christ said, "Why call me good?" (Mark 10:18). Then He says, "There is none good but one, that is, God." However, Jesus was not talking about His nature as the eternal Son in the Trinity, but rather His humanity as a vessel that had no goodness of its own, just as any human vessel has no goodness of its own but must be energized by God's goodness. Jesus was teaching us to live as proper humans—dependent upon the Spirit, dependent by faith. This puts the axe to self-righteousness, and well it should.

Dealing with Unmet Needs

Galatians is about freedom, and how Christ is the author and sole proprietor of it. The only access is crucifixion with Christ, which put the old man to death, so that he might be buried in Christ and rise in Christ as a new creation. God's justice would never be at fault for letting a guilty race perish, each and every one, but His love was greater: He desired to bring us back into Himself the only way possible—in the Cross and resurrection.

As newly created beings, joy and fulfillment come from union with God. That sounds impractical, however. What about needs? No one can go long in a day without thinking of a need or hearing about a need. Need is basic, and God created the balance of need and supply.

He also created situations in which needs appear to go unmet. This stirs anger and resentment when God's ways are not known. God loves patience, waiting, endurance, and faith. Thus, He put Adam and Eve in paradise where they were tested on the level of need. The forbidden tree looked like a holdout, and the serpent exploited that situation to pull them away from their real need, while God stayed back and quietly by His inner voice drew them toward completeness in Him.

God created us to be in this world but not of it. Even when need is experienced on an earthly level, no one has to live in spiritual need. This sounds like second best, but it isn't. Faith keeps respect for the self and knows its completeness, even when the outer senses or lack of connection with others screams that lack is mocking and winning. It is a costly battle when having to live without something or someone that once seemed impossible to live without.

To be sustained in a situation like this is proof of the resurrection in us, and is what joins a man to heaven and keeps him from being only of the earth. This does not denigrate humanity, but elevates it to glory that only suffering accomplishes.

Dying to Reflex Responses

God is refining the appetite for faith—a much more important appetite than natural ones. This means seeing the unseen and knowing the unknown. To flesh, this is impossible, but where flesh fails, Spirit life begins, and continues, as a way of life in faith. The cost is great because it is unpleasant to endure need, which can be dire. By appearances, God is not there or does not seem to care. However, His care runs deeper than we thought. To enjoy Spirit respect for ourselves in the supernatural, a loss occurs on the natural level. Need is felt on one level, while supply is affirmed on the higher level.

When Adam and Eve fell, they traded spirit for flesh and heavenly wisdom for earthly wisdom. Thankfully, Jesus Christ reversed this by making present trials the school of faith. It is a gentle ride on the inside if we let it be despite a rough ride to soul and body. Routinely—harsh, reflex responses get stirred up at something we do not like. In our old life, these would then manifest on a word or deed level. But the new man is dead to these by the Spirit. Faith is the constant practice of knowing this.

Reflex responses, therefore, are not a reason for you to take condemnation. We live tempted, which is the daily fare of what we do not like. It is natural to feel revulsion at that and want to control things and restore a pleasant equilibrium. However, unpleasantness often so outweighs the pleasant that this is impossible, which is what God means. The unpleasant may be excruciating and unfair.

However, God did not create us to respond impulsively with harsh, retaliatory ways. These get taken routinely to the Cross. Even when justified in a harsher response, the Holy Spirit may indicate a softer and more measured response. Moses angrily struck the rock when God told him to speak to it. Beware of being so right that you become wrong. Intercessors take others' wrongs to the Cross before others know how.

When Others Are at Fault

It is easy to be outraged at sin. It is another thing to operate knowing sin as what it is, but being kept from self-righteously saying, "How could that person have done that?" The Holy Spirit reminds us, "There but for God's keeping go I" (Gal. 6). The latter seems hard, but actually it is easy, just excruciating at times.

God desires others to know His keeping. His law (the expression of His nature) sets an impossible standard, thus awakening the need to be kept, or else sin will continue to swamp the struggling self, trying on its own. The one who sees the need for deliverance and experiences it, wants it for others, thinking, "Do you not see that yet? Do you not get it?" It becomes astonishing that others do not see it.

Disappointment in others comes; it is inevitable. As always, opposites present themselves. In comes hurt. Then anger threatens to spoil faith unless faith holds to the Cross and steers past obsession, the nature of which is to harbor resentment because of one's own unmet needs occasioned by someone else. However, is the aim to stand on personal rights or to see Christ formed in that person? Taking up the Cross leads to a word of faith for the other person.

As appearances get worse and time drags on, home base remains—that word of faith even though temptation comes to argue in a logical but self-righteousness way, which is technically correct, but missing the sweetness that suffering works into the man of faith.

The whole thing is impossible for flesh, the very point. Eventually the natural man or the carnal believer cracks, and Satan's lie becomes evident. God means this so that the cracked pot will become the vessel rejoicing in being filled, kept, and supplied. Walking in the Spirit begins, with the new man knowing that the old man died in Christ, as faith learns to enjoy speaking against appearances.

What Do We Do with This Self?

It is a curious thing to be a self. Every person is given one self, plus the opportunity to decide how that self will be fulfilled. The answer to life is not getting rid of the self when the self becomes a burden, but in waking up to how a self is fulfilled. God fulfills Himself by being for others, even when that means the Cross. No human being can be that, but every human being can contain that. The self is a created vessel to contain and express God's nature, manifested by Christ and witnessed to by the Holy Spirit. The obvious thing to do, therefore, is to see this by faith and present the self to God as an "instrument" (Rom. 6).

This fits the whole context of Galatians. The early chapters say that each person lives unto God alone and then secondarily unto other human beings. This fits the Ten Commandments, where God gets the whole heart, and then a man is God's love to his neighbor as himself. No one does this independently of God, which is why God gave the law to prove everyone's failure to keep the law on their own. This leads to the crown jewel—Galatians 2:20—that the Christian is crucified with Christ and no longer lives, but it is Christ who lives. Christ is the enactor in our flesh, meaning in the earthly vessel—the human.

The rest of Galatians is about activation by the Spirit, the member of the Trinity who makes Christ manifest in our members. Otherwise, no fruit will appear since the fruit is the Spirit's and not ours. By walking in the Spirit, a Christian becomes rooted and grounded in Christ, with the Spirit producing the fruit in Christ's body, of which He is the head, so that everything starts and finishes with Christ and His Spirit. Anything else is a false picture of being human, for God's salvation means expressing Christ's life in human daily living. The Cross made this possible by putting Satan out of the vessel and Christ in. This is the Gospel, "Christ in you" (Col. 1:27).

Putting the Heat on God

If a man looks at someone else's sin and thinks, "I would never do that," he still does not understand that self-control is a miracle of faith from walking in the Spirit. A sin that seems remote and unlikely today could be the very sin that continued unbelief leads to. Who can say that he or she has never done anything wrong that at one time seemed impossible? This doesn't mean that God desires people to sin. However, they automatically do sin unless walking in the Spirit. In order to rip off pride's mask, God has to let our false sense of self-respect be shattered to see the lie that says, "I'm good enough." The toxins hidden in the ground have to get pumped to the surface.

When the picture is bleak enough, the cry comes for deliverance. This is sweet music and means that seeing the Spirit's keeping is at hand. This puts all the pressure where it belongs, upon the Lord. "Put the heat on God" is the way Bill Bower says it. Our place is just to receive. Sin is simply refusal to do that, which is why Lucifer fell, and why man fell. Salvation means starting to receive again, which is humbling but reveals God's power in us.

The devil comes against this with every reason why the works of the flesh are not wrong and that no one can hold out against them anyway. The desire to respond to stimuli feels monumental and irresistible. This is why it is important not to take condemnation for temptation and human appetites. They do not represent intent to the one who walks in the Spirit's keeping.

Do not look to feelings and reason to confirm intent. Faith assumes intent and walks as such, even while bothered by contrary urges, which lose their power anyway when faith laughs at them and says, "I hope they get worse. I don't care." This brings detachment. Therefore, let flesh scream all it wants, because the Spirit will quiet it down in due time.

No Other Life

There is no law against the fruit of the Spirit. That is like saying that there is no law against apples growing on a tree. If I were to tell my grandchildren, "No one has made a law against apples growing on that apple tree," they would think me a bit odd. Being a Christian is like being an apple tree. One is just "supernaturally natural," as Bill Bower says.

The argument against this simplicity is the supposed old nature, also called the flesh, which many Christians posit from their feelings, reason, and temptations. Since these constantly get stirred up, the uninformed Christian supposes them to be an alternate identity, parallel to the new creation. They see the self, therefore, as half cruci-fied—if even half. Paul undercuts such a neither/nor view by saying, "those who belong to Christ Jesus have cruci-fied the flesh with its passions and desires." Notice how he says "belong to Christ." If you are born of Christ, you are a son, which does not change day to day according to feel-ings and thoughts.

Paul says that we have crucified the flesh, not that we ought to. It is done. The layer of "should" is the layer that separates. Life, however, is union, so faith says that the old man did die and that the new man did rise in Christ. Soul will not agree, but spirit agrees with God's Spirit. The Holy Spirit draws a believer to agree by the naked will. Later, the Spirit bears witness after one is tested.

We "live by the Spirit" (Gal. 5:25). Actually Paul says, "If we live by the Spirit, let us also walk by the Spirit." This is akin to "If a fish lives in water, it stays wet" implying that Spirit people know their operating turf. The Spirit is life, and is the sea of life, as Jesus said: "The Spirit quickens; the flesh profits nothing" (John 6:63). Flesh apart from Spirit leads to death (Rom. 8), so efforts to live from nature alone miss life, for God birthed us to be the continual expression of His Spirit.

If Sin Occurs

A trespass does not *have* to overtake a believer since every Christian is given the freedom to always walk in the Spirit. However, it can happen that one is "overtaken" in a sin (Gal. 6:1). When a sin occurs, it can be embarrassing and even devastating, not only to the guilty one but to those affected. After hiding for a while, a Christian wants to be discovered because a lie is hard to live with for the one who belongs to Christ. The longing is there for a safe place to be exposed and healed. This is why Paul urges the spiritual ones to handle situations where transgression surfaces, so that the guilty one is not pummeled with condemnation and judgment that hinder putting a sin under the blood of Christ and forgetting it.

This is not to deny the normal and right negative reactions of those affected, but in helping those overtaken in transgression, the goal is the same restoration that we all have needed. Paul called himself "chief" of "sinners" (1 Tim. 1:15), and I have found that I am a chief too. It helps to know that. The peril of judging or condemning others carries blindness to one's own vulnerability to sin apart from the keeping of the Spirit. Not only that, if the blood cleanses, then it cleanses not according to what a sin is but according how great the cleansing agent is, and the blood cleans all stains. The admonition is to clean the stain gently. There is no need to harshly rub the stain.

Who has not needed a safe, priestly person for a confessional? It is assuring that no matter how dark the deed, it can be seen for all its darkness but even more gloriously washed away by Christ's precious sacrifice. It is easy to think, "I wish I had never done that." True—but to beat one's self up and say, "How could I have done that?" is self-righteousness. The better question is, "How could I not have done that?" and the better question shows wisdom about God's keeping as the only safety.

Burden Bearing

It is not true to say, "I will never get over that." This limits God, for whether a man's pain is from himself or others, in Christ there is forgiveness and forgetfulness. When memories pop up, and the devil uses them to accuse, God's greater purpose is the practice of getting settled in His finished work. That is the miracle. Settling may take a while, but it is certain, as the Holy Spirit supplies us with God's memory, not that of people.

Paul says, "Bear one another's burdens" (Gal. 6:2). In a fallen world, everyone carries burdens. The lie of "My situation is unique" does not want to die, but there cannot be refreshing until a person is common enough to be an everyday burning bush in God's appointed wilderness. Then it is no surprise when hurt and anger rise up from supposedly unmet needs, and temptation appeals to wrong ways to meet them. Those settled in Christ know that bearing others' burdens means willingness to affirm with them that Christ not only died to guarantee heaven, but He is their life, their all, now as well.

Being for others has its wear and tear. Burdens also weigh on the one helping. The thought comes, "I have enough problems of my own." True, all have problems, but the settled believer gets through them more easily because faith has proved itself repeatedly, and therefore, the same comfort of faith can be offered to others.

Paul brings up another reason why bearing others' burdens feels scary. Satan proffers the lie, "If others increase, I must decrease." It appears that helping others means less of something for me. Perhaps the most hideous thing about Christian ministry in history has been keeping others dependent so that an elite leadership can pride itself upon exclusive privileges. What is lost is the sense of love that rejoices in loving, because to love is to live. "God is love." He is never less because of sacrificing Himself for others, and neither are we.

June 19

Each Vessel Can Receive Wisdom

To think of one's self as more than a vessel is to think, "I am something," but Paul says, "For if anyone thinks he is something, when he is nothing, he deceives himself" (Gal. 6:3). Everyone starts out deceived. My first reading of Norman Grubb's booklet *The Key to Everything* did not speak my language. He shows from scripture that we are vessels and that the self cannot improve. Those truths did not look like truths at the time, but the arrow had hit its mark to be remembered later since life has a way of wearing us down, and truth's knock on the door sounds more inviting as failures mount.

This is "the law of Christ"—that God created humans as vessels. The law of a vessel is that it contains and is not anything of itself but is defined by what it contains. Thus, the opportunity to contain the Lord Jesus Christ is God's offer to all—not just certain believers. For example, Daniel did not start out being Daniel. He was an ordinary man who saw and accepted the opportunity for faith. His life was in danger because King Nebuchadnezzar was angry at the king's wise men for not being able to tell what the king's dream was, as well as interpret it.

The king determined to kill all the wise men of the land, including Daniel and his friends. They prayed, and God explained the dream to Daniel. Then Daniel says, "But as for me, not because of any wisdom that I have more than all the living has this mystery been revealed to me" (2:30).

Paul makes this same point in Galatians 6—that no one is excluded from the wisdom needed for life's stresses. Therefore, others can help us bear our burdens, but they cannot be a substitute for our own coming to faith, thus Paul's exhortation, "But let each one test his own work, and then his reason to boast will be in himself alone and not in his neighbor." This is the place where we stand alone with God, and He is enough.

Priestly Ways

Hebrews Chapter 5 tells us that pain is a regular thing —not the pain of unbelief or condemnation, but intercessory pain. First, it is Christ's pain, then by adoption ours, but really still His: "bearing about in the body the dying of the Lord Jesus" (2 Cor. 4:10). To embrace pain instead of fighting it is to leave elementary things. It means the end of arguments with God over what He does not remove. Anger leads some to deny God's existence or to turn away from Christ while the carnal Christian continues to stand for the basics of the faith but fails to see that God uses suffering to bring His sons to the priesthood level.

We are exhorted to leave elementary things—not bad things, but elementary things (Heb. 6). This is not a departure from the salvation message but recognition that when someone apostatizes, it is the same as crucifying Christ again, so the thing to do is move on; there is more to life than trying to win over those who reject the basic John 3:16 Gospel—those who have heard it countless times. This does not mean they have to remain hardened, but it is a waste of time to argue on an elementary level with those who taste but never swallow. Embracing suffering at this point means leaving others to God, for He employs a convenient agent to soften those for whom we have spoken words of faith.

A priest gets on with who he is, growing in faith and in the fruit of the Spirit. Jesus had to do this. Look how alone He was most of His life in what He knew of His Father. Later, the crowds loved Him for His miracles but did not understand Him. He could bot base His own depth on the responses of others but had to get His depth from His Father. The fruit will eventually come, so do not get snagged by getting entangled in downward spiraling debates, satanic in intent, with those who show no intent of believing and only want to argue, not believe.

Supernatural Seed

God promises offspring to us, and a promise from God is certain (Heb. 6). The promise is "I will bless you and multiply you," meaning procreation from our spiritual loins. In His miraculous way, God does this, usually out of our extremity and suffering, so that we have to go deep into faith—faith in God's promise. As with Abraham, this means waiting and enduring—hallmarks of the priesthood of Melchizedek. Abraham got frustrated and had to wait and endure. So do we.

The seed has to be supernatural, and Paul tells us in Galatians that Christ IS the seed. Therefore, there is really only one seed, and Jesus said that a seed has to fall into the ground and die (Jn. 12:24). Multiplication works that way, so that as my friend Karen Norris says, "The seed springs forth as something new." God cannot lie, and He gives an oath: "It is our promise as well as Abraham's," Karen says, "We start out thinking that we are fixing something because it looks evil to us, but really we are only in the way." God uses us as priests but only by faith and not as fixers of others. He is the miracle transformer. We just believe, and the suffering is the waiting and endurance. This is the priesthood of Melchizedek (Heb. 7).

Anything but a new birth will be superficial. Satan has his good works too, which lead away from the Cross and give people false hope. The works are good but will fade under pressure when God's insistence on a new birth never changes. The freedom and good works that come from the enemy lead to self-indulgence, whereas those of the Spirit lead to a new creation, with the Holy Spirit as transformer and witness to the necessity of Christ's atonement. There is no fixing of culture and the world apart from sons of God being born and maturing by faith in the realm of the Spirit. Flesh and blood cannot inherit the kingdom of God (1 Cor. 15:50). Only the new creation man, united to Christ, can do that.

The Perfection of Priesthood

Hebrews Chapter 6 emphasizes maturity—sweeping past repentance, conversion, baptism, laying on of hands, the resurrection, and eternal judgment. Maturity means perfection. Something perfect operates how God intends it to. A perfect toothbrush gets teeth clean, a perfect car gets one to his destination, and comfort may or may not be part of those. Perfection in Bible terms means that the instrument does its job, and instruments we are.

Romans Chapter 6 describes Christians as instruments of righteousness, having formerly been instruments of unrighteousness. The Bible does not deal in tools that do not do their job and function as God intends. About that toothbrush or car, they may have cosmetic imperfections yet perfectly do the job. The point is not the appearances but knowing one's self as dead to sin through death, burial, and resurrection in Christ. This also means dead to the law: "the power of sin is the law" (1 Cor. 15:56). Life is not lived by trying, but by the Spirit's keeping.

Any believer can get on perfectly as an intercessory priest. The priesthood of Melchizedek in Hebrews is not to get us dazzled and speculative, but to anchor believers in their one purpose on earth for their few, fleeting years—to intercede for others—to contain and express God's self-sacrificing nature as priests, in order to see Christ formed in others. It is not enough to a priest to know the truth; the priest lives to see Christ alive in others. This does not mean bearing the responsibility for others' choices, as if one can determine those, but rather faith that God will complete His body through His Son in the sons.

This consuming commission does not go out to just a few elite Christians who know "deeper life." It is the inheritance of anyone who presses through to it. Fruit will come.

The Surprise of Being Human

Being human is not what we once thought. Before the Gospel, being human meant soul and body, with some help from God for the person who had gotten as far as seeing that nature must have a creator. Being human, however, meant the finite experience of working on one's self like a tinkerer works on a machine. Half the picture was missing because to be human means that Christ joined to you is your other half. This does not mean two blocks of wood glued together, which lack interchange. Christ in you does not mean next to or alongside of.

It is the invasion of all of you by all of Him. He is you. When the essence of anything is by faith, then faith is the evidence, followed in God's timing by the witness of the Spirit. Just as Mary, the virgin, was overshadowed by the Holy Spirit and Christ came from her body, the Holy Spirit is the secret agent behind our union with Christ to produce a supernatural experience of being human. In the mortal body, this looks and feels like the regular you, but is anointed constantly as John says in his first letter.

John does not mean particular operations of the Spirit on and by us for certain ministry functions. He means that we have chosen the anointed version of being a human itself, as opposed to the once blinded, lost, and darkened version of being human, in which even our good works were filthy rags (Isa. 64:6). Formerly we expressed Satan's nature hidden in us, so now, by having been placed in Christ's death, burial, and resurrection, we are always one with Him, starting with His crucifixion. His blood is for us; that is the atonement for sin. His body is the body behind our humanity, now a new version of humanity because it is humanity expressing Christ. This is safety. More than that, it is explosive life.

Do not look on the outside at appearances by man's wisdom. Ignore the lie that you are just your natural self. You are your supernaturally, natural self.

Living Where Satan's Throne Is

The earth is God's, and Jesus is His appointed king. Presently, rebel forces operate and usurp within the sovereignty of God. However, a time is imminent when the rebellion will be extinguished (Psa. 2). For now, we live "where Satan's throne is" (Rev. 2:13). Norman Grubb regularly said, "We live in Satan's camp; he has a right to shoot at us." These shots are often subtle. Balaam exemplified Satan's strategy that looks friendly at first (Rev. 2:12). It is the seductive appeal to unity. Balaam wanted to win over a group that was holy, and which held itself apart from mixing with what God had forbidden, so he staged events that looked like selfless hospitality. However, they were designed to bring about mergers depending upon things forbidden by God.

But we are in the world, never of it, which would be to apostatize and see Christ as only *a* way and not *the* way, where the goal falsely becomes unity, not Christ as the only way of salvation. Works take over, and any form of supposed, independent goodness draws praise. Also comes the collapse of sexual restraint, as morality becomes what the supposed free and independent self wants it to be. Churches redefine morality and become a false substitute for the Holy Spirit in a believer. Belonging to the group becomes the point, not Spirit-led study of God's word to show one's self approved.

The worshippers now worship a vague God of good will who accepts everybody no matter what the Bible calls sin. Of course we are not to judge people who sin; God does that. His saving way of doing that is by crucifying it in Christ to bring about the supernaturally kept, new creation self who lives in Satan's camp but is not taken in by it. The overcomers eat "hidden manna" and know their unique expression as Christ's new person (Rev. 2:17). They are not taken in by the false religious mix all around, and they remain kept in their faith.

The Open Door to Melchizedek's Priesthood

The priesthood of Melchizedek is mentioned only a few times in the Bible, its full meaning coming out in Hebrews, where the priesthood's purpose is to contain and express God's self-sacrificing nature, so that as priests, we might see Christ formed in others. This does not mean that we bear the responsibility for others, as if we can determine their choices, but it means that we see our purpose as life-quickening and reproductive.

This consuming commission does not go out to just a few elite Christians who know some "deeper life." Sadly, Melchizedek can be relegated to a few curious Christians. Hebrews, however, makes it plain that every Christian is called beyond "elementary" Christian teaching into the fullness of a branch in its vine. The point in Hebrews 6 is that a Christian is a "partaker" of the Holy Spirit, which means settling into supernatural life as continuous reality.

The chapter implies the message of John 15 about the vine and the branch. To be a believer is to spring to life from the dry, dead state inherited through the Fall. The unacceptable alternative is to stay in the dry, dead state as if one can be saved but remain carnal. One's life, then, would hardly be better than the branches which end up cursed and burned. This does not mean that we try to determine who gets cursed and burned, however, simply that we live by living water.

Living water does not get turned on and off according to temptations and trials. When Paul in Corinthians says that weakness is the perfect container for God's strength, he means that. The Hebrews writer, therefore, exhorts his readers to see that the Melchizedek priest sees stress as a battle cry to new fruit in others. In this mindset, two great Bible words, *faith* and *patience* rise up. Faith then throws time out the window, and suffering is expected. In this, God opens up new Spirit dimensions for others.

From Negative to Positive

Salvation means feeding continually upon the Spirit of God, the living word of God, and the power of the coming age—which is ours already to live in, even on the fallen earth that groans and travails in pain, awaiting the hope stored up for it (Rom. 8). Seeing this will spark abandonment of the the lie that the self is partly inspired by the Spirit but still necessarily in bondage to the flesh. Freedom to receive from the Spirit remains constant, like a branch is to a vine, and is not dependent upon outer circumstances.

Faith sees by the inner eye, knowing what we live for—using negative appearances as a reason to laugh and not be moved from the Spirit's witness. As faith holds steady with words of faith that the Lord has incited us to say, the enemy stirs up resistance from those for whom we said words of faith. The prize goes to those who see through and look ridiculous for calling "into existence the things that do not exist" (Rom. 4:17). Faith does this without physical sight yet. Patience waits for the Spirit's "ways and means committee" (the Trinity) to manifest the fruit.

Waiting and enduring sound hard, as if one can live the Christian life only with great difficulty. However, walking in the Spirit is easy; it is just excruciating at times. This sounds contradictory, but the ease of walking in the Spirit does not depend upon comfort, for faith comes easily even when things feel terrible. This is the priesthood of Melchizedek. Our bodies are made to contain Christ's passion, which is the common call of the Gospel and the heritage of every member in the body of Christ.

Opposition is to be expected. This is the realism of the Bible, not "How could this be happening?" When attacks come, say "God, You are meaning this. What are You up to?" The purpose of God remains certain underneath the disturbances.

June 27

Faith Takes on Impossible Odds

"When there is a change in the priesthood, there is necessarily a change in the law as well" (Heb. 7:12). The priesthood changed from Levi's, genealogy-based, to one based on resurrection life. Melchizedek represents Christ, whose power operates the priesthood to see the body of Christ delivered into full son-ship. The means is faith in Christ's perfection in us. The priesthood based on Mosaic Law could never perfect anyone and needed replacing by a new priesthood and covenant.

Abraham's battle to rescue Lot (Gen. 14) typifies the miracle nature of a son's faith to see others delivered. Vastly outnumbered and facing trained opponents, it took a miracle victory by Abraham intervening as a priest-king, Christ acting as Abraham. After the victory, Melchizedek appears, and Abraham pays tithes to Melchizedek, which means that Levi also is paying tithes to Melchizedek since Levi is in Abraham's loins (Hebrews 7). Abraham acts as the father of the family of faith—on behalf of all the delivered sons of God.

Paul tells us why the new race of delivered sons is possible. Adam took all humanity into the Fall, where we were doomed unless a new Adam, not of the first one, would become the new priest-king and birth a race of priest-king sons (Rom. 5). This He does by raising to life those accepting crucifixion with Him (Gal. 2:20).

Then in Christ, like Abraham, we win battles by faith against impossible odds and are "filling up what is lacking in Christ's afflictions" (Col. 1:24). Our ability comes from the New Covenant of Jeremiah 31, repeated in Hebrews. Christ brings us to full son-ship, and we live by God's law written upon our hearts. We see beneath all appearances of reason, emotion, and temptation. We live by the deep inscribed laws of God, really His nature and glory, which are our controller and delight.

June 28

Priests Are not of This World

The book of Hebrews leads the willing believer into the priesthood of Melchizedek, which is only mentioned explicitly in Genesis, Psalm 110, and Hebrews. These define the priestly order of those who see what it means to be "one in Christ Jesus" and "Abraham's offspring" (Gal. 3:28-29). To be a priest is not a human function and never has been, for Christ "did not exalt Himself to be made a high priest, but was appointed" (Heb. 5:5).

Even under the Old Covenant, God appointed the priestly tribe; it was not a democratic process. To qualify as a priest called for proof of one's genealogy as a Levite. Jesus, however, was not a Levite but of the tribe of Judah and the line of David. Yet He is called a priest according to Melchizedek's order, not Levi's. Melchizedek appeared to Abraham after Abraham defeated the coalition of kings that had captured Sodom and therefore his nephew Lot. No mention is made of Melchizedek having a mother or father, or a genealogy. The aura of his priesthood is heavenly and not of this world, thus, not man-made or even derived by natural birth—not even a divinely appointed family of natural birth, as with the Levites. The point is that Jesus' priesthood is not of this world either.

Melchizedek's priesthood means the Spirit-imparted ability to suffer. When he appeared to Abraham, Abraham had risked his life to rescue a nephew who had chosen the best of everything for himself, which Abraham graciously allowed without condemning Lot. When Lot got captured, Abraham could have said, "He deserves this for his lack of faith." But the nobler risked his life for the less noble, and Abraham acted in the Spirit of Christ and as a priest. This is what drew Melchizedek out from behind the scenes to appear to Abraham, for God sends a Melchizedek level priest when suffering is invoked and a heavenly man of faith is needed to intercede for others.

No Surrender of Freedom

Walking in the Spirit brings religious opposition from those who live by externals, while missing the Spirit. This tempts those who do walk in the Spirit to move away from rest and go back into law-driven activity. However, rest is not a state attained by doing. Rest is also not a relaxation or resting technique to calm frenetic thoughts into a state of rest. Instead, no one needs to do anything except receive the rest that is in God. It is based on the fact of Christ's blood and body atonement for us, whereby our sins are forgiven, and by which we are reunited with God through being made the body of Christ.

This happened when we were crucified with Christ. In His death, we died. The old man died. Therefore, identity in Christ is not a makeover version of a self that we already were. We did not get better or improve to become the sons of God. Rather, we experienced a new birth as new creations. A new creation is not an old creation fixed up; it is an altogether new, heavenly self—created by God in Christ. If one looks at the old self from Adam and then glimpses the possibility of a new creation, the old cliché applies, "You can't get there from here."

This also applies to being a priest. In the Old Covenant, priesthood was defined by human genealogy, whereas, the New Covenant priesthood of Melchizedek is defined by being born again, by being supernaturally made a new being that never existed before, one that could not have emerged from the old being by means of rituals, study, good works, belonging to the "right' church, etc.

Reason and emotion cannot validate this. It is Spirit revelation. Once you know that God means for you to live totally against the grain of appearances and flesh-level reasoning, it is possible to take blows without surrendering your freedom in the Spirit that Christ won for you.

Snatching Rest from Unrest

Christians remain immature and unfruitful when they do not mix God's promises with faith. This is the point when the Hebrews writer says that the Israelites fell short of rest in the wilderness, where God tested them on basic physical needs like water and food. Their challenge was to believe God's supply against appearances. The next test was God's call to the land of plenty, but they believed the fearful, unbelieving spies when faced with the possibility of an entrenched enemy that over-matched them in size and strength. The lesson is that one does not enter rest while facing an easy life, but rather a hard one.

That calls for a complete Gospel, saving the whole man. We are exhorted to move beyond the elementary Gospel about the divinity of Christ, repentance, ritual, and eternal judgment—vital as these are (Heb. 6). To remain on that level means falling short of life in the Spirit where a person lives by God's law written on the heart. Otherwise, the false assumption remains that humans are independent selves whose main mission is evangelizing those who have apostatized.

We are not called to do that but to move on ourselves into priesthood to the body of Christ, knowing His life in us as our life, united to Him, with His nature inscribed on our hearts, knowing ourselves kept by faith when facing dire challenges. A full and abundant life of supreme living is in view, and Christ accomplished this for His body, bringing His sons into the priesthood of Melchizedek—not as numerous, mortal priests who succeed each other because of death—but as the one, eternal body of Christ with many members. Rest is obtained where rest appears impossible. That is the best rest of all.

The Indestructible Life

Christ is a priest "according to the power of an indestructible life" (Heb. 7:17) and by Him we are His body—of priests, the operation of which was shown at Pentecost, demonstrating that priesthood is by the Spirit of the indwelling priest, for how can a person minister Christ to others without transmitting Christ's indestructible life? Therefore, we do not merely *speak* of the life: we are *of* the life (1 Pet. 2:9; Rev. 1:6).

The problem in ministry is those who speak of the life but do not partake of the life themselves, leaving them limited by their weaknesses, sins, and supposed old nature. They do not know that they were baptized into Christ's death and therefore also into His resurrection. They will tell you about the water or the symbolism, but not that they died in Christ and were raised.

Insistence on this separate self still stained by sin and under its power contradicts God's word about the New Covenant. God has written His laws upon our hearts (Heb. 8). Therefore, expecting God to do more only brings His reply that Christ's work is sufficient. Laws written on stone did not work under the Old Covenant, but God's laws written on our hearts do, unless interpreted as just another code, relocated to the inner self of an independent doer. The point is this: the living Christ is the doer, as us.

Human weakness, therefore, is the perfect expresser of its opposite—God's strength. Our weakness is called being a vessel, and a vessel's one duty is to contain and make the contents available. This is the opposite of being independent, something not possible anyway and a lie that unsaved people and carnal Christians live in. God's plan is that Christ's indestructible life be manifested in weak human vessels, for weakness is not sin, and never was. The lie of independent self, believed, leads to sin, but human weakness accepted is the perfect vessel for God's strength, leading to glory.

Perfect in Conscience

God created us to live with a clean consciousness. The Fall destroyed that, and since then, everyone fights the battle with conscience. With a clean conscience, one does not obsess, but instead lives in freshness of life, whereas before there was dread and an unresolved list.

Apart from Christ, efforts at a clean conscience include "gifts and sacrifices...which cannot make the worshiper perfect in conscience" (Heb. 9:9). This is because the fallen way of seeking a clean conscience has to do with bodily cleanliness through diet, exercise, and religious rituals for purification (9:10). However, Jesus said that people are defiled not by what they eat but by what is in the heart (Mark 7:15).

The clean conscience can only come from Christ's blood, which does cleanse the conscience. Memories may persist, but the blood is greater. It is pointless to still live with a sin consciousness. This is different from Holy Spirit conviction of a particular sin. Sin consciousness is nagging guilt, and a sense of never being clean and right with God. "Surely I have done something that I should not have or not done something that I should have."

A sin consciousness constantly prays, "Father forgive me of my many sins"—implying a vague, bad self. Looking at self leaves the worshiper believing the lie that there is more to be done, stuck in a sense of unworthiness and shame. We are not to make our sins greater than the blood of Christ and come away imperfect in conscience. That is disobedience. Where the Holy Spirit convicts of a sin, conviction is clear and definite, and seeing Christ's blood restores one "perfect in conscience" (9:9). Anything else is to be rejected as enemy bluffing.

Exploring the New Country

Sin consciousness produces low self-image, guilt, and a sense of not being whole. The worshiper constantly thinks that there is a need to do something, whereas God will not do any more than what He already did in Christ. The worshiper thinks the need is to invite God to "come be with us today," whereas God has invited us to see that He has joined believers to Himself and given them His Spirit.

Fellowship with God is not based on emotion, mental analysis, or physicality—all good created things but not the basis of fellowship with God in "spirit and truth" (Jn. 4:24). Therefore, nothing on any other level is a valid indicator. Even conviction of sin comes from an upward call to life and peace, not torment and condemnation. God convicts, not accuses. Surprisingly, He convicts us also of our acceptance in Christ and of righteousness—the righteousness now yours because Christ made it yours and judged the enemy, not you (John 16:8-11).

No spiritual discipline of any kind brings about the perfect consciousness. As children we receive it from God, who gives the new consciousness. It is not an upgrade to the fallen one, for the fallen one is of the enemy who parades it as a needy, merely human one. The *new* consciousness is the mind of Christ itself. You do not think in order to get to Christ's mind; you cease from your own thinking and hear the thoughts of God. Never mind the noise of the world, flesh, and devil. Underneath these obstacles (that God means) is the voice of the shepherd.

Life gets amazingly simpler. The energy formerly wasted in the quest for understanding gives way to looking at God, who then gives His take on things. Do not expect the unbelieving world to see it, or even the carnal brethren. Holding onto God's view, however, will bring settling and stability, even with the price paid in faith for knowing the real situation.

Done Means Done

A perfect sacrifice removes the "consciousness of sin" so that no other offering will ever be needed. Jesus Christ was that perfect offering, removing the "consciousness of sins." Offering Him again and again, therefore, is not needed. Consequently, a believer with a sin consciousness hangs onto deception, either knowingly or unknowingly. Does God need to do more? To borrow a phrase from Romans, "God forbid."

Hebrews 10 warns not to trample underfoot the blood of Jesus and think that God needs to do more. This is what the writer means by, "Now where there is forgiveness of these things, there is no longer any offering for sin" (10:18). All that is needed is to "draw near with a sincere heart in full assurance of faith, having our hearts sprinkled clean from an evil conscience and our bodies washed with pure water" (10:22). There is nothing more for God to do, and nothing for a believer to do except believe.

Yet Hebrews 10 is a terrifying chapter until seeing this complete work of God. Terror comes from hanging onto separation, whereas God looks at what *He* has done, not what a striving self thinks it does out of a separated consciousness. The latter never seems enough, leaving a dark cloud of condemnation, which is the devil keeping up accusations of a bad, unworthy self.

Taking pressure on the human self to be righteous leaves an open door for Satan to interpret temptations, thoughts, and feelings—all false evidence of an old nature, or an old man not dead, the lie of a dual identity, whereas a Christian is a totally new creation—the human spirit joined to Christ's Spirit keeping us from misuse. Losing ourselves in His divinity, we find our right humanity and start ignoring the devil's interpretation of temptations and soul-body negatives. The new man is not a reformed or amended version of the old man (who died), and the Holy Spirit bears witness to this.

Getting a Bead on Light and Darkness

Nothing a person does can improve or reform the old self. It must die, and die it did in Christ's crucifixion. That is what it took to break the human vessel's union with Satan, for indeed, the old man was the vessel indwelled by the spirit of error (Eph. 2). In Christ's resurrection, we rose as a new creation but still look the same physically, for our earthly body is now the Spirit's instrument. In another sense, however, we do not look the same since the Spirit transforms us into beings of light—light that quickens the mortal body (Rom. 8). No condemnation exists therefore, even when tempted, or when our thoughts and feelings falsely suggest that we are not new.

Norman Grubb often said, "Condemnation is from beneath; light and liberty are from above." Condemnation means falsely thinking that God is wrathful toward us, full of malice. This is Satan's lie. Sin consciousness in a Christian can only remain if you believe the lie of, "I'm unworthy, I'm no good, and I'm wretched." Hebrews 10 tells us, however, that God did a perfect and complete job. Therefore, we do not have to live with a sin consciousness.

Conviction of sin, if a sin occurs, comes from the Holy Spirit and is clear, specific, and without condemnation. Letting go of a sin consciousness also means that sin will be less likely because your focus is now turned to what God has perfectly done in us. There is no more, "I am going to sin anyway, so I might as well give in now."

Instead of trying to do the keeping, faith says, "God, I would be into that sin immediately if You weren't keeping me, and thank You that You *are* keeping me." Know that God can keep you, and then say by faith that He is. This does not mean sin consciousness, but instead, life with the awareness that self cannot keep self. God does the keeping, and He knows His job perfectly.

July 6

God Eternally Wanted to Be You

God says that His name is "I Am." He doesn't need rules because He has a fixed way that He is—a nature—and He is who He is by choice. Eternally He chooses to be who He is: He is Mr. Love; He is Mr. Self-for-Others; He is Mr. I'll-Go-to Hell-for-You. Guess what: He is also Mr. Have-Fun. Everything ends up being about fun; let's not lose sight of that. The Christian life isn't hard; it's excruciating at times, but it is not hard to walk in the Spirit. So I tell people, "If you can unite these two—the ease of walking in the Spirit and life's sufferings—you've got it."

Something be easy and painful at the same time. That's where the fun is. Life is about having fun. A plan like *this*—a world like *this*—we should be laughing. If you see it, you are laughing—and crying maybe a little—but through the tears, you are laughing. "For the joy set before Him, Jesus endured the Cross" for this plan (Heb. 12:2).

What makes it fun to God? What thought, before there was a world and us, excited Him as the most fun possible? The Trinity in Wisdom convened on how to throw the biggest and best party possible. Talking it over, They say, "Let's create an earthen pot—made of clay. Let's do it out of dirt and breathe Our life into it"—"the spirit of wisdom and revelation in the knowledge of Him" (Eph. 1:17).

"Let's do it out of clay; let's make a pot." And the Word says, "Yes!" Let's get clay, then animate it and make it human. Let Us make MAN and live in him. Let's be human! Let's be people." Does that not sound divine? So that was the plan—to be human and live in clay pots. God all along wanted to be you, and He wanted to be everyone that comes under the category of Psalm 139—fearfully and wonderfully made. That is the true human, and it cost God His Son to get such a human.

Made to Be Pots That Contain

We have the treasure in an earthen vessel, or pot if you will (2 Cor. 4:7). About the pot, God said, "Let Us make this pot in Our image." God wills, so the pot is able to will. God desires, so the pot desires. You cannot have any fun without desire. Fun means desire and fulfilling that desire; and if that desire is fulfilled, there is more desire to fulfill. This differs from lust because desire can be satisfied, whereas lust never satisfies.

God experiences incredible desire with incredible fulfillment. This never stops. When Jesus told the woman at the well that she would never thirst again, He did not mean that she would never feel thirsty to drink water: He meant that she would never again know a state of thirst where desire fails to meet with fulfillment. So the pot is going to will, and the pot is going to desire, and the pot is going to know. The pot has to know—be conscious—because God is conscious.

The pot will never be God, but God is going to live His life in pot form, the two as one—that was the eternal plan. Are they two? Yes, but oneness is the excitement. Two are not exciting unless they are being one. Do they cease to be two? Of course not. But life is oneness.

Think about marriage: "For this cause a man shall leave his father and his mother, and cleave to his wife; and they shall become one flesh" (Gen. 2:24). Do you think the excitement is about two-ness? No, it is about one flesh. Paul recognizes this when he says, "But the one who joins himself to the Lord is one spirit with Him" (1 Cor. 6:17). Physical union is exciting, so think how exciting spirit oneness is to God!

His excitement and thrill abound in making man and being man. Man does not become God, but God becomes man through Christ's blood and body. He paid for a full union and desires that we know it. The vessel is holy now because it is God's cleansed and perfect vessel.

July 8

Adam and Eve Go Astray

Adam and Eve lived in glory. What opposites! This was like fire and iron, except it was glory and clay. Freedom abounded in the presence of the Lord continually. Think of what it is like when you get a moment or an hour or a day or a week of anointing—total ecstasy—and what it would be like to know nothing else. Adam and Eve had known only ecstasy.

Imagine someone from the future, saying, "You do not know the hell people are going to go through because of your choice" (our choice too Paul tells us in Romans 5). "You do not know the ecstasy in which you live." They would say, "Ecstasy? What ecstasy?" They didn't know. They had anointing and covering and glory…all the time. What would we do to have that on an experiential level? We do have it, but with suffering too, for now.

In comes the serpent. The devil never changes, does he? He convinces them that they do not really have things so good—they do not have enough and there should not be a forbidden tree. The devil plays that up and does *not* say, "You need to go back and ask." The devil does not want you to ask. He operates from, "Let *me* tell you," while stirring up discontent: "You think God has your best interests at heart, but He holds out on you."

The thought is planted, "It would be great to be like God. What is this about being a vessel for God's glory? Where is *our* glory?" The devil liked that: "Yeah, take control; be all *you* can be." They went for it. Some things, however, cannot change: a vessel is always a vessel—made only to contain God.

One might think humanity was spoiled goods, ruined forever. However, their fall was not from fixed spirit choice, and the pot can be washed and reclaimed for those who receive the blood and body of Jesus Christ as their life. We are revealed in glory with Christ who is our life (Col. 3:4).

July 9

Adam and Eve's Negative Surprise

Some things cannot change: a pot is always a pot—it is made for one thing, to contain. When Adam and Eve fell, therefore, they could not constitutionally become different; they could not become unoccupied humans, being just themselves. God made us to contain Him, and pots remain pots. Scientists say that nature abhors a vacuum, so once they turned away from the Lord, who was going to come into the pot?

Two things happened: Satan came into the pot, and then Satan hid that fact. The devil fuels only one way of thinking as if it is just you: "You can do whatever you want because you belong only to yourself and must get your way regardless of others. Everything is all about you"—a total ME-consciousness! That is the loneliest, most anxious condition possible, one that is fear-filled and lust motivated. After they fell, they experienced this. So what could Adam and Eve do to cover over their choice and get out of the terrible loneliness, fear, and dissatisfaction that filled them and began to drive them?

They turned to activity, meaning performance—anything that would mask or block out what now went on in their center, a terrible condition similar to what we find in the beginning of Genesis: a state without form—a void with chaos and darkness. What was God to do? Did He know the Fall would occur? Yes, He did. Had He already made a plan for when it happened? Yes, He had. Was He surprised—taken off guard? No, He was not. The Fall in no way changed His plan to live in pots as us. It meant, however, that the cost of bringing it about soared—through the roof—because the plan would need the Cross. But that was perfect because that is who God is anyway. He did not have to change and *become* the Cross. He already was, but He would now have to manifest the Cross in order to bring about the plan—the fun plan—for Him and for us. A new Adam would appear—Jesus.

Leaving Your Gift at the Altar

When taking a gift to the altar, what if you remember that someone has something against you? Jesus tells us to go and be reconciled (Matt. 5:23-24). This is no guarantee of another's response, nor can anyone control whether others forgive. Hopefully, the other person will forgive, but if not, you are reconciled. God has reconciled us to Himself in Christ (2 Cor. 5:16-21). Not even God, however, usurps freedom to force others to reconcile.

Many have gone to others and made the effort, only to find refusal. The verse does not demand endless efforts until the other person accepts us on terms other than God's. The exhortation is to obey by faith and leave the results to God (Rom. 12:18; Heb. 12:14). This is particularly painful when dealing with those with whom we have had close fellowship, and where a barrier still exists.

Some Christians base fellowship on agreement with their doctrines and inclusion in their group, losing sight of John 3:16. Church rules on behavioral matters can cause brothers and sisters to ostracize others who disagree or leave. The supposed sin is leaving that church or group. Therefore, no reconciliation is possible until the one who left repents and returns.

What is there to do? In *The Way to Christ,* Jacob Boehme paraphrases Matt. 5:23-24: "reconcile yourself to your brother" (p. 77 Peter Erb translation, Paulist Press). The emphasis is reconciling *yourself* to your brother. This means that the self that *you* are is reconciled to your brother. You are not holding onto an independent view that keeps you from yielding yourself as a servant.

Boehme says, "He who wishes to pray correctly and by prayer to reach God's power and Spirit should forgive all his enemies and put them in his prayers, and ask God to convert them, and to reconcile them to Him in His love so that not a serpent might remain in his heart and hold him back and tear the power of prayer from the soul" (77).

Performance or Promise?

A problem loomed after the Fall because fallen humanity resists the idea of anything being wrong. "Something wrong with me? I'm fine!" Never mind the turmoil and rage underneath resistant protests. How would God get across to these fallen, Satan-filled pots some inkling of their true condition? That was planned already in a three-letter word: L-A-W, and yet, even before the law, God gave the promise, beginning with the promise to Adam and Eve, of the messiah. He also gave promises to Abraham and the patriarchs. Believing in God's promise is justification, but because of the Fall, we do not cling to God's promises until the law eliminates hope for justification based on performance.

Our performance goes back to Adam. Romans 5:12-19 says that when Adam sinned, we sinned. The text does not say that when Adam sinned we were affected by it. Rather, when Adam sinned, *we* sinned. That does not seem fair, does it? We would like to say, "Well, Adam did that, and I wasn't there. I would not have done that!" Sure. But what he did, we did.

Scripture shows a parallelism, however. Salvation's plan hangs on the Last Adam doing something that, when He did it, it was also we doing it: "I am crucified with Christ." Jesus, not I, hung on a Cross 2,000 years ago, but Paul says, "I am crucified with Christ" (Gal. 2:20). Therefore, when Christ died, I *did* die. What He did I did. Yes, what Adam did we did—but much more, what Christ did we did. When He was crucified, so were we.

A person does not have to be born later and do a separate, individual act to have done it. The Adam that one is born into is the point: when the head of the family line acts, everyone born in that head acts. By Adam, the pot (vessel) is born into sin captivity, with Satan indwelling. By crucifixion with Christ, however, the new man is born into righteousness. Satan goes out and Christ comes in.

Lost Spontaneity Versus Saved Spontaneity

God means for us to see that the pot (vessel) indwelled by Satan is the "old man" that Paul describes (Rom. 6). This old man cannot be reformed but must die, crucified with Christ. The holdup on humanity's end is the deception related to the Law. Lost people think that they can keep it, and carnal Christians think they should be like Jesus—the same thing. Mired up in deception at first, we think that God gives the Law so we will keep it, or at least get a passing grade, or perhaps God will grade on the curve.

But only a perfect score passes. This is shattering but necessary conditioning since God always knew that we cannot keep the Law. He is laughing His head off and has been over what non-Christians and Christians alike think about the Law. He is laughing, thinking, "They think they can *keep* it! Let's pour on the commandments even though they never seem to wear down."

God must convince us of our need so that He can save us. Everyone battles the law, and God means that because the Law (holy and good as Rom. 7 affirms) awakens us from our self-satisfied view of ourselves. Even Paul's testimony says, "I was alive without the Law once" (Rom. 7:9). But was he really alive? No, he simply felt good because things went his way in his deceived state of thinking that he was keeping the Law.

Dan Stone often told about the spontaneity of lost people—a spontaneity that he enjoyed in his carefree days before the Law. He then became a Christian but spent years trying to be like Christ, while secretly jealous of the non-Christians who lived spontaneously. After years of wearing down under the Law, Dan discovered that a Christian *can* live spontaneously—by trusting Christ within to keep His own Law. Dan saw that God uses the Law to condition us away from self-effort and into Christ's life in us as our supply. So there is a spontaneous version of the spontaneous life for a Christian.

Legalistic Thinking

Everyone longs for spontaneity. John says, "His commandments are not burdensome" (1 John 5:3). Living by law instead of the Spirit does not have the same ring as what John says. One might think that John had special powers not available to the ordinary person, but John speaks for the ordinary person, the everyday person—the person who is simply a vessel of clay. Every human is that, and it is just as possible to express Christ spontaneously in a life of faith as it once was to express Satan spontaneously in a life of sin.

However, we all started out thinking, "I can do the Law." Life is one resolution after another, in the secular world as well as in the religious world. Look at how advice columns dominate media. Look at the political emphasis on legislation as the answer to change people. The world is trying to be like Christ on its own, which sounds holy and good, but turns out to be the definition of sin.

Seeing the Law's purpose makes that clear—that the transgression might abound (Rom. 5: 20). God will never tell you that you can keep the Law. He gave the Law and commanded obedience, but He will never tell you that you can do it. Anyone telling you that you can do it is deceived. Actually, Satan is the one behind, "You can do it," and he is the one bewitching Christians under law. Paul calls them "bewitched" and "foolish" (Gal. 3).

The Law only serves to bring people to Christ, aware of their sins. Law is not meant to remain our mentality—because law presumes an independent self; but we were never free people that God interrupted with the Law. Satan was the master behind our supposed freedom. Therefore, God gave impossible standards as a wrecking ball to any honest person—a mirror worth looking into until one says, "God, if You do not do it, it does not get done." Until not one piece of the cup thinks that it is one drop of the coffee, the Law will do its work.

A Good Little Lesson on Sin

A casual or unconcerned attitude about sin will not do. The Holy Spirit has to open the Bible to us to think about sin because that does not come naturally. Honest Bible reading brings a shock until one realizes: "I am not anything like what this book says." Then we learn of the savior to forgive sins. But there is also deliverance from the inner turmoil and enslavement of continuing in sins. Until seeing this, problems mount as the seeker intensifies trying, while getting worse as the Holy Spirit's conviction deepens. Dishonest Bible reading diverts into little self-improvement schemes and pats on the back for trying.

It is not unusual for the Bible reader to discover increased disillusionment with the self, as the gap between the natural and the supernatural is increasingly perceived as infinite, along with the need for a drastic change. Awareness becomes, "I do not resemble and have never resembled what this book says, not ever!" This is honest and admits, "I experience flashes of victory, and I believe John 3:16; and an occasional Bible verse lights up; but when it comes to living life, there is more guilt than glory."

Satan's lie is, "Well, nobody is perfect." But to go all out and honestly say what God says, and do as God does, leads to saying, "This ship is sinking." No more lists of principles and effort to keep them will help because the need is for deliverance at the self-level. This is not the issue of a onetime sin, but repetition of it and powerlessness to escape it and get free. A sin gets put under the blood. Then it happens again. No wonder the sin consciousness hangs on.

Deliverance comes with awareness and acceptance of powerlessness. "Who will deliver me?" (Rom. 7:24). Deliverance is not from being a self, nor is it change in the human constitution. The self remains what it is, but the Holy Spirit takes over the living of life. Soul and body still clamor, but they are not the boss.

July 15

Satan Out Christ In

Listen to Paul: "But shall we sin that grace may a-bound? God forbid." Then he says (this is amazing), "Do you not know that you are dead to sin?" What? More likely, people read Paul and make him a liar like I did the years when I said, "That cannot be right. That is not right, because I can still sin, and if I can still sin, then I am not dead to sin."

The Spirit is radical, and so the meaning is radical. If sin originated with the devil getting into the self at the Fall (remember, the self is a vessel), the solution means getting the devil *out* of the self. Devil in—devil out. If he is in there, God must get him out. Now we did not know that. We thought about law, commandments, particular sins—acts, deeds—all well and good. But as you know, when cutting down a plant, everything grows back until the whole thing is out, including the roots.

Thus, God's plan meant pulling sin out by the roots. God already knew how He would get the devil out of the vessel and put Himself in. He had to crucify the human vessel by making Christ become, on the Cross, the vessel with the devil in it—which is you and I—Adam— the first Adam. That is who Christ was on the Cross. He was Adam and everyone born of Adam—the devil in the vessel. That is who He was on the Cross.

Christ poured out His precious blood for the for-giveness of sins. But crucifying the devil in the vessel is what got the devil out because God and the devil both want to live in a human body. Something fascinates any spirit about living in human flesh: God wants to do it; the devil wants to do it. Heaven wants to do it; hell wants to do it. It is cool to be human. It is all right! If God and the devil both want to occupy your body and live through you and be you, and yet you still know that you're you—that speaks of an incredible plan.

God's Recapture of the Human

In order to recapture the human body, and us as persons, Christ became sin, apart from doing any sin Himself (2 Cor. 5:21). Romans 6 tells about the body side of the Cross. There is a blood side, and there is a body side. The wine in communion is about our sins, but the bread is about the body. The mystery behind the bread starts with the devil in the human vessel on the Cross and ends with Christ in us. But suppose you go up to somebody in your church and say, "We just had communion today, and we just had the bread. Do you know that the bread means Christ being made sin in order to get Satan out of you?" The listener might consider you mad or blasphemous.

Grace does not mean that God accepts sin; it means that He freely gives us His life, one that is dead to sin by causing us to die in Christ, to rise in Christ, and to be operated by the same Spirit that raised Christ from the dead—all the way to the right hand of the Father. Life is hard, but on the supernatural level it is not that hard. God's plan is really pretty simple. Self-improvement is the big lie, because the self that is joined to Satan and sin died. Therefore, the self does not need to improve but to simply live by faith as a branch in the vine and as the body of Christ, Christ being the head. You are a new creation.

We died in Christ's body when Christ's physical body died, and the devil lost a body to live in. We died to sin. However, there is more. A dead person will not sin, but a dead person does not live either. Death cuts us off from the sin spirit, but for us to *live*, we rose in Christ's resurrection. This is experienced by faith, which means not helping God. When a thing is impossible, only God can do it. If only God can do it, say that He did do it.

Why Do Christians Still Sin?

Seekers say, "Why do I still sin?" One reason for sin continuing is not knowing that every Christian died in Christ to sin (Rom. 6). However, when believers remain ignorant that sin lost its dominion in the Cross, sin will take advantage of that ignorance. A greater knowing of Christ's completeness in us is needed. Jesus living in one's heart is more than a broom in a broom closet, or to put it more elegantly, Christ in you is more than a jewel in a jewel box— precious and holy, but hidden away except for special need.

Christ is in us for more than a role every now and then in a crisis. After receiving Christ, however, most get diverted into the "Be like Christ" outlook. A good dose of Romans 7 helps sort out that lie unless there is a diversion into the misconception that Romans 7 asks a Christian to concede to having two natures. The two nature theory runs counter to what Paul meant by deliverance. He was delivered from sin by faith, not by trying. Further, he did not experience this because he was special but because he desperately cried, "Who will deliver me?" Anyone can receive.

Until that cry goes out into the night, the seeker keeps trying, and trying ends only when the desperate person's energy fails and leads to the cry, "God, You can deliver me, but You will get no help from me." This is radical faith. Then when temptation comes, which is all the time, you might think at first, "This is sweeping me away; I am helpless!" Yes, but do not stop there. Tell the Lord that you will do the sin unless He keeps you, but then thank Him that He *is* keeping you by the Spirit.

Sometimes I do not feel like I want to be kept. That is normal. It is temptation 101, and there is no cause for alarm. A quick review of what life was like *not* being kept is enough to get the faith muscle pumping again. The real you does not want to sin—that is a fact.

Faith Is in Something, in This Case, Someone

Faith by itself will not save a person. The evangelist Bill Bright said, "Do not put your faith in faith; that is like casting your anchor inside the boat." Faith must have an object because faith can only operate when something is available. So, what is available? Christ is available, right there in you, all the time. Being dead to sin, knowing it, and walking free from sin are available! That *is* your life. Christ *is* your life. "As He is, so are we in this world" (1 John 4:17). When it appears ridiculous, say to God, "I did not think of it; You did."

People panic and protect the freedom to sin, which is there, but sin is not compulsory. Why mandate sin? Walking in the Spirit overrides that. Overzealous insistence that a Christian must sin daily makes a provision for sin, when God says that any Christian can live out the Romans 6 declaration that Christians are dead to sin.

How bad are your sins? Maybe taking them too lightly makes them easier to hold onto. When people want to protect the necessity of sinning, I think, "Are you ignorant? Have you not gotten to the point where your sins might snuff your life off this earth?" Or perhaps you have not gotten out of control yet, but devastation is nonetheless at work in your life, impacting others as well.

Many say, "We are going to sin, we are going to sin." Who says that you have to? Sure, the freedom to sin is there, and some will choose to. They are on the law treadmill and probably will sin because they think that they have to, so they will. However, what if you said, "I do not have to. Since I am not under sin's dominion, I can be kept. Keeping is available." Faith is based upon something's availability. If a man does not believe that freedom from sin is available and that it is possible, he will never go for it. A living Christ is in you. He, by the Spirit, is the freedom from sin, and the freedom unto all that is good.

What You Take Takes You

It is tempting to think, "I can never hold out. I am going to end up doing the sin anyway, so why torture myself? I may as well give in and do it. God will forgive me." It is wonderful to be forgiven, but what does it say about the Cross—to live in defeat, relying on a pattern of sin and forgiveness as if there is no remedy for dealing with temptation?

For those desperate enough to think, "I can't go this way anymore; is there a way out?"—yes, there is. A way out is available, and the availability of deliverance opens the door to faith. Once the possibility of rescue is realized, desire for it can quicken. God's keeping power looks better than it ever did, while going the same old way again looks futile. Then desire intensifies to know human powerlessness and *divine* strength—God living through human weakness. Being a vessel looks sweet, and the desperate person thinks, "I cannot do it—only Christ can do it in me." Then through Him you do it. It is you doing it, but it is He doing it—as you.

Desire alone, however, is not complete faith. Desire will move toward faith through increased tension, which God uses as the set-up for us to take Him. What you take, takes you. This is the law of faith, even when it does not appear that you have been taken by what you took. Hold on—God is testing your faith. Do not back down, but rather stick with what God says. Agree with Him that He *is* keeping you. This is the taking.

By faith, thank God that you *are* dead to sin. Thank Him that He *is* keeping you—and doing a perfect job of it. Do not worry about apparent delay of the Spirit's witness or the sorry voice that says, "See, you took 'dead to sin,' and it is not working." The witness of the Spirit will come in God's timing, which is always perfect. Do not try to get the witness; just know that it is coming.

What Is Sin?

Sin is not primarily a deed, a nature, or a principle deriving from ourselves: sin is fundamentally a person whose nature is self-for-self, deriving from Lucifer, the highest of the angels, who led a rebellion and wanted to be like God. Satan, therefore, is the one who lives in fallen, human vessels. We are all born fallen, as Romans 5 declares, which is why Jesus had to be born of a virgin—so that He would not be born a minion of Satan, already indwelled by the spirit of error from birth (Eph. 2:1-3).

Sin did not make Adam an empty vessel or free him from being a slave as he had hoped. Romans 6 reveals that we are either slaves of sin or slaves of righteousness, but always slaves. God gives us a multiple choice question with two options: slave of sin or slave of righteousness. Not liking these answers, we politic for a third option, "I want to be my own boss." Repeatedly, we have tried to pencil in this third option, never offered by God. The "be my own boss" option comes from the devil, who continues in this deception himself.

We were slaves of sin as unbelievers, not recognizing the hopeless enslavement by sin. This is true even if life appears well mannered and basically upright. When a *believer* does not walk in the Spirit, the former slave owner, Mr. Sin, plays around in that believer's members even though he has no right to, and he does this by the lie that we do our own evil or good.

No wonder Jesus asked the ruler, "Why do you call me good?" Jesus knew that to commend or condemn people as if they originate their own deeds, misses the point. God created us to contain and express Himself, and in the Fall, Satan took over the indwelling rights to humanity, so that man began to do Satan's lusts (John 8:44; 2 Tim. 2:26). God's saving plan, therefore, included expelling the false indweller by crucifying us in Christ and restoring His glorious presence in us.

Vessels Are Powerless and Meant to Be

We are accustomed to praising people or blaming them, seeing people as just people and ourselves as just ourselves: we are all about being human. Christians celebrate the incarnation of Christ, and rightly so, for the mystery is that Christ, equal with God in eternity, became flesh and blood. Where would we be if He had not? So we have every good reason to celebrate our humanity, since the Son of God took on humanity and now reigns as a glorified, ascended man.

It is good, however, to examine how Jesus said that His humanity worked. A man came to Jesus and addressed Him as "Good Master," to which Jesus replied, "Why callest thou me good? None is good, save one, that is, God" (Luke 18:19). Jesus picked up the self-righteous tone of the ruler, as if men are just men who do good things. Nothing could have struck Jesus as more heretical, for He emphasized that He lived from His Father abiding in Him and did only what He saw His Father doing. Jesus knew that God's purpose in creating humanity had eternally been to contain and express Himself—as us—vessels, branches, temple, body, and spouse. This means that God created humans to be powerless, including His incarnate son!

Many consider powerlessness to be the province of only those in society prone to addiction. Acknowledging powerlessness is the first step toward recovery. The larger picture is that God created all humanity powerless, even before the Fall; and in heaven, we will be powerless forever. Adam turned away from this, becoming the first addict, and all of humanity with him, excepting the virgin-born savior. This did not change God's plan but meant that humanity became enslaved to Satan, and that redemption could only be by Christ's death, resurrection, and ascension to free those who believe, cutting them off from Satan and uniting them to Himself as a family of sons who live in their right powerlessness.

From the Impossible to Intercession

Confidence comes from a sense of bedrock at one's center. Everyone has times of feeling like life is a slippery mud hole without footing, from which rescue is necessary. In our old life, impossibility meant impossibility, whereas the new man acknowledges such but moves anyway by faith into seeing what God plans to do. My friend Sylvia Pearce has a quote on her wall: "Faith laughs at impossibility." God presents us with one impossibility after another. How fitting that is. In response, faith quickens with a spark about how God will show the way through. His Wisdom reflects it in the mirror, backed by the Father's will. The Son then walks out the Cross in us, with the Spirit as the power and witness.

All that is needed is a healthy sense of impossibility, plus faith in God's moment-by-moment manifestation of Christ in our members. Those for whom we intercede grow weary of hearing with fleshly ears that live in the lie, "Anything you set your mind to, you can do." God's intercessors have already been well-placed lambs, ready for this.

The Intercessor in us is The Lamb, who paid the cost of taking sin upon Himself to rescue lost Adam, and no man adds to that. However, Paul speaks of "filling up what is lacking of Christ's afflictions" (Col. 1:24). Jesus is the atonement once and for all, so what remains is sharing in Christ's sufferings as the body of Christ now, meaning the individual intercessor who absorbs the shock waves of resistance from others while remaining a messenger of God's deliverance in Christ. Though excruciating, we say, "death works in us, but life in you" (2 Cor. 4:12). This turns suffering into glory for others by faith.

Two Mirrors, Which One?

Nothing about the self tells us who we are because self cannot be its own mirror. It tries and fails but knows nothing else to do. Sensing incompleteness, the self looks to others as mirrors since God created man to need approval. However, until God is known as the mirror, others take His place. The chief lie of the enemy is independence, and others are viewed independently as well, so Satan suggests their reactions as the measure of wellbeing. According to Satan's lie, the physical universe and human reason rule the day when interpreting others' responses, making a person a hero or victim according to the highs or lows produced by the response of others.

But though the mirror behind the lie of independence, and behind the highs and lows of flesh responses, is the enemy, there is a freeing mirror, which James calls the perfect law of liberty: "where the Spirit of the Lord is, there is liberty." Paul says that we are "beholding as in a mirror the glory of the Lord" and being "transformed into that same image" (2 Cor. 3:17-18).

When the countenance feels like it will fall because of hurt, it makes no difference. That same mirror of liberty is there, never moving, with one image: the new man. This is not produced from an accumulated file of ideas that a Christian must collect in order to imitate; rather it is the unique, living image of you—created and energized by the Spirit. The image is not only a judicial position based on the atonement but also your new self. All you do to experience it is to look in the mirror and take what you see—the new self, created by God and maintained by God.

Faith accepts this by the will. When the old mirror tries to sneak in, say, "I don't take it." Say it with all the force that a refusal could have. Jesus despised the worst shame that the enemy tried to force upon Him using every kind of mocker and tormentor (Hebrews 12:2). Nowhere does He expect one of His to do anything less.

Silent

Being heard spiritually by others is not guaranteed even though the Bible emphasizes that the declaration of truth calls for boldness. Situations arise where silence around others is the only escape. One face of evil is busyness that occupies itself with its own plans and its own goodness. Good deeds and self-satisfaction in those deeds get promoted as if the meaning of being human or a Christian consists of merely doing good works and cheering others on who do the same.

The Spirit man feels stifled and frustrated, not with evil, but with good that is not credited to God as the doer. Norman Grubb called this "good Satan," which sounds contradictory to the young Christian. However, those who do not sin flagrantly but merely go on with good works as if those works are independent, resist hearing that it is not we who live the Christian life but Christ who lives it—"not I but Christ."

This is why Psalm 39 pictures someone reduced to silence in the face of resistance from others to the Spirit. No word or deed from the Spirit-led person will help, because the listener continues to interpret your words and actions as the self-congratulatory kind that you are actually contradicting. The situation is maddening, so The Psalmist retreats into addressing the Lord for three things.

First, he asks the Lord to keep him mindful that life is transitory. The maddening world will pass away and the saints remain. He also asks the Lord simply to keep him straight and true. We are who we are unto the Lord, not because others notice. Last, since it is such a bitter pill to swallow that he must endure in silence the false good of others, he asks the Lord for serenity: "Turn your gaze away from me that I might smile." He has seen the Lord's revelation of "good Satan" but also wants to keep the joy of the Lord. Seeing sin need not take us down so far that *we* lose joy. Keep smiling, for God is in control.

Rejecting Shame

Adam and Eve felt shame when they disobeyed and fell. It was inevitable, even in their ignorance, since God is the only shameless one. Separated from God, no one can do more than make a pretense of having no shame, but this pretense is a sorry mask. Shame hides underneath, for only God is pure and shining light, and only He can cleanse His fallen vessel and shine the same light out from us so that we do not live in fear of shame turning up.

It is a mistake to try to rid one's self of shame. Such trying is insanity, and the process becomes endless, finally turning into outer religion with various dry rituals. Trying accomplishes no more than Pilate's obsessive hand-washing after sending Jesus to the Cross. This remorse obsesses, saying, "How could *I* have done that?"

The mind of Satan is the source, and nothing but shame and condemnation, which is fueled by the spirit of independence. Those deceived by him try to keep outer law instead of walking in the Spirit. By faith, however, Christ's life is manifest by the Spirit in a clean vessel, the blood of Jesus having made it clean. If sin once again dirties it, the same blood does the same cleansing.

The vessel is the house and home of the Lord by which the shameless life is manifest by the Spirit. The mystery is God the Person within, even though believers look like ordinary humans, which is meant for now. But faith knows that the glory presently hidden will someday manifest in the new body as the norm of the new heavens and earth.

For now, this glory is hidden but radiant in the countenances of those in the light. Nothing mortal can steal it; no stirrings of the flesh need cause alarm as if those represent who you are and as if sin must manifest. No, those flesh stirrings are the constant pulls of temptation that every Christian can easily use to replace the lie and unmask its seduction back toward shame. Do not take it. As a son of God, you do not have to.

Not Pretending

Good manners are commendable. They are taught, but are also fake for many. The person learning to make proper responses does not want to be fake but learns what wins favor with others. The faker guts things through, thinking, "I think the opposite of what I am saying but dare not acknowledge it." Though the disparity is loathed and the secret hypocrisy regretted, manifesting the real self is risky and could mean a loss of favor and position.

The saint takes a different approach. All of those ugly thoughts and feelings inappropriate to express are not suppressed by force of will while thinking, "This is my real self that I am suppressing." The saint acknowledges all of this negative but miraculously does not manifest it, calling forth the Spirit response instead—the fruit of the Spirit. The saint says, "This is my real self, the self in union with Christ and His Spirit." Ugliness that is unworthy and not useful to manifest is recognized as pulls on the flesh that are not sin because temptation is not sin.

Pulls toward the works of the flesh are not recognized as identity. Instead, Spirit responses are recognized as true identity, not that they come from the human self as the originator but from the Spirit as the originator. Our part is faith, and no condemnation is necessary when faith labors to call upon Spirit responses. These are a high privilege and God-given freedom even when the labor of faith makes life at moments seem not spontaneous like usual.

What then of venting? God gives us healthy space to vent, and He certainly knows how to check us when it would become sin to continue expressing the negative. No rules can cover this. Sensitivity to the Spirit shows the way through, moment by moment, making life great when negatives can be faced without pretending and without false identity. Moreover, dying to certain responses is not pretending, but rather death on one level, giving way to greater life on another.

When Appearances Contradict God's Promise

Here is the story for the ages of a shipwreck. Yes, it is a detailed account taking up a whole Chapter (Acts 27), with the drama carrying over to the end of the book as Paul reaches Rome. The lesson is that when God wants to get you somewhere, you will get there despite all the efforts of hell. The backstory is Paul, who had been jailed unduly long. Finally he appealed to Caesar, which prompted the voyage. The ship was at Fair Havens, past Crete, and the ship's owner and captain both wanted to avoid wintering over in an unfavorable winter port. Paul had warned that to continue the voyage would mean loss of the cargo, lives, and that great damage would occur.

The centurion aboard disregarded Paul's warning, and Luke narrates the intensity and ferocity of the storm that beset the ship for many days. No human hope existed for rescue, but God had bigger plans to show His glory in this disaster. An angel appeared to Paul and said, "You must stand before Caesar." Paul announced this and that the Lord had given Paul the crew as well. But Paul was considered inconsequential in this vital decision. Who is a political prisoner, with no qualifications, to decide about ship navigation? However, God has His way of bringing total desperation upon all involved, in order to clarify who is hearing the voice of God.

God had already promised Paul before the voyage that he would "witness at Rome also" (Acts 23:11). God spoke this to Paul back when the Jewish opponents first swore to kill Paul, and he was taken into custody. Not even a shipwreck could change God's promise. God orchestrated everything to save all lives, and later continue the voyage without the original ship and cargo. God destroyed all the plans for this transport except the preservation of lives: "God has granted you all those who sail with you" (27:24).

Sometimes we are protected from the storm, other times in it, as God transports us along.

Peer Pressure

Peer pressure is the saying that equates to the Bible's command not to be man pleasers. One morning I dropped by to take our son Carson to pick up his car. Mindy and the three boys were at the breakfast table, and she said, "Poppy, would you like to read the boys their devotional?" They use a book with youth stories, accompanied by a scripture. Wesley read 1 Peter 4:1-5, and then I read a story about two boys who talked their friend with a removable cast on his foot into joining them in a swim in spite of doctor's orders to do no such thing. Unfortunately, the boy gave in, even while his conscience was telling him no.

No one outgrows this kind of pressure. It comes from what scripture calls the world, the flesh, and the devil. These become specific the moment you go counter to what others want. No one likes to be on the outside looking in. It is normal to want to be in unison with a friend, a group, a team, even a culture. This is not wrong, just like the good things of the world that God provides are not wrong, and normal appetites are not wrong. God, however, sets up many scenarios in which we cannot obey Him and at the same time go along with what others want. To give in will lead to being used by the enemy as instruments of sin. In our old life, we would have given in, but we are new—having died with Christ.

When God gives a specific prohibition, we may not know how we will get through under pressure. It is good to say, "I don't know what I will be doing, but I do know what I will not be doing." This closes the door and makes no provision for a change of mind about what is a settled no. It is not necessary to know what will happen, just what will not happen, by God's keeping, and that the new path will open up one step at a time.

The Psalms 46-48 Trilogy

Psalms 46-48 are a trilogy telling how the world will end and the city of God will appear. The beginning of birth pangs is cataclysmic, natural disasters. Faith will not fear but will see this as the prelude to the end. Mountains will slip into the sea, and the earth will experience so much apocalyptic damage that wars will by necessity cease because the universal concern will be survival.

After mention of natural disasters, the scene shifts to the eternal city (Psa. 46). It is present now in the invisible, but cannot be revealed until the world is silenced and all but destroyed in order to get the attention of world leaders. The description of the eternal city is simple and beautiful: "There is a river whose streams make glad the city of God" (46:4). The picture is serenity eternally existent but revealed to those ready to make the crossover to the Spirit world when the earth falls apart.

This signals a worldwide decision by leaders and nations of whether to cross over to the new world or stay in the one being destroyed. The present world dies so that those wanting to live in God will see that only rebirth into God's new world will get them across the otherwise uncrossable divide between the temporal world of the Fall, and the city of God, which is Spirit and which cannot be entered except through death and resurrection.

Finally, the King "has ascended with a shout…with the sound of a trumpet" (47:5). The tone is regal and calls the shattered earth to recognize God as its King and move into the manifestation of God's rule, with the vanquishing of all rebellion. The only weapons left are Spirit weapons. Nothing carnal survives. The leaders and people who have submitted begin to marvel and assemble: "panic" and "anguish" signal the last chance for "childbirth" (48:6). Then begins the celebration as those who accept the new birth on a world-scale see God's manifest kingdom arrive.

Law Catches Those Who Need to Be Honest

God knew that we could never see our fallen condition without first encountering the law. This is because the deception that we do our own good or evil runs so deeply in us that it we do not easily admit that we have broken God's laws. What is law? God Himself does not live by law. One member of the Trinity never says to another, "What shall We do? Let's pull a law book off the shelf and see." This is ridiculous to think. God's nature is self-for-others: He has made the eternal choice to be love. God is love. Therefore, He does not live by law but by His nature.

We, on the other hand, as creatures, and fallen ones, were born with the deception from the indwelling spirit of error that we can do our own good or do our own evil. We either commend or condemn ourselves and view others likewise, commending those we esteem, and condemning those that we disapprove of. We do not come into the world thinking that we break God's laws and need a savior to keep us from going into eternity separated from God. The Bible warns of this destiny for the unbelieving, and asserts that many take this path, yet these warnings go disregarded as hysteria and unworthy of a loving God, despite the unmistakable, plain word of the Scriptures.

God's first order was to convince us that we have not kept and cannot keep His laws: we cannot generate a life like His by imitation. Thankfully, through the Bible and the Spirit, many do come to see that they have sinned and need a savior. They accept Christ's atonement and know that their sins are forgiven. This is unspeakably wonderful.

Being a forgiven sinner, however, is not enough. God does not mean us to express thanks that our past is forgiven and heaven awaits us in the future, yet live trying to be like Christ in the present, with a never-ending sin consciousness that leaves us feeling like dirty saints who never measure up. In the Spirit, we live complete, competent, and clean. That is a total plan.

The Self Is Operated by an Operator

The fact that Christ is in the Christian's heart is not new news. Every Christian knows that "Jesus is in my heart." The newness of the Gospel, when we see it, is that God put us in union with Christ, whereby the two are one, and we stop asking for God to help us as if we are living independent lives and need help occasionally. That lie of independence is Satan's lie. It posits a big "I" still carrying the load and needing a little help from Jesus. An earnest seeker will eventually see that he needs total help. Christ must do it all. The seeker might conclude, however, that there is no human self in the equation at all, but this is not true either.

The Gospel is all of Christ in all of you, with you as the vessel, branch, and temple. We live by "Christ who is our life" (Col. 3:4). Our humanity is in focus as the receiver, container, and expresser, with no more commending or condemning the human self as the originator of good or evil. Commendation and condemnation are evil twins, for we are operated by a master, either sin or righteousness, which means either the spirit of error or the Holy Spirit (Rom. 6; 1 Jn. 4:6).

A letter from a brother commended a fellow Christian for good works, and by implication took shame for his own deficient works, which implied seeing good people and bad people, or good people and not so good people. The emphasis smacked of works and trying. However, trying must go on until trying can try no more. Then the seeker is ready for miracle territory where life is supernatural, and the seeker lives by, "God, You and I know that I will sin unless You keep me, and thank You that You *are* keeping me!" Saying "God You *can*" turns to "God You *are*." Let us add to that, "God, there is no good work that I will do unless You do it in me, and thank You that You are doing Your works in me."

Go Ahead, Try to Keep the Law

For all of the talk about "born again," what understanding is there about this radical sounding phrase? Jesus told Nicodemus that he must be born again, and the same holds for people today. Born again means more than being a forgiven sinner, for as wonderful as forgiveness is, if the mind does not change, and new actions do not follow, then we only reckon ourselves the same old person, just forgiven, when the truth is that we are now saints.

Do not misunderstand here: knowing that we need forgiveness and a savior is the door into the kingdom of God, for thereby we accept that we have all broken God's law and that no amount of reform, resolution, or good intention on our part will get us into the kingdom of God. We do need a savior, and we cannot save ourselves by any works whatsoever that we do; only the blood of a savior come from heaven, only the blood of God come in the flesh can save us.

God has quite a task to get us to see that we have broken His law. He has to put the Law before us repeatedly until we agree with Him that we have broken it and need His forgiveness. God Himself, however, does not live by law but by His nature, which is love. When He gives us His Law, He mirrors to us in an external way, what to Him is internal. The Law that God gives us describes the divine nature but does not describe any nature or actions that we can generate on our own.

Therefore, we cannot be like Him because He is the only one of His kind and always will be. This is what we must find out. Why then does God have to give us His Law? He does not give it to us because He thinks that we can or will keep it but to prove to us that we cannot. We are the ones who have been deceived by the enemy. In no other way can God get through to us that He created us to be branches and not trees—the cup, not the coffee.

Position without Condition Is an Imposition

In Paradise something went wrong that affected everyone born of Adam. God created man to be branches of His one eternal tree, but the devil deceived Eve into thinking that she could be her own tree, not needing to live as a branch of God's tree. After Eve fell, Adam saw what happened, and he made the conscious choice to follow Eve's path. The result was that they became branches of Satan, expressing Satan's self-for-self nature. The law, therefore, is what God uses to show us that we come into this world expressing the opposite of who God is.

The fact that Satan got into our first parents and took over, expressing his nature by them, might make Satan sound like an equal rival of God, but nothing could be more erroneous. Satan is a creature too—from the highest angelic realm—but nonetheless still a creature, for all his power. Not only that, Satan keeps us from knowing that he runs the lives of the unredeemed because he wants people to think that they are just independent, human selves who do their own good or evil. This fact is well hidden until the law has worn down those who are honest enough to see the impossible demands of the law—that they mirror what only God can be.

No amount of reform can change what we have done or alter our works to make them acceptable to God. Here is where the difficulty comes in living the Christian life. Many know that God reckons Christ's righteousness to us as ours, but they see it as a positional righteousness instead of righteousness flowing out of the life of Christ in us. Instead of the living God being Himself in us, they see righteousness as a bookkeeping entry credited to us but not actual in our experience. Nothing could be further from God's intent, for He expelled the enemy from us and restored His presence and total life in us so that we do not have to live with a sin consciousness. Sin consciousness comes from the enemy: reject it!

The Old Man Died in Christ

All around is the maddening dilemma of those who either do not admit that they have sinned or those who will not stop hammering away at sin to Christians. Sure, a Christian can still commit a sin, and thankfully, forgiveness is ample: "and if any man sin, we have an advocate with the Father, Jesus Christ the righteous" (1 John 2:1). However, it is not enough to know ourselves as forgiven sinners, for which reason John says, "My little children, these things write I unto you, that ye sin not" (2:1). John tells us exactly what the other Bible writers also say, that we can live in victory over sin! We do not have to repeatedly fall into sin, with no hope of deliverance.

Yet many stay in ignorance and mistakenly try to repay God out of gratitude for His forgiveness, trying to be like Christ. But if we could keep God's law, why did we agree with God in the first place that we needed a savior? The truth is this: we need a savior for our living as much as we need a savior for forgiveness. What sense does it make to realize that we have broken God's law and need Christ to forgive us, only to turn around and try to keep it now? Reform did not bring forgiveness, and reform does not bring Christian living. Only Christ can live the Christian life. Notice the simplicity and completeness of that statement.

God's purpose is to live His life in us as vessels, containers, and branches, and He planned this as His purpose even before the Fall; so the way that He created us to function is not a byproduct of the Fall, but the way that He created us. Whereas reform means trying to fix the old man, renewal means that we died and were born new creations in Christ. Nothing about the old man gets fixed up or improved; instead the old man died on the Cross in Christ's death: "I am crucified with Christ" (Gal. 2:20). This is the fundamental of the Gospel—we DIED.

August 4

Don't Let Time Fool You

Time as we know it leaves reason baffled when reading Romans 6 and Galatians 2:20. Flesh says, "I could not have died 2000 years ago. Christ lived then, and I live now." However, eternity means beyond time: to God, anyone saved in all of history is crucified with Christ. Reason cannot compute this; it can only read the words on the page. The Spirit gives the revelation that outside of time, every Christian in history died in Christ when He died, and rose in Him when He rose (Rom. 6).

Death became our sentence because of the Fall, when Adam and his seed became the "old man." The old man is empowered from within by the spirit of error (Eph. 2:1-3). No wonder the old man had to die. God put us into Christ's death, which is a mystery revealed to the church through Paul. Faith receives this fact and stands on it. At some point, the Holy Spirit bears witness when faith has been tested, and the believer does not get shaken and fall back into the natural mind. Falling back to external reason can only lead to seeing the self the same way that it was before conversion—what the Bible calls "consciousness of sins" (Hebrews 10:2).

God, however, calls us to see the completion accomplished on the Cross when He put to death the old man and raised a new man in Christ: "Therefore if any man be in Christ, he is a new creature; old things are passed away; behold, all things are become new" (2 Cor. 5:17). This means that a Christian is an entirely new creation. Though the body looks the same, and though one's personality is the same, God has birthed a new being, united spirit-to-Spirit with God through Christ, who takes on all responsibility to produce the qualities that He requires. If a Christian continues in sin, it is not because God failed to cause us to die to it (Rom. 6:3) and supply us with His Spirit to walk in.

Operating the Operator

The Bible is so sweet in how it says to receive. Life is receiving and expressing what is received, or in this case, expressing *who* is received. God forces this upon no one; He offers it to all. No wonder Norman Grubb said that there is "one person in the universe." False mystics get the oneness part right, but they do not get it right about whom the oneness is with—that it cannot be apart from the Lamb slain and the Lamb's atonement.

Yet when God trusts us, He tells us to command Him. Norman put it like this: "operating the operator." No wonder Psalm 82 calls us gods (little "g") or that God said to Moses, "I make you as God to Pharaoh" (Ex. 7:1). Of course, people think you are saying that you are Jesus because they think they are Jesus, but they think it in the wrong way, as if flesh is God. They call their flesh Christ.

They started out unhappy with their flesh and wanted relief, so they started to die to flesh level seeing and came alive to expressing the Spirit. Then the devil came along and twisted the meaning as if union means calling flesh Christ. Then one has the original nightmare; only now there is no deliverance because now one has to call flesh Christ, when God all along was saying that we come alive in His Spirit and then rule our earthly members by faith.

We have all had to go get beaten up some more, drinking the same old cup of frustration and futility until the condemnation is bad enough that we are ready for Light. Sometimes, we just have to let people go the way of Satan's lie and trust that it will be a good whipping to drive them back. Waiting for that is excruciating, but God honors the suffering that we endure, and the long wait until He, in His time and way, completes the work, which to Him is complete, but does not appear that way to those who do not yet agree with God about who a Christian really is.

All of Life is Containing

Adam craved to enter into nature on a flesh level and know on that level, rather than stay outside of it, and be in it, but not of it. His craving was temptation, but his choice to go with it took him down, and us—as if knowledge of good and evil can be known by flesh. Jesus said, "I have meat to eat that ye know not of" (John 4:32). If we are only of soul, he would not have said that. The will needs to go against everything natural, not because the natural is evil but because it is evil to be ruled by the natural.

To be human does not mean to be ascetic: "touch not; taste not; handle not" (Col. 2:21). It means that your central person-hood is beyond time, space, and all that is merely soul and body. Everything about being human is related to being a vessel. The body contains the soul. The soul contains the spirit. Body and soul contain your spirit. Your spirit is joined to the Lord, really containing the Lord. Mimi Anderson used to say that faith means being "mixed with" God. He is in us, we in Him. One might even say that we contain Him, and He contains us. However, who is uncreated and who is created? Who is Lord?

Nothing in life has any meaning apart from containing. Even the devil wants to swallow everyone up and contain them, but for what reason? We know. And he too is created. If you are in Christ, then God contains you. His Spirit contains you because you are in Him. Impersonal religion sees this but calls God a force, whereas God is a person, meaning one who desires, wills, and knows. This is man's rebellion, trying to escape the person who is uncreated and who has the Cross in His heart. The world's version of containing is a big blob of fleshy, feel-good stuff—all on a soul/body level, and all self-for-self. God's version is His incarnate Son crucified for us.

God's Pattern for Being a Self

God desired to be a self. Would He be a self-for-self, or a self-for-others? He desired to fulfill Himself, but how would He do it? A self must fulfill itself and will do so by one of the two opposites—satisfaction at others' expense, or Christ the Lamb slain for others. We know God's choice—the Lamb slain. From will then, comes knowing; there can be no knowing without will. This is where the outer, flesh world has it backwards, wanting to know first, and then choose. This is no faith in that. God says to operate by faith, and then knowing follows.

This is spirit level. Soul and body make up the instrument and manifest the variety of the One person. Soul and body left to themselves would choose according to what they are and not make spirit choices because they are not spirit. If will were in the soul/body, when you died, your spirit would go to be with Christ, but you would have no will. It would be in the grave.

Bill Bower says, "I *am* a spirit, I *have* a soul, and I live *in* a body." Why would God step down to our souls for our faith level operation? Why would He speak into your spirit and have union with you there but leave your decisions to the soul? That would be asking for fleshy living. God desires us to rule over our souls and bodies with a higher capacity, namely spirit, where the will is. What is the most important thing a person does? It is faith. How can the most important thing a person does be anywhere but in the centermost part of you?

People in unbelief live in their souls and let their souls and bodies rule them, which is why Hebrews Chapters 3 and 4 say so strongly to discern soul and spirit, or else no entry into rest is possible. Holding onto the lie that will is in the soul makes provision for the flesh. Seeing will in the spirit opens up possibility for the Spirit's division of soul and spirit.

Persons in the Person

"God is spirit" (John 4:24), which means that spirit is the seat of God's desiring, willing, and knowing; and He created us in His image, giving us those capacities in a created way for fellowship—like unto like. He created us to be in union through Christ and not act independently, but only by choice. The will must be free to choose its indweller, either Christ or Satan. But who wants to be a vessel of Satan? Therefore, Satan's ploy is that choosing independence defaults automatically to Satan's consciousness—a sin consciousness.

Freedom is God's risky gift for us to choose a master, either sin or righteousness (Rom 6). Though born in sin, we do not have to remain slaves to sin, but can choose a new master, Jesus Christ. The error is to think that self alone is the doer, which is why Paul says, "it is God who is at work in you both to will and to do of His good pleasure" (Phil. 2:13). Faith is based on the will, and in proper function expresses the will of God, so faith therefore means simply agreeing with God and not resisting. With rebellion out of the picture, our faith becomes the faith of Christ. Freedom is implied, for everything starts with the freedom that is in God, and out of which is all freedom. Freedom then makes its choice, which for a created spirit being is which master to serve.

Spirit is your center. Soul and body have a will, each on its own level, but the human spirit is the center. Body would choose body, soul would choose soul, but spirit chooses its spirit master. Paul says, "he that is joined to the Lord is one spirit" (1 Cor. 6:17). This is why Paul says that only the spirit of a man knows his own thoughts (1 Cor. 2:11). The spirit is the command center, the dwelling place of God to operate our members, which must obey their spirit master. The ultimate answer to "Where is the will?" is to say, "My will is in my Father."

Spirit Is the Focus, not Matter

Under the Old Covenant, the Lord dwelled away from His people, in the tabernacle or temple, above the ark in the Holy of Holies. Intimacy with the Spirit of God seemed foreboding because of the law's condemnation, and only pioneers of faith found intimacy. The writer of Hebrews refers to the Old Covenant as a "blazing fire" and "darkness and gloom and whirlwind" and "the blast of a trumpet and the sound of words, which sound was such that those who heard begged that no further word should be spoken to them" (12:18-19). Familiarity with the Spirit of God such as that known by Noah, Abraham, David, and the prophets was the exception and the hint of a mystery that Christ would later unveil.

The apostles clarify the mystery: man is God's temple, and He conforms us to the image of Christ by forming Christ in us (Gal. 4:19). The word *spirit* overtakes the word *soul* in significance because the part of man corresponding to the Spirit of God comes into focus. Man is a spirit-being with a material body and corresponding emotions and thoughts—soul. The spirit of man is the seat of union with Christ because to be a spirit means three things: to desire, to will, and to know. The issue of life on the spirit level is the choice to be self-for-self or self-for-others, which is the decision God made. Thankfully He is the eternal will that loves unto His own death.

For believers, God and man become one spirit through Christ (1 Cor. 6:17). Soul and body discover that Spirit joined to the human spirit is the master, and life becomes inner-based, not outer based because the Holy Spirit is the interpreter of earthly life and puts it in perspective compared to eternal life. The things of the Spirit cannot be obtained through the emotions and thoughts, but only by revelation (1 Cor. 2). This is humbling, and those who know this, know what a waking up it is to enter in. The sleeping world does not know.

Three Parts: Spirit, Soul, and Body

The question, "Who are we?" invites the discussion of spirit, soul, and body. Good Bible minds debate whether man is bipartite or tripartite, some thinking that spirit and soul both refer to the immaterial part of man, some seeing them as distinct. Others distinguish them but see them like circles that overlap. Although some overlap at first appears reasonable linguistically, the New Testament's focus is spirit as our center—leading Paul to speak of spirit, soul, and body with reference to sanctification (1 Thess. 5:23).

The Old Covenant, now superseded, was a covenant of separation from God, emphasizing the here and now before an indeterminate Sheol after a person died. The Old Covenant celebrated life in the body with regard to health, sex, food, property, wealth, government, international supremacy, while at the same time making the body unclean because of disease, death, bodily emissions, and certain animals unclean to eat or offer as sacrifice.

The New Covenant reveals us as spirit-beings in union with God through Jesus Christ, who has prepared the real kingdom for us in eternity. The word *spirit* overtakes *soul* in significance. A part of man corresponding to the Spirit of God comes into focus, and the two become one spirit (1 Cor. 6:17). Soul begins to convey more the idea of our earthly components of emotions and thoughts (the kind of feelings and logic based on body chemistry). In contrast, spirit directs itself God-ward as the vehicle of knowing, willing, and desiring—as opposed to the reflexive needs and emotional/physical complex of the body.

Enjoy all temporal blessings God gives you, but know that present earthly life is filled with devastating losses that we see as opportunities for glory, sacrifice, and praise. Our bodies are mortal, thus still attached to the Fall, but the former bodily uncleanness of the Old Covenant is replaced by "bodies washed with pure water" (Hebrews 10:22).

No Condemnation When Tempted

Why would God complete a plan for our forgiveness and new lives that leaves us in the mindset that we always fail on some level? Surely the Bible argues against trusting for keeping from some sins but not others. Can we fail? Of course we can, but we do not have to. You can have victory on whatever level you live in faith for; everything is available. This does not mean a proclamation of instant perfection as interpreted by those who see the self as perfect in and of itself, maybe with a little help from God.

Perfection is a person—the person of Christ, and we can walk in Christ all that we wish to. All the perfection in the universe, Christ Himself, is available to us every moment. Why settle for less, and the Bible makes no place for settling for less. It is also true that if perfection means no disturbing thoughts or feelings, then not even Jesus was perfect. The fact is that normal appetites and thoughts get pulled into what James calls lust (1:14). By this James does not mean settled intent but the strong drawing of an appetite or thought, which is why he uses the word "conceive" to describe when sin occurs (1:15).

The enemy sees when natural attraction occurs or when a normal feeling or thought can get twisted to an interpretation of accusation or condemnation. The enemy even puts his spin on scriptures, especially anything that can get used to foster law and guilt. Pretty soon, Satan has people thinking that there is a law against having a soul and body with appetites and thoughts that can even be *pulled* toward misuse.

Perfection, therefore, means reversing the direction of temptation. Instead of using the drawings of lust for self-for-self, the perfect thing to do is affirm that the Spirit means to be for others and build them up. The devil is foiled, and God is glorified in our mortal bodies and uses them as His instruments, expressing His perfection. Fear gives way to faith, which is perfection.

How Much Victory Is Possible?

Dead men do not keep God's law or even try to. They live by the fruit of the Spirit—meaning the delightful flow of God's life in us so that He is all that He commands us to be. There is no need to live by law because Christians live by God's nature, and the Bible is the beautiful description of how God is expressed as us.

What then about the "consciousness of sin" (Hebrews 10:2)? No Christian has to live with it. Why say that we still sin every day? Certainly it is possible to sin every day, and who can deny that such is the experience of many Christians. But who is to say that there must still exist sins that we cannot be kept from? Who is to say how much victory is possible? In frantic concern, some do not want to wave a wand over themselves or others and proclaim a state of sinless perfection because that usually means attempts to baptize carnal responses as if they are the life of Christ in us. However, it is equally true that Christians often take needless condemnation for temptation when basic human appetites are pulled toward what *would* become sin if carried out.

Natural impulses from our humanity need not cause guilt, nor lead anyone to call them the life of the Spirit. The point of the Spirit's life is that it is Spirit life. As the Spirit quickens the mortal body, condemnation drops away for being human. Hebrews 4:12 tells us that the word of God is living and active to reveal to us the difference between our souls and our spirits. Our souls consist of our thoughts and feelings—our natural desires. Often, we get to enjoy many of life's pleasures—moments in which Spirit and soul rejoice together. It is equally true that the Spirit leads us to extreme discomfort and some level of death in our earthly members, which naturally would run from the Cross. Only a mind set on the Spirit finds life coming out of death on a soul or body level so that Spirit life can flow forth to others.

Dead to Sin also Means Dead to the Law

Christians who do not know that Christ is their life continue to sin because Satan, now kicked out, grabs their members from without. Satan can never be lord of the castle again; he can never re-enter a son and be the boss. The most he can do is to manipulate one's members, and he does this by his chief deception, which is to keep Christians unaware that they are only containers and branches. Not knowing this leads to continuing in the false notion that humans act independently, with God's help.

However, the truth is that to receive Christ means to belong to Christ; the enemy got expelled. In Romans 6, Paul calls this being "dead to sin." Faith causes the flow of Christ's life out into our earthly members by His Spirit, with Spirit discernment of the difference between old flesh impulses using neutral thoughts and feelings, and Christ's new mind in our members—whereby He quickens our members and produces rightly operated humanity in these earthen vessels, making them alive with glory even in this groaning, travailing world. We see who we now are by this new birth and by faith take that as our identity and life source.

Knowing that we are "dead to sin" necessitates seeing also that we are "dead to law," for sin gets its power through the law. Romans 7 is our primer on law, for if we are still trying to be like Christ, we will only get discouraged when we fall back into sin. We will think, "I know that I died; I am dead to sin, but why do I still sin?" The reason comes from *trying*, which means that we still live by law. Paul tells us in Romans 7 his own history of trying, his passionate first person narrative about his past experience of trying to keep the law, only to find that trying kept him doing what he did not want to do and falling short of what he did want to do. Romans 6 and Romans 7 are the twin emphases on "dead to sin" and "dead to law."

Three Astonishing Things

Jesus said that He had to go away, but that this would lead to three astonishing things (Jn. 16). These would be functions of the one known as the Paraclete—most often translated as advocate, comforter, or helper. However, my favorite translation is counselor (RSV) because of the Isaiah 11:2 connection to the sevenfold Spirit of the Lord.

The first function is to "convict the world concerning sin, because they do not believe in Me" (John 16:9). All sin comes from not believing in Jesus, even behavioral sins since a particular sin against any of God's commandments gets resolved in one way—by Jesus Christ, whose death is the only atonement for sin and whose resurrection life is the only keeping from sin.

The second function is "concerning righteousness because I go to the Father and you no longer see Me" (16:10). This sounds odd at first—being convicted of righteousness. We are to be convicted by the Holy Spirit of our righteousness in Christ because Jesus did everything needed to make us righteous, and He in His person is our righteousness. No wonder He could go away and send the Helper; the job was finished. The Cross and the burial were enough to cleanse from sin and cut us off from the spirit of sin, making way for Christ living out His righteousness by His Spirit in those who believe—based upon including us in His resurrection and ascension.

The third function is "concerning judgment, because the ruler of this world has been judged" (16:11). Satan is no longer our ruler, no longer our indweller, and no longer the determiner of our fortunes. Though the world still lies in the power of Satan (1 John 5:19), believers do not. Satan's power is broken and over for us, and he can only bother us on a temptation and suffering level, but never in the inner citadel of who we are. There is every reason to stand as one who has overcome the evil one and all of his lies.

Resurrection Power in the Body

The New Testament warns against rejecting the body as unimportant since God desires to live in our bodies as temples and vessels. We do not live by mandates of "taste not, touch not, handle not" (Col. 2:21). Christ's indwelling life manifested through our bodies pleases God and manifests His self-for-others nature to others by us.

The agony of Abraham and Sarah over her barrenness illustrates this. God promised Abraham an heir, but Sarah was barren, and the couple's aging became a factor. Soul and body could not produce God's promise by natural means, so God would have to birth Isaac supernaturally, apart from any flesh ability. This becomes Paul's metaphor in Galatians and Romans for the new birth and the Spirit's fruit in us by faith. Just as Abraham and Sarah could only conceive by the miracle-working power of the Holy Spirit, we too can only conceive our desires by the miracle of the Spirit in us. We want to see things happen in our lives; we want results. Waiting and repeated trying to produce these results, without success, heats up the fires between soul and spirit. Soul and body are not wrong (we are fearfully and wonderfully made) but represent what Abraham and Sarah saw and felt naturally, whereas spirit represents God's promise that He will fulfill, despite appearances. This tension leads to either the choice to try things again the natural way, or the choice to believe in miracles.

Just as the incarnation of Christ brought deity and humanity together, our union with Christ means great significance for the body. The resurrection in us makes holy what before was unholy. Instead of Old Testament commandments about bodily uncleanness, we now have "bodies washed with clean water" (Heb. 10:22). We freely accept our human selves without suspicion or the desire to escape from our humanity. God loves to live in earthen containers as us in our ordinary daily lives. Someday, even mortality will disappear.

Seeing through Soul to Spirit

Ordinary life offers plenty of opportunities for daily dying as we discern between soul and spirit. On a feeling level we feel threatened or hurt, or on a body level we think that we cannot live without food, sex, or some kind of comfort. Hebrews 4:12 sorts out how to see underneath who we are: "For the word of God is quick, and powerful, and sharper than any two-edged sword." God easily sees how to make things clear by "piercing even to the dividing asunder of soul and spirit, and of the joints and marrow, and is a discerner of the thoughts and intents of the heart."

The Spirit knows how to cut beneath fear and make clear how to walk by faith in a world that is always falling apart. Notice the mention of soul, joints, and thoughts in contrast to spirit, marrow, and intents. The Israelites failed to enter God's rest in the wilderness because they majored on food, water, and escape from conflict—allowing lack on a soul and body level to turn them to unbelief (Heb. 4). They insisted on physical provision and security at the expense of stepping into the unseen world of faith.

Though the body is important and God's temple, there is no point in fussing on a body level and missing the opportunity to see through in the Spirit. Underneath turmoil is rest. There is no need to take condemnation for negative thoughts and feelings; use them as the opportunity to live in God's rest during times of physical and emotional hardship.

Sometimes those hardships come about from how others treat us. Intentionally or unintentionally, people always do things that irritate us, go against our will, and deny us what we want, even tempting us to think that we do not love them. If we reason according to soul, we will think that we really do resent others. If we reason according to God's fixed nature of love in us, we will say, "I feel like I hate that person, but Christ loves that person perfectly by me."

We Live Tempted

We live tempted, and God means this. Therefore, it helps to understand temptation and how to get through it. Lack of clarity brings unnecessary, nagging guilt. Torment and anguish can result. James tells us that God cannot be tempted with evil and does not tempt anyone (1:13). God does, however, have a convenient agent to do the tempting. If God did not mean for the devil to do his job in this present age, he could not do it.

God pointed out Job's righteousness to the devil. Some might say God even incited him, and God certainly turned the devil loose on Job, with specific limitations. We see the same with Jesus: Mark's Gospel says, "And immediately the spirit drove Him into the wilderness" (1:12) where Satan tempted Him for forty days. The writer of Hebrews, stressing how Jesus as a human was like us in all things excepting sin, says that Jesus experienced all the temptations we do (4:15). So we have plenty of company when it comes to temptation, even the Son of God.

God knows that we will fail at first if we are still living out of our own supposed strength and not settled in Galatians 2:20 living. Jesus said to Peter at the Last Supper, "Simon, Simon, behold, Satan has demanded permission to sift you as wheat; but I have prayed for you that your faith may not fail; and you, when once you have turned again, strengthen your brothers" (Luke 22:31-32).

God exposes us to opposites because He knows that true faith is a tested faith. Love must undergo the test. In this case, Jesus knew Peter would fail in his initial temptation, but then repent and use his experience to help others. The answer to temptation is not a strong self-will and new resolution. Those take us back to self-keeping. Faith is as simple as Paul's word that we consider ourselves dead to various passions and lusts since we died to them in Christ and are alive to Christ's pulls amid contrary ones.

A Little Wisdom Helps with Temptation

A little wisdom goes a long way when tempted, but that wisdom may take a while to learn. Paul says, "For I say, through the grace given unto me, to every man that is among you, not to think of himself more highly than he ought to think; but to think soberly, according as God hath dealt to every man the measure of faith" (Rom. 12:3).

In grade school, it was time for a go at swimming lessons. For several days the instructor led the class through different stokes to practice in the shallow end of the pool until one day he said, "Everyone ready to dive off the board on the deep end go on down and line up." Almost everyone scurried off to the deep end. I felt sick because I still could not swim or even tread water but also felt embarrassed by what others would think, so I got in line behind the board on the deep end. Jumping in, I immediately floundered, trying to keep bobbing high enough to gasp for air. Mercifully, the instructor came to the rescue and had a word for boys who need more wisdom.

In addition to what we are not qualified for, there is the matter of what we cannot have. Who has not tortured himself longer than needed before accepting an already settled verdict? The tempted one hopes that God will say yes to what He has already said no to, yet desire remains unabated and continues. It is like the child with nose pressed to the candy store window after his parents have said, "No candy!" Finally, it is time to walk away.

There is a world of unnecessary guilt among Christians about even wanting what is not permissible. Strong desires, however, are not sin. It is in the will where sin is conceived (James 1:14). Beware of just confessing negative thoughts and feelings (or positive ones) as sin, hoping they will go away, because often they do not, and it is not our fault any more than coughing in smog is our fault if we are stuck in smog.

The Safe Human

We live with more ease when we stop condemning ourselves for our God-made, strong appetites. The tempter certainly will solicit us through the same avenues that God means to use for His purposes. James tells us not to dread this, but to "consider it all joy" (1:2). Every temptation is common to man (1 Cor. 10:13)—common like the cold we might say. Nothing in the way of temptation should shock us or lead us to condemnation. God made us with strong appetites for His right use, and those appetites are just as alive when the tempter seeks them for wrong use.

Trying to get rid of human desires can't work and will only lead to feeling rebellious and thinking, "God, why did You make me this way?" "Why am I human?" Here again, God means for us to go through temptations. Dan Stone always said, "Do you know when you won't experience temptation? When people look over at you and say, 'Doesn't he look natural?'" Lust that pulls is not sin; lust that conceives by the will—"I will do it"—that is sin.

The answer to temptation is not a strong self-will and new resolution. That takes us back to self-keeping. Faith is as simple as Paul's word that we consider ourselves dead to various passions and lusts since we died to them in Christ. Faith says, "I am dead to that." I often start laughing when I realize, "Oh, it's only lust," or, "It's only the devil trying to make me think I want my own way."

Sometimes our thoughts and feelings shock us. "How could that cross my mind?" or, "How could I feel that strong of a lust?" Fear not, we might experience any imaginable thought or feeling, and we walk through easily in faith unless we tangle ourselves in condemnation and do not thank God that He is keeping us. The point is not the thought or feeling but knowing that we are spirit joined to Spirit and kept. The keeping is everything, even if not to our comfort level.

Satan's Trick to Make You Think Temptation Is Sin

We might experience any imaginable thought or feeling but walk through easily in faith unless getting tangled by condemnation. James tells the secret: "Every man is tempted, when he is drawn away of his own lust, and enticed" (1:14). The emphasis is not on bodily appetites, but on lust that demands its own way. The real temptation is not the soul or bodily avenue, but the temptation to self-will that conceives by saying, "I will take that for myself, regardless." This is where lust becomes sin. Until then, lust is strong desire through a normal human faculty stirred up to intense craving. It is the enemy who tempts us on a will level, hiding in our first person thought, "I must have this" or "I can't resist this."

Sin is always that way. When we were lost, we did the lusts of our father the devil (Jn. 8:44). As Christians, we are safe at center, united to Christ, but sin is always the same old thing—Satan's lusts not recognized and refused by knowing that we are dead to sin and law (Rom. 6 and 7). Temptation says, "Will I wear down or will I eventually give in?" It is about endurance. That is why the only thing that works is the moment-by-moment faith that we no longer live, but Christ lives in us and is keeping us. God's greatest purpose with us in temptation is not about the temptation, but His keeping of us.

Acceptance of temptation goes a long way toward serenity. We live tempted. Not to recognize this means that we still long for a "La-La life" not offered in the Scriptures. Faith considers temptations and trials all joy and as everyday occurrences, understanding that God encourages us on to endurance as He provides an escape hatch, custom-made for every situation. The ultimate escape hatch I have discovered is the one that says, "Lord, I will commit any sin unless You keep me, and thank You that You are keeping me!"

Circumcision Is a Deep Bible Concept

Circumcision culturally is for health reasons. In the Bible, however, it is a sign of God's covenant with His people. In the Old Testament, it meant cutting away the male foreskin. In the New Testament, it means the Cross of Christ cutting away the body of sin. The fact that males start out covered with a foreskin of flesh represents Adam's fall into trusting the flesh. Originally, the glory of God covered Adam, not a layer of flesh. Adam's fall in the garden plunged us into darkness and the dominion of Satan, so that we began to trust only in what the flesh can do in its own supposed power—instead of what God can do by man in the union of His Spirit with our humanity.

The first Biblical record of circumcision is Genesis 17, where God reaffirms to Abraham that Abraham will "be the father of a multitude of nations" (17:4). He is now ninety-nine years old, yet God commands circumcision as the sign of the covenant, and also declares that Sarah will bear the promised son. Abraham "fell on his face and laughed" (v 17). Who wouldn't do the same? God's plan is ridiculously impossible to flesh. However, what flesh cannot do, God easily does by His own power; in fact, His plan for us was always that He be the power in powerless vessels created by Him to contain Himself. What we call miracles, God always intended as our normal way of life.

Abraham came to see this. God meant circumcision as a sign that Isaac's birth would be supernatural, not by the normal conjugal means of a couple in their 90s. Circumcision told everyone that each member of the covenant people came into the world because of a supernatural conception that started the covenant line of Abraham and Sarah, leading to the nation of Israel.

The new birth in Christ follows the same pattern. Because we were dead in sin we were unable to produce the fruit of the Spirit. Therefore, Christ crucified the old man in Himself, then birthed him a new creation.

Results

No one likes to work at something without results. That is normal. In the physical world, if one lifts weights but never sees a muscle get stronger, after a while, the pain of the gym will not be worth the expenditure of time and energy. An investment that never pays off will lead to cashing it in and trying something else. Life is about increase.

God certainly concurs with this, but His ways look backward to us until we know them. Death comes first, and then life out of death which sounds scary. First God gives a promise, and the promise likely brings hope and exhilaration as if the fulfillment will happen soon. Wrong, we find out, as time drags on. Nothing changes, and moreover, situations get worse than ever. Did God promise, or did a lively imagination conjure up that word of faith you said?

Add to this looking foolish, or even in error. The flesh cries out, and the devil is hotter and more accusing than ever. This is excellent—the heat and suffering that build faith—and faith is the first result. God's promise is a result, but the result that He seeks first is faith. Faith is its own substance, followed later by the eventual manifestation embedded in God's promise.

The process puts a man onto God alone since nothing human can bear up under the inner death, and nothing human can raise one up from it. Fear drops away and ascension life is built within as God Himself forms Christ first in the intercessor and takes him or her all the way. When things do not go as hoped, God is the one meaning every delay and the mounting sense of impossibility.

He is hammering out certainty in us. Then we know and step forth to say that we are on a perfect schedule and pace for the harvest. Nothing less will do. Instead of backing off, faith gets bolder and laughs at contrary appearances.

Outer Versus Inner Circumcision

Physical circumcision cannot produce a heart of faith, which is why Jeremiah quotes the Lord: "I will punish all who are circumcised and yet uncircumcised" (9:25). An outer act can't produce a condition of the heart, and thus Paul tells us, "For indeed circumcision is of value, if you practice the law; but if you are a transgressor of the Law, your circumcision has become uncircumcision" (Rom. 2:25). But can someone uncircumcised become as one circumcised? Paul answers yes (2:26) and then adds the radical revelation, "Circumcision is that which is of the heart, by the Spirit, not by the letter" (2:29). The New Covenant did not eliminate circumcision but redefined it in Spirit terms according to the Cross as the instrument circumcising one's heart. Circumcision is now the "removal of the body of the flesh by the circumcision of Christ" (Col. 2:11).

This makes it applicable to females as well. "For we are the true circumcision, who worship in the Spirit of God and glory in Christ Jesus and put no confidence in the flesh" (Phil. 3:3). Gentiles in the church grasped this radical, new understanding more easily than many Jewish believers. To Jews, not circumcising a male Jewish baby brought terrified feelings, for the Old Covenant threatened being cut off from God's people for not being circumcised. This fear was so deeply implanted that only a new, radical thought could replace physical circumcision.

Paul gives that. Our circumcision is "the removal of the body of the flesh" (Col. 2:11)—"having been buried with Him in baptism, in which you also were raised up with Him through faith" (2:12). These two verses are a miniature of Romans Chapter 6. God unzipped Jesus on the Cross, put us into Him, and then zipped Him back up so that everything that happens to Christ happens to us: death, burial, and resurrection. And now what happens to us happens to Him.

What Is the True Circumcision?

True circumcision is not what anybody would have guessed. God revealed it to Paul, and Paul to us. Not only did God put us into Christ on the Cross, He made Christ to be who we were as lost people. Ephesians 2 tells us that the spirit of error dwelled in us from birth as a result of the Fall (see also John 8:44 and 2 Tim. 2:26). We come into the world as slaves of the enemy who indwells us. Therefore, God's plan of salvation had to take Satan out of us so that Christ could come into us. This is why God made Christ on the Cross to "be sin" (2 Cor. 5:21). This does not mean that Christ sinned but that on the Cross, He became sin, meaning that His body became our old man, the man indwelled with the spirit of error.

Uniting to Christ's death makes us dead to sin, for death to sin means that God took the sin spirit out of us as our indweller and boss. When Christ's body died (as ours), the sin spirit went out, and the empty body went into the grave. This body is dead to sin, but it is also dead to righteousness: a dead body cannot sin but cannot do anything righteous either. It is simply a dead body.

For the body to become an instrument of righteousness, your spirit must rise from the dead joined to Christ's Spirit, so that you, the new man, can take charge of the whole you and walk by faith in the sanctification of your spirit, soul, and body. Even your mortal body must obey you until the day when the new body will replace it as your manifest body. This is the true circumcision and the radical truth revealed to give all Christians, including Jewish ones, the courage to let go of physical circumcision as an element of salvation. It is always challenging to move from outer ritual to inner reality because it feels safer to stay on the outside, but God replaces outer safety with inner safety.

Sabbath Keeping: Outer or Inner?

The church has discussed through the ages which day is the Sabbath and how to keep it holy. For a Christian, is Saturday really the Sabbath, or is it Sunday? Also debated is what constitutes work on the Sabbath. However, maybe this kind of analysis misses the point. The argument from the book of Hebrews shows that Joshua did not give the people rest, meaning that Christ, as the Joshua of the New Covenant, must give us rest. The writer warns against failing to enter into this rest.

The Old Testament Joshua did not fail in his mission. God meant that he lead Israel in battle, conquer a land, govern by the Law of Moses, and give the nation prosperity and peace in the land with a theocratic constitution. Even today, God may assign a Gospel people a land, with just and merciful laws, all with a view to their prosperity. None of these, however, brings rest to the inner man because only Christ's blood and body death can do that by the Spirit as a believer sees Christ in you the hope of glory.

The Hebrews writer describes rest in the Spirit whereby we do not look to the work of man's hands for the source of rest. The argument is simple; God finished His work of creating the world, according to Genesis, and He ceased from that work. All that remained was to enjoy it. In the same way, God completed the work of His new creation when Christ rose from the dead and ascended. Nothing remains to do except that we enter into that rest from our own works and enjoy His righteousness.

In both instances—the physical creation in Genesis and His work of salvation for those who believe—God was the sole worker, with the view that we simply enter by faith and enjoy Christ as our life. We did not take part in the creation of the physical world but were placed into it, and so also, we did not take part in the new creation but were placed into it.

Why Would Man Think He's an Ape?

Adam and Eve fell and then sewed fig leaves together to cover their nakedness. Animals, however, are not naked, because nature provides their covering, while man has to make his own. Yet before the Fall, Adam and Eve were clothed by the One who later resided above the Ark of the Covenant in the holy place of the Jewish temple. This was a sad separation that awaited Christ's blood and body to restore Shekinah as the new man's radiance, to be manifested fully at the final resurrection.

The Fall plunged man into bondage to Satan, and the lie that flesh is the truth. We became enamored with wanting to be an animal instead of God's son. Without Christ's mind, there is only blindness that keeps people enslaved on an animal level, separated from being born anew into the Holy Spirit's kingdom through the Cross. Nature is not evil, but nature is mortal, penetrated with Satan's lie, and awaiting subjection to redeemed man as regent. Thus, nature is wild and self-serving, which appeals to fallen man, who then would like to see himself as differing from animals only in superior intellect by rising randomly through an evolutionary process to heights of technical genius. This allows fallen man a sense of grandeur in working his way upward to his present scientific accomplishments.

This also allows self-flattery in applying the same idea to social sciences, by which humanity thinks that it can be an animal but also a noble creature that simultaneously removes social injustice and ushers in a day of equality based on being a highly evolved, loving animal; but there is no salvation in being a mortal, loving animal. Salvation is only by the blood and body sacrifice of God's incarnate Son, which can birth a fallen man out of the lie of being an evolved animal and into knowing himself as a son of God in spirit eternally through Jesus Christ.

Abraham's Seed Is Christ

Salvation means forgiveness of sins, but it also means restoration, by miracle, into union with God. Many, including non-Christian sects, believe in union with the divine, but only Christianity offers the valid means of return to our original union, since the Bible is clear that we cannot obtain salvation by any works of our own. This is why God's incarnate Son had to die on a Cross for us and as us. This is what it took to put us into His body and to put Himself into us. God unites us with Himself through the death, burial, and resurrection of Christ.

There is no such thing as just believing union with God and entering into it apart from Christ's work on the Cross. All we do is believe Christ's work in order to know union with the divine. This belief is not a work but simply receiving by faith Christ's completed work. Abraham saw glimpses of these truths. Certainly he saw that God meant circumcision as a sign that Isaac's birth would take place supernaturally and not by the normal conjugal means of a man ninety-nine and a woman not far behind him in age.

We, as new creations in Christ, fulfill the promise to Abraham, a promise not only of physical descendants of Abraham, but a promise of the seed of Christ. In fact, Paul says, "Now the promises were spoken to Abraham and to his seed," and that seed was "Christ" (Gal. 3:16). How could Christ be Abraham's seed? When Abraham and Sarah could not sire a child, God circumvented the flesh—putting His supernatural life (seed) into the procreation process, meaning Isaac's birth, but even more into our new birth as new creations from the seed that is Christ.

This was His plan all along. He always wanted to produce Christ, the seed, in us so that we could live as incarnations of Him, whereby we become a race of new creations in Him, expressing His being in our human forms. This is life divine and eternal, which the Cross circumcised us into.

Works without Faith Are Dead

The Christian life begins in the Spirit, continues in the Spirit, and finishes in the Spirit. Human works never enter in as the way to live. The only works that count are those of the Spirit in us, as we walk by faith. This might sound too easy. Already, some are rushing to James to underscore that faith without works is dead. Yes, but do you know also that works without faith (works not produced by the Spirit) are dead, human works, no matter how good they look? Worse, they have bewitching as their source (Gal. 3:1) and are set on fire from hell (James 3:6).

The Hebrews letter deals with adversarial pressure to return to the old treadmill of self-effort and return to law. This would mean retreat from Christ, but if we can keep the law, Christ died for no reason. Why return to what the self thinks it can do to improve itself and work for God? Faith is not needed, and human toil becomes the measure of good. This is not rest, and the honest heart knows it.

Hebrews Chapter 4 exhorts to let the living Word separate soul and spirit—finding rest in the Spirit despite miserable outer circumstances. This sounds dangerous. What will we do? Fear of not taking care of ourselves leads to more fear—that if we stop to rest, it will only increase our sense of lack and leave us dry.

Hebrews is not cold-hearted but affirms that Christ sympathizes with our weaknesses when we are faced with temptation, since He too was tempted. He means us to live from rest in what He has done and is doing by the Spirit in us when things are rough. Jesus Himself looked worse and more incongruous to His world than we realize. Think of how it threw the world into a mad rage that Jesus waited upon His Father and only did the works that His Father did in Him. Therefore, He perfectly understands our discomfort and suffering when we do not conform to the militant expectations of works according to the world's idea of self-preservation.

August 29

Commissions from God Are Unique

Uniqueness is a gift. Trying to be unique will not work, and the one who tries shows the wear of trying. Everyone can see the person dripping with effort. Uniqueness is a gift received, not achieved. Looking away from self to Christ, you see yourself in the holy mirror—a self you would not have thought of to invent, and would not have the know-how to maintain. Then you know yourself from a detached view from the mind of Christ and not from natural reasoning.

Commissions from God are the same. Usually, we start by imitating what mentors do, seeing their acts but not knowing their ways yet. Thus, others seem special and not like regular humans, which is why imitating them looks like the way. It does not seem possible that they are ordinary humans endued with the Spirit's manifestation of the fruits of the Spirit in a unique way by them. Then comes the day when models, schemes, and trying to be like others, get tossed aside, and the seeker, worn from trying, is now willing to stand alone and say to God," I am just looking at You." Then the seeker sees himself as he really is. It is the Spirit's gift, and the viewer hardly lingers to dwell on it, but gets right out into life in the joy of that real self.

The will of God becomes an easy flow, even when placed into difficult situations. Those situations are a lot less difficult when knowing, "I am supposed to be here." It is one thing to choose a road; it is another to have had it chosen for you and to get on walking it. It is always tempting to look at others' roads and compare, rather than walk as God called you. All roads start with the Spirit's witness, and no road is the right road until that is settled. When it is, every road is the right road, no matter how curious or odd it seems.

The Biggest Mess Is the Right Mess

God made man to incurably seek social connection, yet because of sin, socialization turns out to be either sharing the self that one wishes to be, or the self that treads water in one mess after another. There is always something wrong, a problem, something to be figured out and fixed; and usually things and relationship-thinking drive one's interpretation. This is the natural or carnal mind, which means trying to fix things but not yet seeing to the heart. No one starts life any other way, and God does not condemn us for this but grieves when someone stays there.

The real issue is the self that tries to be what it thinks it should be, while enlisting approval from God and others. The desire to understand and to be understood still rules, and the source is the enemy, who hides that he is the perpetrator. The Bible certainly exhorts us to understand God's ways, but equally says that only the mind of Christ knows them, the mind we received when the old mind died (Rom. 6). The new mind is "the eyes of your understanding being enlightened" (Eph. 1:18).

Then light is the norm. What, or rather who, is this light? John says it is God Himself: "God is light" (1 John 1:5). Everyone has natural eyes, but these are not of concern here. The point is the eyes of the new man, which God has made to be our eyes of faith now. The Spirit opens these eyes, bringing conviction. A new experience occurs —God's own seeing through us.

This is why Christianity is not a change of mind in the ordinary sense of human reason. Some crisis finally alerts the desperate person that nothing is working—everything is dead, futile—never destined to work in the world of constant messes. Trying to fix enough messes in order to approach God is not what God seeks. He says, "Come to Me with whatever it is, and I will be the One in you who is not a mess." Mess consciousness gives way to opportunity consciousness.

How Does Self Analysis Work?

In a self-help world, problems lead to seeking help from others. Someone struggling will find a person with insight and counsel. This sounds good at first, but the flaw comes if you think that truth is apprehended by natural reason, which is soul, instead truth apprehended by the human spirit quickened by the Holy Spirit (Heb. 4). On the surface, the battle appears to be standing with reason against ever-fluctuating emotions, but this only puts one part of the soul against the other in seeking stability.

Moving the arena to the human spirit but not as quickened by the Holy Spirit, one still faces the challenge of discerning lies and coming up with willpower to believe what is true. This cannot satisfy because the self retains the sense of being a self that tries to believe correctly and modify its view of itself. Where is the miracle?

God sees us according to His nature, expressed by the Cross, and this is true regardless of what we do. His nature is constant because of His fixed choice, an eternal choice, to be love. He is for others at the supreme cost of the Cross. Therefore, His only disappointment—even His wrath—can only occur when a person fails to see with His seeing. Even then, wrath is only love's grief when someone remains in darkness. In the Cross there is no torment; outside of the Cross there is nothing but torment.

No human ever sees as God sees unless God is the seer in the human. The Holy Spirit awakens the seeker into God's very seeing. To see one's self becomes a detached experience, in which seeing one's self is experienced as if another is doing the seeing. This *is* in fact, what happens. Yet the experience of seeing is still experienced by the human who sees. It is you seeing yourself, but it is God doing the seeing by the now detached you (Gal. 2). No man can judge himself properly without this miracle. All that is necessary is the willingness, and God even quickens willingness in one who desires to believe.

Dealing with the Impossible

Everyone needs a dose of the impossible. It is already there, but since the Fall, Satan deceives the carnal mind with two extremes: either there is no hope, or "You can do anything if you stay at it." All is either doom, or all is a challenge that any independent self with some dignity can master. Life is full of suffering. That is a fact, and hiding from it does no good. However, holding a positive attitude without the eternal offers nothing beyond the grave.

No wonder God means evil to overrun the supposed independent self. God means evil for good. He never does evil, but He does not prevent it. This may be the world's biggest offense with God—that He does not remove evil or prevent it. Even His children suffer just like everyone else. When people ask, "How is the world treating you?" I reply, "I am more concerned with how I am treating it."

Even for Christians, evil comes roaring in from every side because God has not lifted us onto a cloud removed from its outer effects. Grief and pain are normal, but God means them for good, despite how others intend them. The Bible even says to hate evil. However, it also says to love the good that God is working, first in us, then in others. God's greatest good in us comes by seeing everything under His control and meant by Him as a call to faith. He who calls us to endure something, endures it in us. Therefore, we are never alone, and what happens to us happens to Him. Not only that, what happens to Him has a clear purpose. We just may not know why.

The point is faith and its awareness that it is impossible to produce God's light by any human agency, or any agency other than Christ Himself. All roads lead to death working in every Christian to produce life for others (2 Cor. 4:12). Heaven's streets are made of this.

Pulling the Teeth out of Evil

We are afraid of evil until we know what to do with it. In this present age, God has not removed it from the world, and He even assigns His children to live in the midst of it but says that evil is not in them. Fearing evil means thinking that enough evil perpetrated against even a Christian will penetrate and elicit evil in the one seeking to suppress it. One stays stuck in fear of what he or she will do. No wonder God does not whisk evil away when someone becomes a Christian. Instead, the "accuser" accuses "day and night," nonstop, and God lets this happen, or rather actually means it to be for now (Rev. 12:10). This is because faith in God's keeping grows stronger against resistance.

Think of the worst thing that you have ever done, or that anyone has done to you. Plenty of room exists for shame. The devil uses what we or others have done to rub our faces in it with torment and condemnation. It is relentless, cruel, even murderous—devoid of forgiveness, plus no amount of confession can ever cause Satan to back off. Neither will confession or restitution toward others satisfy the determined, angry accuser. Only one thing can triumph over the accuser. What conquers is the blood of the lamb and the "word" of your "testimony" (Rev. 12:11).

The devil brings to mind shameful things that we have done in order to accuse, and he brings to mind shameful things that others have done against us, fueling blame and resentment. But when these are seen under the blood of Christ, they lose their sting, causing forgetfulness to settle in except to testify of the miracle of a clean, fresh new life. God's greater purpose becomes the point, which is making whole what appeared destroyed beyond hope. Nothing in God's universe is greater than His ability to create abundant life out of ruins. The ruins are the before; the resurrection is the testimony.

It's not as Complicated as It Appears

Walking in the Spirit is easy but not what many think. It is not the gifts of the Spirit, though these are real, as well as specific task anointing. When Paul writes about walking in the Spirit (Gal. 5), his mind is on the fruit of the Spirit, which is a list of what the world mistakenly calls character qualities. Nothing could be farther from Paul's intent, however, than trying to imitate love, meekness, and patience—as if they are learned by practice. The fruit of the Spirit is the point, and the fruit comes from the normal connection to the Spirit as one walks in the Spirit. This is routine, not the stuff of heroes. Every Christian has the Spirit (Rom. 8:9), and the normal thing is to live from it. Therefore, instead of trying to produce character qualities, the Spirit *is* those. Trying to be what only the Spirit is would be like a cup trying to be the coffee it contains. However, the point of a cup is to serve others a drink of the Spirit that lives in us.

Believers are free to do that, and the devil cannot prevent it but only intensify crazy thoughts, put false spin on emotions, and continually lie as if the truth is hard to know and off in the distance away from easy access. Truth is never far away; it is "on your lips" and "in your heart" already—quietly there underneath (Deut. 30:14, Rom. 10:18). Just know that as you open your mouth or move to do the next thing, the Spirit will perfectly manifest Christ, and not only that—as you, because once you see that the cup is not the coffee, the pleasure of being a branch of the vine makes us wonder why we ever thought abiding was impossible or rare. Do not wait as if one has to remove soul and body distractions first. These are not the problem—not even enemy lies. Go straight to the Spirit, for God's currency is always faith, and faith depends upon operating against what appears true. The same human instrument that appears too defective for walking in the Spirit is the very instrument that God has cleansed and occupied.

Fretting Accomplishes Nothing

Fretting accomplishes nothing; well, it can wear you out. We are commanded not to fret over wrongdoers (Psalm 37:1). Fretting, therefore, is more than just natural dislike. Things to dislike pop up constantly, and reactions to them are as normal and reflexive as "ouch" to a pinprick. However, in your spirit, where you will and know, interpretation takes place—not the obsessive head-weary analysis that the enemy loves to promote, but the discernment where one decides according to what the mirror of the Holy Spirit reveals.

The dictionary offers a range of definitions for the word fret, the main idea being to wear down under continual exposure to something that gnaws away. The idea is akin to the distraught person who says, "If you do that one more time, I will lose my mind." Fill in the blank with any script of desperate, and now justified retaliations based on unrelenting provocation from an irritating source. It is the cliché, "I can't take it anymore."

God means this to happen. He does not mean for us to fret, even when a situation surely gives permission to fret. Not to, however, would require a miracle, and this is what God is always after—the miracle. Everyone has a situation in which another person or a scenario is so awful to experience that the desire is finally to get rid of the irritation or leave. Leaving can be prudent. Those with boundaries (Spirit ones) know when it is time to leave others to what they are doing and go elsewhere.

Other times, God traps us so that no external escape is possible or sanctioned. In these scenarios, since God means us not to escape externally, He has provided a door of escape internally. Often, the escape is as simple as thanking God for the difficult person or situation. Just when fretting would occur, there is the door to refuse it— a door of the Spirit's rest. Others will say, "Why don't you do something about this?" We have: we are not fretting.

Seeing Through on Evil

Seven trumpets sound forth in Revelation. When God forecasts doom, it is a warning to awaken, and trumpets sound out the call. Underneath all of the complicated or cryptic description is a simple story. A child can see that God uses physical hardships and satanic attacks in hope that hardened people will become disillusioned with lost or carnal living and come to the pure streams of living water. God is so merciful that He will set aside judgment until a person, or the world, has had every chance to drink of futility enough to see Satan exposed and Christ revealed. Hell, then, is only for those who love their hell.

The pattern in Revelation is that outer need intensifies. Quarrels and wars break out over lack of supply. As conflict heats up, Satan appears more boldly, and Chapters 9 and 12 show Satan as the driver behind accusation, anguish, and torment. When Satan is loosed to do more, God's purpose is desire for tormented ones to awaken and cry out to Him for rescue. Though it appears merciless to loose Satan, it is merciful to do so because God says, "Is this what you really want? This is coming from within *you,* where you are trapped in a lie."

In Chapter 10, John hears thunders but is told not to write them down. Why? Thunders signal the end, and God does not want that. He has a little book for John and us to read—sweet to the taste as God's word is—and this book exposes Satan's lie that the lost world lives in and that carnal Christians have not seen yet. The point is to preach the book. This is depicted by two witnesses in the Spirit exposing the lies of religion that keep people deceived when they know religion but not Christ. The lost world and the religious church attack the messengers, but again, the attacks are God's mercy to let His messengers even be killed if others would believe (Rev. 11). Nothing stops the messengers; they know that death for them only means resurrection.

When Reading Revelation

It is 95 AD. John is banished to an island—a solitary figure apparently with no say in how the world is going. The Roman Empire rules in full force, no longer a republic but an emperor-centered power. Christianity appears to have failed, with Rome emerging as the victor. John lives as an exiled apostle in solitude who knows who he is but looks at a world that does not know who it is except for scattered pockets of believers. Suddenly he receives a lesson in world history, an overpowering vision (and version) from above. At John's lowest, he sees the highest. That's the way it is. When your world falls apart, God shows the new world like the butterfly coming forth. That cannot happen without the old version dying. John could have told this already, being a seasoned apostle and father, but now this little man who appears set aside and minimized, becomes the vessel for how gloriously and completely God endures the worst that the enemy can do, only to bring to our seeing the most eternal that God is, and God starts within against appearances.

Not only is God not defeated, but the deciding battle is ridiculously one-sided. For all the fearful threats and attacks, Jesus Christ emerges victor over the vilest enemy possible, but He does so first in the hearts of those whose world has been crushed—outwardly that is. For John, God Himself is the architect of the plan all along, no matter how bad the plan looks. How bad the plan looks, turns into how good the plan looks, and how total. When you have been set aside, even cast off, when everything you worked for has been minimized and an enemy has stolen the stage and exalted himself, these are only the birth pangs of knowing that the eternal stage is Christ's—and yours. When the curtain comes down, you will be the one making the bow to the thrilling audience of heaven, and then earth as well.

When Christ Begins to Reign

The kingdom of the world has become the kingdom of our Lord and of His Christ (Rev. 11:17).

God looses Satan against those who are not sealed. This is for their salvation if they will see God's merciful hand pointing to the hell that they are already in but do not see because the pretender of light has masked it, even a hell that God means—to intensify inner torment in the hope of desperation and awakening. The saved, however, find God's book sweet to the taste but then bitter in the stomach, which is their great stress of intercession as they point to the futility of self-made works that see no need for the Cross, and which undermine Holy Spirit messengers who witness to Christ's blood as the only remedy for sin and Christ's body as the only tree whereby one may be a sanctified human and branch.

When your world falls apart, there is comfort in the coming new world—the kingdom of God—His worldwide manifest presence and rule, which includes judgment on evildoers, and their exclusion from the kingdom by their own choice. However, we do not see the kingdom of God only when it manifests outwardly. Jesus told Nicodemus that to be born again is to see it—an instant view differentiating it from the world as surely as the Spirit divides soul and spirit.

It looks foolish to proclaim as real and triumphant what has not manifested outwardly, but such is faith? Hope is faith that does not question if a thing will manifest, but while waiting, sees it as guaranteed and complete. We long for manifestation, but first comes the age of faith, in which Satan's greatest fear is a race of sons birthed of Christ, and this is the reason for the woman with child in Revelation 12. Not even Satan's worst can stop the creation of the new race that She carries to birth. He cannot kill Her or prevent Her children from being birthed from Christ the seed.

Satan's Lamb Imitation

Satan does not know how to be a lamb, but he needs a lamb imitation to deceive people into mistaking evil for good. This does not seem like it would be possible, but evil can look good in its works and masquerade as light. The works themselves help others to meet an outer need, while underneath, the motive is a godless system of control and uniformity. This is fleshly religion with no Spirit. Forms and rituals are there; the scriptures are all there, but followers do not recognize that they are letting themselves be stripped of hearing from God themselves. In fact, they are taught not to trust hearing from God themselves, but to go only by human intermediaries, who supposedly are more qualified to hear from God.

One day, the unsuspecting worshiper wakes up and finds himself worshiping a leader, a code, and a group. It is not that God does not establish these secondary entities; He just demands to be the shepherd of the sheep individually so that each believer, no matter how new and untaught, can perfectly trust to hear the Spirit's voice. "My sheep hear my voice, and I know them, and they follow me" (John 10:27). Even when we listen to others, we listen for the voice of the Spirit—in them and in us. There is "one body and one Spirit" (Eph. 4:4).

The wisdom of the Spirit is unity that baffles us on how it could be unity except by faith and by God's declaration. The inner Spirit is the same, the worshippers are free and know it, and the enjoyment of fellowship is without paranoia. With Satan, however, one liberty after another vanishes in ever-increasing religion without the Spirit of God—without the Cross. Instead of the leaders sacrificing for those they serve, the leaders shun in every way anyone who does not promote their agenda. But when Christians know who they are, they weather each other's differences by the true shepherd in them.

Blessed Are Those Who Die in the Lord

Revelation never says that there is no independent self; it simply never makes a place for one. A child can read it and see that Jesus Christ is Lord, refusal of whom automatically defaults a person to Satan's camp, where the state of mind is always self-commending or self-condemning, both of which are slavery. Just like Christ does, Satan asks for a fixed and final choice to be in his camp and receive his mark; and just like there is a heaven, there is a hell.

Hell is not a safe retreat from the consciousness of God, however. In hell, there is no consciousness of God such as is the mind of Christ. Instead, the experience is the consciousness of God experienced as one who is refused but still omnipresent. There is the torment of refusing the one person who really is love. Hell is using every bit of one's energy resisting that love. The one in hell knows that God is and that He is a Lamb, but he can never rest because he tries to imitate what only God can be. Thus, the one who insists on independence experiences God in wrath form.

God can only be worshipped as an other-than, who is all in all. This is the ground of safe oneness with Him— oneness that God offers anyone in the blood and body of Christ, mediated by the Spirit. The rebel, however, says, "If I cannot be God Himself, I will not accept Him at all." No rest is possible, or relief from condemnation, only Satan's regret internalized through law-consciousness.

Satan appears to be winning in the world. Not only is the prevalence of evil (called the beast) suffering to God's children; they are persecuted as well, many unto death. Yet Christ pronounces a blessing to those who "die in the Lord" because they have seen both sides and made their choice to stay with the Lamb no matter what. All the world can do is hurt or kill their bodies. Spiritually, they are ever and always united to their Lord, and this is hope eternal.

Hell and Heaven Contrasted

Hell is the place where a person is locked in time. No sense of eternity exists but only the endless obsession with time. Heaven means that time is a measurement but not the consciousness. Heaven is always fresh and in the moment, without enslavement to a sense of time. Hell is being locked into the material world, unaware of spirit. Heaven is the place where matter exists but reflects the Spirit that created it. Hell is conflict never resolved, or where resolution carries the fear of it breaking out again. Differences necessitate conflict, and argument is sought for its own sake. Heaven manifests endless differences, all in one Spirit where tensions are simply the stuff of opposites that make for rhythm and balance in the particulars expressing the same Holy Spirit. Heaven in you means that conflicts get resolved in you, even if not in the other person while the present earth is still with us. You do not have to have negotiation or agreement with others to settle your inner conflict. The single eye is possible now, and your body can be full of light now.

Hell is the world of self-improvement. The self is seen as an entity to work on and improve as if a human being improves by means of self-derived resolutions and trying. Heaven drops all that and sees human beings simply as vessels and branches to express the trinity. One experiences perfection by containing and being in union with the one perfect person—God.

Hell is the world where finally no one can get beyond the borders of his or her own self. It is the sense of isolation and being trapped in the self alone, where loneliness has taken over completely. The common grace of relating to others has been forfeited by choice, and the blessing of staying interested in others has died out. Heaven is where escape from the self has taken place by the Cross, and staying connected to God and others is the normal, easy way that God expresses Himself in His vessels.

September 11

Our Joy Is Greater Than Our Trials

Life is not easy, nor is it supposed to be. It is a misconception to think that we are only to experience the positive side of life and not also its hardships. Jesus was "a man of sorrows, and acquainted with grief" (Isa. 53:3). God did not shield Him from suffering but kept Him through it. Suffering is not something Jesus wanted, but He went through it anyway for us, and He still does in the sons—like vine, like branch.

As sin drops off in our lives (which it does once you see that you died to it), relief comes, not being entrapped by various lusts and passions. They still assault us daily, but we know God's keeping, with joy and satisfaction over walking free of what formerly kept us in bondage. This relief goes a long way, accompanied by much peace and victory.

While life becomes infinitely more manageable, as it should since one fruit of the Spirit is self-control, trials never cease. We still are pilgrims in "this present evil age" (Gal. 1:4), Jesus being the pilgrim of pilgrims, who was understood by no one until the Spirit came. Some loved Him while baffled by His responses; others could not take Him at all, wanting Him out of the way, even dead. He is the same in us.

Though it would be wonderful to scoot on off to heaven, when we think about it, the Spirit's urgings inside trump the desire to go home too early to be with the Lord. Instead, a will to endure hardship far outweighs the desire for being removed from the plane of suffering. This is God's desire in us yearning to give ourselves to seeing others come through no matter what it takes.

This does not mean thrashing around in self-flagellation or being morose; it does mean that it is clear how hard life is and that the joy of being a laborer in faith and an overcomer makes it all worth it.

Readiness

Jesus emphasized readiness (Luke 12:35). In this passage, the view of us is slaves serving a master. Paul will also point out later that everyone is a slave, either of sin or of righteousness (Rom. 6). Honestly, the only person who does not render account to another is the Father, for even Jesus lived according to His Father's will, which will is always the Cross. This is the great liberation, when we see that God asks no one to be or do what God Himself is not by nature, first in His only begotten Son and then in the redeemed sons.

The sons will inherit the earth despite the world's opposition. The master expects us to expect His bodily return even though time seems to drag on and the evils of the world argue that He never came from heaven 2000 years ago and certainly never rose from the dead, and therefore at most was a moral teacher but will not return as Lord of all. The waiting slaves, however, know the inner transformation of the new birth into slaves who love their slavery so much, and know the nature of God, that they are now friends and sons.

Our master lives in us, and we are the rightful heirs in Christ of His kingdom, being now united in spirit to Christ who is our constant life now and forever, knowing that He will at the climax of history overturn the excuses of those who deny that there is a master. God is love, and in His Wisdom knows when that day will reveal all and display openly that Jesus was not just a moral teacher of followers evolving from cosmic randomness. Only an enemy comes in to undermine the simplicity of what Jesus said, and thankfully that enemy has no place in us anymore.

When Does the Thief Come?

Imagine a thief who lets a household know when to expect the robbery. The household will be ready to repel and enforce justice (Luke 12:39). It is having to be on guard that marks this present age. The devil does not just have certain times that he is the devil. He is the devil all the time, which God means for good in this present age to stir alertness and watchfulness. This is the age when the battle is on and the age of establishing in the sons of God that they have overcome the evil one (1 Jn. 2).

In sports, players need to know opponent strategies, and so, much more in life where the stakes are ultimate and eternal. No one with wisdom avoids defensive awareness. Some people talk about the devil too little, some too much, but the point is to know who the enemy is, that God is in control, and that we overcome by faith. The devil is doing his job all the time, but God is much more doing His job all the time, and those who live in the love of God do not care if they need to be watchful all the time, doing what their master needs done. They see about the needs of the household. To them, there is no separation, no doing one's own thing. All of life is God, and God only. They have the consciousness of God because they have been born of Him through the Son, and they think as the Son, because they are the Son in born again son form. Christ is formed in them, as Paul puts it (Gal. 4:19).

When their flesh wants to resist, which is normal and most of the time, they know that this is not who they are, and they walk on in the Spirit despite feelings of resistance from the flesh. They also know that the devil does not take vacations, and so they do not think of life as having long periods of safety away from attack just because the enemy does not appear overt. The Bible is a book of settling into faith that gets us through moment by moment, day by day, which is equally the opportunity for a steady walk in the Spirit despite the enemy.

Sabbath Rest All the Time

The priesthood of Melchizedek is not based on law-keeping, but on the New Covenant, wherein by faith we recognize that God has written His law upon our hearts. God promised this by Jeremiah, and through Christ, God has brought it about for those in whom Christ lives, which means that like Moses, who was the type of the new man, we experience the glory of God face-to-face. Moses enjoyed this kind of fellowship on the mountain, while those who were under law fearfully only saw the quaking and consuming fire. Yet Moses experienced glory and light. Clearly, the Lord did not deal with Moses the way that He dealt with His people still consigned under the Law. Thus, Moses is our picture of the new man in glory.

This all has great meaning for the Sabbath, which in Hebrews is the rest of ceasing to live as if believers can do any work of their own. Rest means that Christ does all the work, which is the death of the believer but rebirth as well. When a person gets too tired to try anymore, life requires a constant miracle to continue. I for one became ready for someone else to live my life. Oddly, by coming to that, I popped back into view as a self that I had never seen before. Life formerly meant trying to be like a self that I pictured in my mind—the self I thought I should be. But this picture was a lie and satanic in origin. Trying to be like this presupposed-self also took enormous work and led to exhaustion. Satan was behind all this, authoring the lie and producing the dead works.

When Christ does all the work, then comes the discovery of the real self, the new creation. Suffering and laboring in faith continue for others but not trying to produce self-generated works (really, satanic in origin). This is the continual stream of inner resurrection, because the new self is the miracle-self. There is nothing to do but believe. The Sabbath, therefore, is all the time, and works iresistibly come from rest in a "can't help it" life.

Loneliness Is a Lie

Loneliness drives much of human behavior. People thrive on social connections, wondering what others are doing and who is with whom. Relationships drive life, mostly romantic, followed by family and peers; yet out on the crowded streets of life, where activity continues to escalate, loneliness still hides inside, unresolved. The first lonely person was Adam in the first pages of the Bible.

God saw Adam's loneliness and created Eve as his companion. Did she meet his need? The Bible does not offer hope that romance and marriage satisfy loneliness. When Jesus shocked His disciples with the standard for marriage that a man not divorce his wife except for fornication, His disciples answered, "If the case of the man be so with his wife, it is not good to marry" (Matt. 19:10). To youth, and to those who never mature, the disciples' view is cynical because of infatuation with fairy tale hopes in literature, television, and movies.

Moses let husbands divorce their wives because of displeasure with them, leaving men open to find a new wife. On and on the succession might go, and so it is today. Lose one, find another; get rid of one, get on a high with another—with women free now as well to divorce. Many think the answer lies in finding the right mate, the one of God's leading, and that this will terminate loneliness. The scriptures do say, "He who finds a wife finds a good thing and obtains favor from the Lord" (Prov. 18:22) and "A prudent wife is from the Lord" (Prov. 19:14). Add to that Proverbs 31 and *The Song of Solomon*, and the case appears fixed for marriage as the answer to loneliness.

Jesus' disciples knew, however, that things are not so simple. Surely Pascal was right when he said that there is a God-shaped vacuum in every heart, and only God can fill it. The New Testament reveals the complete human— Christ in you. Whether married or single, in a group or not in one, every Christian is whole and complete.

How Does Jesus Spread Fire upon the Earth?

Jesus came to spread fire upon the earth (Luke 12:49). Fire can mean judgment, but when it is the burning bush or Pentecost, it is the fire of God that is life. God is a consuming fire (Heb. 12:29). The point is that fire cannot be ignored, and such is God. Those who do not know God will be consumed to their dismay, whereas those who receive Him become fire-safe and love how Christ makes fire to be the delight of fellowship. Give me fire, fire, and more fire since God is the fire of self-for-others love.

Before Jesus could spread fire on earth, He had to undergo a "baptism" that would crucify our old self and cut us off from the dominion that Satan gained over man in the Fall. Only then could the Spirit come as fire because the Spirit is the gift to the resurrected human, not an addition to the old man. Jesus says that this baptism and fire divide households, setting family members against other family members. This means that the new birth is more important than even the connection of blood family.

No one is to refuse birth in God's bloodline through Christ in order to keep favor with earthly family. Yet, Jesus did not mean that Christians should be hostile, divisive, or contentious toward their earthly family members. The idea of dividing households and removing peace is not intended to promote hostility in Christians toward family, but to convey the hostility of family who resist a savior from sin.

Where unsaved family members act out of ill will toward their Christian family members, or where carnal Christians act in the same way, those on the receiving end can weather the attacks by knowing that Christ in them sustains these attacks and even turns them to a higher purpose of believing for the hostile ones. They let their roots go deeper into Christ in them, even as them, and they stand in faith and love for those who do not see the true love fire from the baptism (Rom. 6) that Jesus underwent for us and as us.

Bye Bye Loneliness, Hello Christ

After an exciting courtship and start to marriage, surprise hit early when low-level depression crept in. Hungering for a spirituality forgotten during the energized time of courtship, my wife and I searched for answers in the Bible. The one that came quickly was how no one can know the things of God except by the Spirit of God, and how God has given us His Spirit and mind to know Him (1 Cor. 2). But like a foolish Galatian, I soon plunged into the mentality of law to seek perfection. I had not yet had a Romans 7 awakening, but soon would. I began trying to be the Christian I had never been, but now would strive to become. One day I read, "His commandments are not grievous (burdensome)" (1 John 5:3). I blurted out, "That's a lie." I was caught. Professing to believe God's word is inerrant, I found myself arguing with the Scripture.

God has His way of boxing us in. Jesus' disciples had caught this, and noted psychiatrist M. Scott Peck in his best seller *The Road Less Traveled* voices it with the riveting three-word sentence that begins his book: "Life is difficult." At first I was not prepared to hear, not really accepting life on God's terms, with all its suffering and temptation. Finally, after enough wretchedness, snagged in Romans 7, the truth was sweet and desirable that the Christian life is not we living it, but Christ living it in us.

God created us to contain and re-express His nature of self-giving love as opposed to Satan's nature of self-for-self, false love that enslaved us as non-Christians and even kept us in bondage in our days of deceived carnality as Christians. The awakening is to see Christ in you—a total Christ in a total human—the meaning of the completed Christian. There is no place then for loneliness in union. Sure, there is a desire for fellowship, but not neediness that keeps people in the lie of living by human relationships. One relationship does it all, from which fellowship abounds with others.

Trading Relationships for Fellowship

God tests us with others to bring detachment from human relationships. Until detachment comes, the rise and fall of sanity hinges on how our relationships are doing and not our relationship with the Lord, which is a fellowship in union, with the two as one. Marriage is a severe place of learning, and God means it to be. Without grounding in who we are, marriage will be a constant expectation that the other person will bring fulfillment.

Marriages go through severe trials, even separations, during which important decisions get made. All the while, there is a shortcut to the Promised Land called "Christ plus nothing." This might mean solitude, even years of it, but certainly no more loneliness. Emotions, hormones, and craving for companionship feel as strong as ever, but a settling comes inside of joyful completeness in the Lord.

This appears strange to the world. Someone will say, "You need a life." However, the reply is easy: "Christ is our life" (Col. 3:4). He does not give us life; He *is* our life. Detachment means that you have only one relationship—with God. Everything else is fellowship. This can sound a bit inhuman, but it is the most human thing because true humanity is Spirit-driven, with soul and body being the perfect instruments of Spirit.

This is the simple truth for anyone open to discover it. Loneliness can drive anyone there who lets it. Those living by the law will appeal to Moses, who allowed divorce for those hardened of heart. Those questing all the way, however, will find their completion in Christ that satisfies, even in their deepest marital pain. The truth gained here will generalize, and what used to be burdensome human relationships will become opportunities for fellowship in faith. Interest in others will be driven by "What does that person need Lord?" rather than, "Why isn't that person being what I want?" Intimacy is surprisingly enhanced by detachment because flesh is no longer the master, Spirit is.

September 19

No Longer Victims of Dysfunction

My mother-in-law, Mimi, called me about a letter she received from an inmate who attended the jail Bible study that we led. He was reading a therapy type book on getting in touch with anger, experiencing anger toward his earthly father, now dead, but an alcoholic while he was a child. Mimi asked me what I thought, and I could only answer from my experience, which included rage toward my own father until I was forty-five. I lived constantly angry at my earthly father until he abandoned our family when I was eleven, never to come back as we slowly discovered. He completely disappeared for fifteen years until a younger brother located him through a genealogy book.

As a youth, I felt relief over his leaving, but then came pain as I observed those with regular families. Pain later turned to anger and rage, so that by my adult Christian years, I faced the need to forgive him, which I did by faith, through persistent affirmation of forgiveness, yet the distress continued. My own sins finally brought me to a miraculous place of experiencing God's forgiveness toward my father, no longer holding him responsible for my own choices in life. No lingering resentment remained or lack of resolution. Then came a surprise. The Lord made it clear that no Christian needs to attribute anything in life to the actions of family in the past, because He has taken us out of that earthly family, placing us in a new family, the family in which God is Father and in which no dysfunction exists. This is the inheritance of a new blood line—Christ's—and now everything comes from Him.

Some may protest at this that we need therapy to get in touch with past hurts. This is true where denial and re-pression still exist, but always dredging up memories may hinder settling into Christ's new bloodline where "old things are passed away; behold, all things are become new" (2 Cor. 5:17). Satan says no closure is possible; God says it is.

Clearing the Rubbish Away from the New Birth

Unfortunately, many see Jesus like a jewel in a jewel box—a treasure hidden away to bring out and wear occasionally for show or in a pinch. Otherwise, life goes on, changed, but still with the idea of a wonderful new add-on to a life still pretty much the life that was. But in the new birth, the life that was, died. Yes, God could find nothing to salvage in the life that was.

He had to crucify the old self to raise up a new you—cut off from sin and the spirit of error producing it. The enemy had mostly remained hidden as the operator of the old self. Death in Christ brought severing from the old operator. This is what most Christians do not get, that they died. They did not just receive Jesus. They died. Then came burial, resurrection, and ascension in Christ.

Christ in you does not mean Christ in the old man, but rather Christ in (even *as*) the new man. The Gospel is not Christ added to the self that was, not Christ added to the old self. God put that self to death in Christ. He does not even add Christ to the new self, for the new self is the human and Christ as one, while both remain intact. This is a mystery. How can you be you, and Christ be who He is, and yet Christ be in you, even as you? Only God knows. But since He tells us that this is how we are made new creations, we take it by faith and walk in the Spirit.

The first half of Galatians tells us who we are. The last half tells us how we walk, which is in the Spirit. This is supernatural and never gets old. It is not information but the Spirit of wisdom and understanding guiding the new man and setting forth the path and works ordained for us to walk in.

To see what the new birth is means that it is no longer appealing to see life as God adding Jesus to a self who just needs forgiveness and help. No, life is a miraculous new self, created in Christ Jesus, and led by the Spirit of God.

Freed from Dysfunction

Being of a new bloodline in Christ means no longer tracing any effect upon us from the first Adam. Instead, we take all family input from the last Adam. Blame toward parents and family departs in the light of God's grace. Does this negate earthly families and ties to them? No. We still acknowledge our earthly families and our responsibilities to them for provision and support. They cannot, however, meet our real needs, for now the Holy Spirit supplies all needs based on union in Christ's death, burial, and resurrection.

Paul says in Galatians 2:20, "I am crucified with Christ; nevertheless I live; yet not I, but Christ lives in me." By identifying with Christ's death, burial, and resurrection—we see that God unzipped Jesus on the Cross, put us into Him, and then zipped Him back up. This took us out of the first Adam and his family line, and placed us into the blood and body line of Christ.

Are you still trying to dig through endless memories and continually rehearse them—feeding anger that anyone can let go of by seeing oneness with Christ? Perhaps holding on to anger is in ignorance, not knowing the futility of such guilt and blame—not knowing that the new man in Christ is not imprisoned and bound to anger because of a dysfunctional family. Only Satan feeds the lie that even a Christian is held back by past dysfunction.

Enjoy the grace of God in your new, heavenly family, and let go of the past. If the need exists to consciously bring the past to light, go ahead, but then place it all in Christ, no longer as a victim of dysfunction—no longer as one in bondage and helpless as a consequence of the dysfunctional family. "And because ye are sons, God hath sent forth the Spirit of his Son into your hearts, crying, Abba, Father" (Gal. 4:6). Now you can walk in the Spirit and be for others.

September 22

Woman at the Well

The woman at the well was living a confused, religious, and immoral life—having had five husbands and now a boyfriend (John 4). She was Samaritan, meaning roots to the ten tribes that long before had split in rebellion and set up a worship center other than Jerusalem. Jesus was tired and thirsty, so He asked a favor, but not as if to despise her or treat her like a servant. He needed a drink, and she needed living water, not as a barter, but simply that each had a need.

Jesus does not let her social status or sin be a reason to act as if she is not there. She likely has the momentary thought that for Him to speak to her means more trouble from men, but He mentions living water immediately. She heard something, and a part of her that was not quite dead, quickened in interest. Despair had not destroyed the spark of hope that life could be different and God could be knowable to her.

Like many, she thought, "What church would I go to and where?" The complexities of religious debate confused her, so Jesus affirmed that Samaritans and Jews both went back to the same patriarchal origins, but what would simplify that?

All truth hinges on not being a lie. When Jesus probed her moral life, He did not want to shame her about living out-of-wedlock; He wanted to know if she would lie about it. She didn't. Then He pointed her to worship God in spirit, which is not geographical but based on intent. She was ready to worship the one who is the center of the universe—incarnate at that!

Then she had to decide if God would really have arranged a personal encounter just for her to meet and receive the messiah. If for her, then for any.

September 23

Seeking the Kingdom of God

Jesus said that no one even sees the kingdom of God without being born again. This implies more than being saved, great as that is. Being born again means operating as a son of the kingdom within the kingdom. A switch of worlds took place from the domain of darkness and the old man, into being a new creation who operates by the Spirit, not by natural means. The Christian life is a supernatural life, in which we find ourselves doing routinely what was formerly impossible. The reason is that we do not live according to nature, but by the one who created nature and who energizes it by His resurrection Spirit.

Life has its way of crowding in with demands, plus more to do than time. Needy people press in from all sides, desperate with their needs, which feels overwhelming. God means it to feel that way to the flesh. Why would life not feel like continual crisis in a groaning, fallen world?

So, now you are a son of God with all of this pressure in a broken world but with a new consciousness that is not a sin consciousness but the gift of the cleansed, energized mind. Then comes temptation: "How will I get everything done? I must seek food, clothing, business, meetings, and attend to endless stressing and wearing details. There is no time to refresh, to relax, to look into the mirror of God's mind." Yes there is. At times, I feel like I cannot stop, relax, and take care of a thing God has set in my path. That's when the verse pops up, "Seek ye first the kingdom of God, and all these things shall be added unto you."

This is the Spirit of efficiency, saying that if we walk by faith in what we think there is no time and energy for, He will work out deferred needs in some other way.

I find that when I go God's way, which is by faith, that the Holy Spirit can get more done in less time than seems possible. It is a miracle of the Holy Spirit's efficiency, and that is what the Christian life is.

Beat the Hurry

There is a time to hurry, but in the Spirit, there is rest even then. Whereas most people work to rest, God teaches us to work from rest. As a young man, I went to hear Norman Grubb but didn't understand a thing he said. He seemed to make life sound too easy, so I asked him, "How do you feel about hard work." He said, "I do as little of it as possible" and went on to the next question. I was livid.

It took a few years for me to see the riddle and that he had answered my question. Hebrews Chapters 3 and 4 talk about laboring to enter into rest. Our fear is that if we do nothing, nothing will happen. This is based on the lie of trying to do what God has already done. God created the natural world in six days. He did it all. Adam and Eve only needed to live in what God had already finished. There was nothing more for them to do except live in what was already there. The same is true for salvation now: God has created the new man, and there is nothing to do but walk as the new man by faith, step by step, in the works already custom appointed for each child of God.

What about the fear of missing His will, not being on schedule, or not achieving what God intends? Nothing can be known by fear, plus human will power cannot drive off fear. But the new man can any given moment say, "I am walking at the perfect pace, in perfect timing, and in perfect achievement." God loves faith and bears witness to it. Fear turns to faith, which is the normal walk of replacing the negative with the Spirit led positive. This is not just another form of the world's positive thinking. This is the new man walking in faith against appearances, enjoying that God is on time and bearing fruit by the one who has accepted rest in the Spirit as a way of life. Then, whether double timing, or casually stepping along, anxiety is gone. Work is never the same again because it is the supernatural fruit, as always, of God, who never ceases to amaze us with what He can do, as us.

Pointing the Way

In his first letter, John says that we do not need someone to teach us because we have the anointing. That is John's way of saying that we have the teacher within us. Yet teaching is one of the New Testament ministries. The point is that there is no independent self who teaches other independent selves. That would only be pride and a lie.

I have sat under many mentors and teachers and have learned much from them, but the reality is that the Spirit speaks through them, and the Spirit bears witness to the listener. Most of us have had the experience of getting concepts down on an information level first, perhaps even with some quickening and receiving by faith. But we know what it is like to have the nagging sense that what is supposed to be liberating is not yet what we hoped it would be. The haunting voice of "head knowledge" still speaks the lie of, "This does not really work."

You know it works when it works, and it is plainly a miracle beyond one more effort, like so many in the past, that ended in disappointment. What is the difference when one finally knows? The difference is that you say, "The life that I am living is beyond anything that I imagined; this is beyond anything human. This is miracle territory."

Instead of defeat, defeat, defeat—life is victory, victory, victory over old besetting sins. Then past teachers take on a new light. God is first, and our teachers a distant second, but our respect for them is more than ever, and they appear as those planted by God along our way over the years—pointing the way until the day when the teacher within is truly our teacher, and we know it.

The New Birth and Glory

The new birth is not imitating Christ but Christ being Himself in us. This is the hope of glory (Col. 1:27). Where God's glory is, there is not any law—cannot be, for in the glorified realm, all is from the urges of grace and love, where now your inner longing is to do what is commanded. It is not law, but God as a magnet, calling His sons unto His divine and delightful way, even when that means first taking up the Cross. Thus, the Spirit of glory changes how we see law. Law, then, is simply the description of how God directs things to operate, and a son flows with glory in his inner man, disregarding fleshly urges to the contrary and not mistaking them for the true self. He who is born again discovers who he is, and knowing who he is, he knows his true desires.

Temptation of course causes suffering, and at times, temptation brings moments of doubt: "Do I really want to do what is wrong?" But he who is born again does not look to reason to find an answer. He also resists the urge to interpret his desires from emotions or sentiment, no matter how noble. Rather, he remains in a state of inner spirit rest and only moves or stays still by what Christ in his inner man is doing.

Neither does he try to make himself look like what he thinks Christ would look like, remembering how that image was false and how the enemy used the lie of imitation, which comes from blindness to creatures being vessels and branches, not imitators.

So then, we do not go about measuring ourselves and putting ourselves up against standards, even divine ones. The standards are clear, holy, and good—just not attainable by us. Our passion is being absorbed in the person of God, while living from glory fire within through the new birth—which is to say—we are irons molten from the fire that is not of us, but glowing in union with that fire.

Moving to Spirit

Even Jesus was not recognized outwardly as from another world; thus, it is not outer things that tip off the realm we live in. The issue is inner—how we see. To expect others to discern with natural eyes is unrealistic; that will lead to discouragement and falling back into how the world sees. Only a new Spirit and walking in the Spirit open the eyes. Therefore, we do not judge ourselves according to human standards or wilt when others judge that way, painful as it is.

It just does not work to view success outwardly with anxiety. Neither does it work to question God's provision, or whether others will esteem us. The needy consciousness never knows enough. It is stuck in the lie: "I can't go forth and succeed." This puts problems above provision. God looks at faithfulness and a whole heart. Everything else is results, which may not show up outwardly until deep things are brought to light and shallow ones cleared away.

Sin has blinded the world, also holding Christians in bondage when they do not know the miraculous life of rest—ceasing from one's own works. The foremost job is "it is no longer I but Christ"—free of anxiety despite constant temptation to the contrary. If the soul/body life is taken as an identity—thoughts and feelings—life will always seem slippery and loaded with condemnation. To discern soul and spirit is to laugh off the lie; the point is spirit union with Christ.

Clarity releases energy formerly tied up in condemnation and efforts at control. Temptation is seen for what it is. Instead of being fooled, life is lived on the deep level of God's keeping in whatever situation the will of God places us. It is not hard to know the will of God: once you walk in the Spirit, the trail is clear, strange or ordinary as it may look. You bring heaven to earth in disguise, after being the first to see through your own disguise.

September 28

Opposites Wrongly and Rightly Seen

The universe runs on opposites. That is how we know a thing—by its opposite. Otherwise, everything would fold up into one, ever-contracting ball, or else expand forever and never be approachable. There must be both attraction and repulsion, or else an atom would not stay together, with all its particles knowing when to approach and when to push away. Though we think of love mainly in terms of attraction, we also see Spirit led boundaries, where the Spirit says, "Do not touch that!" This is love too.

Christ is the glue: "by him all things hold together" (Col. 1:17). Within God's established boundaries, oneness is the order of the day. For all the repulsion in an atom, the overall picture is of the atom's oneness. Flesh cannot take this. Soul or body attraction is exciting, but when it comes time for repulsion and boundaries, flesh interprets this on a self-for-self level as, "You are not meeting my needs" or "I am done with you." No wonder all the splits, divorces, and wars take place. How can flesh be any different?

It cannot on its own. That is the point. Satan is the hidden deceiver behind all the wrong use of repulsion and boundaries, never making a place for the Cross, or daily dying, or servant-hood. In a fallen world, no sooner does the present love interest become boring than the seeker says goodbye and looks elsewhere. The problem is that we are self-for-self apart from union with Jesus Christ.

He alone is love, and the scripture says, "God is love." God is the only self-for-others person in the universe; apart from Him, no love exists nor can. We love by faith, not by our emotions, or hurt thinking. The Spirit in us says, "What is best for that person?" This does not come naturally, but it does come supernaturally. Look for it when it seems contradictory and flesh wants one thing, but spirit another. The flesh way looks easiest, but the Cross is the true oneness, and the sanctifier of the whole person: spirit, soul, and body.

Love Makes Knowledge Safe

"Knowledge puffs up, but love edifies" (1 Cor. 8:1). The reason is simple; knowledge is brain based, whereas love is spirit based. Everything has an operator, and when love ceases as the operator, knowledge turns prideful, and the enemy is at work. Awe of God as both creator and sovereign over the earth humbles us when we have gotten things backward. To know that God can do what no other can do gives a sense of security.

Even in this evil world, it is safe to be a vessel to contain God—His plan for us. That makes us expressers of the Cross, which looks unsafe, but it is the safest place to be since who else but Christ in us can be forgiveness and hope for ourselves and for others. When evil has done its worst, only the Cross ends the wheel of commendation and condemnation, Satan's evil twins of obsessing on self-performance.

Knowledge alone is knowing *about* a thing or person, but love is "being mixed with" as my mother-in-law, Mimi, said. To know is to experience the grace of God at the spirit level, where knowing isn't mere mental assertion and mastery, but the sense of being held and driven by someone living at the center—as us. The compelling One has compelled us, and surrender finally comes easily and naturally without resistance.

Trying to surrender is over. As the ground receives the rain, and as the plants receive the sun's energy, the sons of God receive God's love in Christ from within, even when others do not understand. "God is love" is the central passion, making knowledge safe. When love operates knowledge, the two mix, and knowledge becomes the manifestation of the Holy Spirit, but not the source. Those who touch your knowledge sense a well of living water they may not know exists—yet.

How God Uses Depression

We hate and fear negatives until awakening to the fact that they are not an identity unless made into one. To say, "I feel depressed" is different from saying, "I am depressed." The feeling might be recognized as a soul or body thing, or it might be recognized as Satan's depressed spirit tempting us with a lie. Satan is Mr. Depression. He is depressed, and he has a lot to be depressed about, and he wants to share it with you. Don't take it.

Before I knew my true identity, life piled up. One grows up hoping for education, job, and family; then, after the new routine, life's harsh aspects intensify, and depression can be a good wakeup call. God uses it, so we might as well use it too. "What's going on Lord?" is a good question. The Lord might reply, "Stop obsessing about your problem and look at Me" or "In all things give thanks."

These are not the solutions we had anticipated, but they open the door to Spirit, where peace, joy, and love hide out by faith. Crooks are not the only ones who need a hideout; saints need one too. The Bible talks about being carried on eagle's wings, standing on the high rock, and entering the fortress. Negatives bring the invitation to say, "I want more than a Savior to forgive my sins. I need life."

Until we know who we are—that we died to sin and are one spirit with the Lord (1 Cor. 6:17)—life is the lonely self, trying to solve its lonely problems, and usually wallowing in a lonely sounding lie from the devil, that ingested enough, will lead to depression. This sends the ailing saint to Dr. Jesus who is our life. (Col. 3:4). You get to trade your life for His and then see the vine as life, not the branch on its own. Life becomes living His life while enjoying His life as your branch. That is deeper than depression, especially when recognizing that Satan is just mad that he lost the power to stop our full awakening.

How to Forgive Sins

When I was wee small, my mother tied my shoelaces. Then came the awakening; she was not tying my dad's shoelaces. He did that for himself. Under her guidance, with a little practice, I learned to do it. She had let me know that it was time to learn. God is the same about our past sins: He must teach us how to be kept from tripping over accusation and condemnation when sins come to mind, either ours or those of others, so that a sin committed is not always a loose string, guaranteeing continued unresolved pain.

The simple answer is the blood of Christ. That blood stands apart from everything I or someone else might feel about something I did or something another person did. Without the blood, one is helplessly open to any lie the devil can say, either directly or through others; therefore, floods of shame encounter no walls to keep them out. How can this be the joy of having a savior?

Salvation also means deliverance from the consciousness of sin. Sins get forgotten as well as forgiven. When an old sin does come to mind, the practiced believer recognizes opportunity to see the sin as under the blood; and having done that—tied the shoes—there is no snag. The obvious thing to do is get on with life as if the sin does not exist—because it doesn't. It may be recorded in history for testimony purposes, but it is not an untied shoelace.

Suppose someone comes along to say, "You have not dealt with that" or, "You have not acknowledged the pain you caused others." Be careful about pulling a sin up and out from under the blood. The devil will sting you, as well as others who do not see the sin under the blood of Christ.

Just Say No

Despite continued troubling thoughts and feelings on a soul level, and despite attacks of temptation, Spirit life is easy and not self-conscious. Spontaneity rules the day because God created us for spontaneity—not for fear and second guessing. The human will does not get discarded but operates normally by the Spirit to discern truth from error. This does not stop soul and body from being what they are—registering outer stimuli—but God's Spirit lets you know what is real and pure, so that by your knowing, you do not bog down with anxiety and obsession. The devil's lies get exposed and refused.

Satan uses countless avenues of temptation because our humanity is rich with opportunities. Everything that God sees as good, Satan sees as something to misuse, and then use to accuse us about. When he finds a place to entice, and then condemn, he intends for it not to be only about the pull to a particular sin. He is after the bigger thing of a sin consciousness: "There is something wrong with me!" This becomes the dragging, accusing atmosphere of life. Soon everything is one big guilt trip over not doing enough, accompanied by fearful cringing over any little thing being a pathway to sin.

This self-conscious, anxious mode thrives on the constant fear of too much or too little of whatever comes along, and the drift is ever toward trying to manage outer behavior by law and resolutions, instead of enjoying inner Spirit freedom. The conscience becomes a big courtroom, with life lived in the face of an unrelenting prosecutor who questions the motive behind every move. No wonder the saints drag and fade under the lie of "I'm no good" and try to flip over to compensation by good works.

No saint has to take this. Just say "No! I don't take it." We are not the devil's boss, but neither is he ours. Order him and his consciousness away. He never gets tired of trying, but we never get tired of refusing. It's that simple.

To Worship Is Built into Us

One either knows God or not. To know Him is to be "mixed with Him" as my mother-in-law, Mimi, put it. This is what union is, not the self and Christ as separate, airtight compartments, but like a branch expressing its tree, and how else can a tree express itself except by its branch? One life does not end and another start where the branch is connected; they are one life.

Before we can safely know this, we must be humbled to know that we are created beings and not God. We do not worship ourselves or others, only God, whose visibility became known by the ultimate expression of human life—His Son, Jesus, who expressed the Father in human form. Then the Son made believers one body with Him to express the Son in human form. Paul says, "I am again in labor until Christ be formed in you" (Gal. 4:19).

The lie is living as if we are mere human beings living by a code of honor. To live in the lie of independence leaves a vacuum that must be filled, and the only option apart from God is to worship someone. Who? Paul says, "when you did not know God you were slaves to those which by nature are no gods" (Gal. 4:9). In our lost or carnal state, we worshipped other people, idolizing them. We lived or died by our worship of heroes, none of whom was God—each only another created being. All of life was peer pressure and conformity to others.

At root this is self-worship, and under that is worship of the enemy—the devil who hides this fact for as long as possible, so as not to scare people to Jesus. Everyone is created to worship; it is inescapable, and the only safe option is to worship God. Everything else, by default, is worship (and slavery!) to those who cannot set anyone free. Only Jesus Christ sets anyone free, because only He is free (John 8:36). Christ, therefore, does not give anyone life; He *is* life (Col. 3:4). He *is* what no code can produce—life itself—for others.

Mother of All the Living

Adam named his wife Eve "because she was the mother of all the living" (Gen. 3:20). This at first sounds harmless, even noble, but Adam is naming her this from a fallen state. He has heard God tell the serpent that the seed of the woman "shall bruise him on the head" (3:15), so Adam has hope that Eve's offspring will defeat the serpent, but he does not know how, and indeed this is a mystery. Only with God's revelation to Paul do we see that Christ is really the seed of Abraham, and thus the seed of the woman (Gal. 3:16).

Adam stops blaming Eve enough to echo God's promise to her, but apart from faith, he can only see her in a human way and love her with an earthly attachment. Eve cannot produce life; she cannot author the new birth or be the womb of it. Only natural life can come from her, and this is the bitter lesson that both she and Adam will learn, and all of us born of them. In our fallen or carnal state, we think that life is in the natural—meaning earthly appetites and self-for-self. This is because the Fall extinguished Spirit life and left the human race in Satan's darkness, totally outer oriented except for a longing within that can awaken to God's redemptive call.

God would need to come in the flesh as the seed to redeem man, and though the Virgin Mary carried the seed in her womb, it was the divine womb, the "mother above" who really birthed Jesus (Gal. 4:26); and it was the Father who gave Him the nature of God. The divine womb is the true mother of all living, not Eve. Adam had this mixed up, and there has been a mix-up ever since.

To be redeemed means to be born again, of a new creation—to be born of God—made new and "partakers of the divine nature" (2 Pet. 1:4). The divine nature cannot be attained humanly but only received by the new birth as an eternal gift.

The Knowledge of Good and Evil

What a deep thing that the Lord would say, "the man has become like one of Us, knowing good and evil" (Gen. 3:22). Man had sinned, and yet he is "like one of Us." This means knowledge of opposites, for something is only known by its opposite. Prior to their fall, Adam and Eve were untested on opposites until solicited to disobey a command through temptation. The Bible does not say that the only way to know good and evil is to do evil, for God made the eternal choice to say no to self-for-self and yes to self-for-others. Therefore, evil is only a potential in Him that never manifested and is eternally swallowed up by good. God knows the evil that He died to being, not by doing it, but by seeing what it would mean and saying no to it.

Eve was deceived, so her choice was not eternal; similarly, Adam's choice, though by the will, was not eternal either. Neither made a fixed choice, so they were redeemable if such a thing as grace exists in God. And it does! This does not mean that the way was easy; the consequences of sin were spelled out, while beautifully, the promise of redemption began their hope.

Now both God and man knew good and evil, but from opposite poles—God being fixed in the good, but the race of Adam being enslaved by the serpent's nature. The question for us became, "Who wants deliverance?" Anyone who does can be redeemed—bought back.

In the meantime, man was driven from the Garden, and cherubim guarded the tree of life with flaming swords until the time would come, through Christ, for the redeemed to eat of this tree again, but not until being made safe to eat it. It must be eaten inwardly and not just outwardly, or else the tree will be misused as a means of perpetuating evil. Thus, the Cross is the only safe way to eat of the tree. When one approaches the tree of life with the blood and body of Christ, Spirit access is immediate.

Christ the Master, Me the Slave

God only ever intended that we be a slave of one person—Him. Slavery to anyone else is evil. Listen to Paul: "at that time when you did not know God, you were slaves to those which by nature are no gods" (Gal. 4:8). In other words, we are not to be slaves of anyone who is not God Himself. What could be clearer? Cultures more noble in their view of humanity eradicate slavery, yet no one can escape slavery's root apart from the Cross.

The reason is simple. Anyone who is not a slave of God is Satan's slave. Romans Chapter 6 says that we are either slaves of righteousness or slaves of sin. Thus, there is no middle place of being free as an independent person. Not even Satan is free; he is enslaved to the self-for-self darkness that is inevitable from rebelling against God. For humans, God determines that those who do not serve Him, serve sin, and that means serving sin's author, Mr. Sin.

No wonder Satan tries to stay under cover and hide. His slaves might wake up and flee to Jesus Christ, who, though the only legitimate master, nonetheless operates the kind of slavery that makes us free as He is free. Christ is the master who gives us everything that He is and has—makes us one spirit and body with Him, whereas Satan takes away everything for himself and leaves his followers empty and hopelessly lost in the loneliness of narcissism.

There is no being an independent self—unless you are God. Good luck on that. To accept our creature-hood is sweet bliss and union with the Creator, who expresses His unknowable self in knowable forms. That is, He manifests Himself through infinite variety on the human level by His one Spirit expressed in countless human forms. The form is never God, but God makes Himself known by His forms—by being in union with them.

No sooner does a man accept his slavery to God through Christ than Christ says, "You are my friend." And He means it.

Look not to the Right or Left

Next to keeping silent when that would be wise, the hardest thing is to plow one's own row. It is ever tempting to look at what others do and compare. If indulged, this lets law back in, and the "I should" is no longer the free, easy leading of the Spirit, who both gives a command and fulfills it in the one receiving it. Back comes the heavy yoke of the self that thinks it is independent.

God made you uniquely you, with your calling, uniquely yours. Maybe it looked glamorous at first, but then daily dreariness set in, namely routine life—life in the ordinary. But that is the way God works; life in the extraordinary gets lived in the ordinary. This is no crime. It does not mean any less of the extraordinary, just that life is made up of opposites, including therefore the ordinary, so that mystery is preserved.

Everybody likes the extraordinary and wants to march off, arm in arm with others, in a glory cloud and constantly feel euphoric. Then when each is placed by the Spirit into an individual trench, the feeling is a bit dirty and grimy. Maybe others did not have to go into a grimy trench. If not, maybe something is wrong; "I have misheard and should be feeling loftier." The truth is that trust and trenches go together. God needs those who stay where He puts them to do the ordinary work of being for others.

Looking at the task, or comparing, is deceiving. Seeing others as God sees them, daily grind and all, is what elevates our seeing. The people in front of us are the ones we serve, not the people in front of others in their rows to plow. When Jesus was getting ready to ascend, he told Peter what to expect. Peter naturally was curious about John and asked, "Lord, and what about this man?" meaning John (John 21:21). Jesus made it plain that this was none of Peter's business. Our business is to follow the personal word of the Spirit and be faithful in that.

Irritations

Irritation is an early form of anger and common to life. When things do not go as hoped, or when hurry threatens tranquility, irritation arises. Planning is excellent. In fact, spontaneity gladly salutes planning because spontaneity is a spirit, not an action, and can therefore spontaneously carry out a plan. It can flourish with planning or without it, and even make scattered plans into beauty.

When a rub arises to interrupt things, irritation is a normal feeling, no sin there. The only problem would be refusal to see God still in control, and the human self still His perfect instrument for His perfect plan. Perfection to God does not depend on everything going right in the conventional sense because to make the perfect response to inconvenience or even suffering is the perfect plan.

Irritation has a lot to do with timing. Satan is always in a hurry because he does not have much time, whereas the saint has an eternity. This is not an apologetic for procrastination or laziness, but it is one for not letting Satan's brand of hurry crowd out meaning in the moment. Traffic on the road is a good metaphor: millions of people are in a mad rush to get somewhere, only to then madly rush to get somewhere else after that. Such misuse of speed is a false cover for simply not enjoying wherever we are.

No moralistic "Slow down and enjoy life" is intended, just the Spirit's freedom to let others' plans and timing act as God's call to stay in the Spirit, where perfect timing and perfect pace are the norm. This awareness will never come by outer observation but only from inner rest, arising from faith. Look chaos and hurry face on and say to God anyway, "I am in the flow of your perfect timing and pace. I am achieving perfectly." An amazing sense of rest comes out of that.

No matter the emergency, irritation will not fester into anger and then rage. The Cross keeps the believer alert and aware when temptation turns out to be God's call to faith.

Life Is Temporary, Eternity Is Not

If life is harsh and hard, at least it is temporary. If life is smooth and easy, it is temporary as well. The fact is this: life in the mortal world is temporary. Deterioration and death are certain, even with God's gift of science that enhances quality and prolongs years on a limited scale. The lost person can enjoy the good things of life in an outer way, which masks the need for eternal life, yet no matter how good this life is, it is not paradise, nor can it be. The Bible message is that God means good times to draw men to Him in gratitude and bad times to draw men to Him— both to awaken the sense of emptiness that every person experiences without being filled with God. Since He made man to contain Him, man cannot rest until that is realized.

The Bible tells us that we are like a vapor or a breath— or like a flower in its moment, followed by wilting and corruption. This does not speak of inner life, but of the outer life in the physical world. But what about the inner world of the spirit, where a man's spirit is the candle of the Lord? Everything that God does is to drive home the temporary nature of this world and to awaken fallen Adam to his enslavement to the enemy—darkness the Bible calls it—so that each individual has the opportunity to come under conviction, die in Christ, and be reborn eternally. Failure to be reborn in Christ constitutes the second death— refusal of Christ in this life and thus for eternity. There is that fearful possibility. That is freedom.

Two men can look equally prosperous, yet one be in darkness and the other in eternal life. Two men can look to suffer equally, yet one be in darkness and the other in eternal life. We live in the moment, but if that moment is not eternal, then on a spirit level, there is no hope: all turns to grief. In Christ, all turns to an eternal weight of glory.

Not Only When I'm with You

The Galatians pulled away from the Spirit after Paul had been gone. The acceleration came from opponents introducing religion and law to undermine pure Spirit freedom. When someone draws back from the Spirit, a vacuum occurs because God created us to worship, and where worship is not of the living God and in the Spirit, ritual takes hold, based on separation from God rather than union with Him. Instead of enjoying pleasurable rituals spontaneously, built up from a unique brand of the Spirit, ritual becomes the worshiper trying to lessen the separation while trying to gain approval already there in Christ. It makes no sense, and frankly, how can it?

The Galatians were regular folks—like us. The fact that they lived in Turkey 2000 years ago and knew Paul personally is no more the issue than Jesus' disciples living then and knowing him personally. The goal is always to have Christ formed in us so that we know we are the same, no matter where or when we live. Paul stated this clearly, "I am again in labor until Christ is formed in you" (Gal. 4:19). Apart from that, one can only get built up inside when a mentor is around and then fall back when the mentor is away. Somehow, we get past that, discovering that identity and freedom do not change according to mentors, even the savior Himself, being around us.

God locks us in—into the fact of Christ formed in us, so that when the mentor is not around, life goes on the same. Sure, we miss certain special people, longing to enjoy them face to face and experience the oneness of the body of Christ, but never do we say that our completeness or freedom is impaired by geography or time. Nothing about getting fixed by faith in who we are minimizes the enormous contributions of others in our lives as vessels of the Spirit to us. That is never in question. But neither does their absence change who we are as complete and free, or cause a "fall from grace" (Gal. 5:4).

Taming the Old Man or Birthing the New One?

When a believer draws back from the Spirit, only self-made religion is left, with rules about the body and the environment as if they can be managed and brought into submission. God finds this humorous, also ridiculous since He mocked Job for not being able to subdue the wild animals. James says a man cannot even tame his own tongue. What luck then will one have in battles with various lusts, or with anger over an unjust world?

This is where religion is at its finest, appearing refined and disciplined, while turmoil rages within. However, the worst deception is Satan masquerading as an angel of light (2 Cor. 11:14). Thus, discernment cannot operate by outer appearances but only by fellowship in the Spirit, first with God through Christ, and then with those born of the same. This cannot be faked because Christ is our life (Col. 3). He does not give us life, as if life is an additive to a life we supposedly have of our own. No, Christ *is* our life, and His life is known by His Spirit.

No wonder Paul talks about walking in the Spirit. To be a Christian is to be born of the Spirit and to have Christ formed on the inside. The Spirit forms Christ within the Christian. When the blinders fall off and a Christian sees the larger picture of Christ formed and Christ keeping, the possibility of sin is understood in a different way. Sin is recognized as a move away from the Spirit and away from one's core self, where self is now one with Christ.

The battle against sin is not a battle against one's own body or even one's own self; it is the awakened stand by faith against the appearance of still being the old man. That man died (Rom. 6; Col. 3). Satan did not die, but union with him did. Therefore, when sin beckons, the new man does not answer because he has been discharged from obligation to sin and knows only Christ as master and keeper.

Lust versus Spirit

Eve saw that the forbidden tree was "good for food" (Gen. 3:6). However, it was not necessary for food since all of the other trees were available. Somehow, this tree stirred lust in her, not just hunger. It was "a delight to the eyes," and she lingered to become fascinated with longing. The more she looked, the better it looked. Through her stomach and through her eyes, the serpent's lust found a gateway for temptation toward the unlawful. All that Eve needed was justification to partake, and the serpent's offer of wisdom sealed it for her, enticing her will to experiment dangerously, leading to catastrophic consequences.

Just because something appeals to bodily appetites and engages the natural eyes does not make it a good idea. God created man a spirit to operate earthly appetites only within Spirit prescribed boundaries. Never are we intended to become enslaved to mere appetites, no matter how natural and normal they are.

James tells us that in temptation, lust gets stirred up. Since life is a constant stream of what is attractive or repulsive to body, emotions, and reason—lust is common daily temptation and not sin unless conceived by the will.

There is no need for condemnation; but neither is lust something to indulge, which is what Jesus meant when He said that to lust is already to have sinned. Jesus meant refusal to move to the Sprit when lust tempts, not the initial enticing of lust. Conception occurs by the will when one agrees to follow through instead of turning back and fleeing (2 Tim. 2:22). Temptation's lust is a surge of energy that does not stand still, forcing one to either follow through or retreat. No stationary lingering will work since lust is not the point, but the decision about our source of life. To follow through escalates lust and, as always, brings satanic darkness to the spirit, whereas saying, "I am crucified to that" keeps the Christian on an identity level with refreshing living waters of Spirit life.

October 13

Various Lusts

No sin can spring up without lust since lust is a form of desire. Without the movement and energy of desire, no oomph to commit sin would be stirred up. In temptation, desire is solicited toward self-for-self lust. One who knows who he is sees himself dead to sin (Rom. 6), so that the Spirit will express itself from the Cross. The Cross is in the heart of God by His eternal choice, and therefore in those born of Him.

Life is built on opposites, and consciousness comes by a thing swallowing up its opposite. Two such opposites are flesh and Spirit, and all too often Christians see flesh as evil and Spirit as good, whereas the Bible celebrates our humanity in its Spirit operated use. The dichotomy is not evil flesh and good Spirit, but which one is the center of operation. One has to rule over the other and swallow it up, so that the swallowed up opposite serves the master.

When Adam fell, fleshly lust became man's realm, not because flesh is evil but because it is evil to choose flesh over Spirit. Adam chose evil and let Satan into human flesh as master, and the race became enslaved to various lusts, and thus various sins (James 3:3). However, through the Cross, believers died to being enslaved by all forms of lust. Temptation challenges this truth by saying, "I can play with this pleasurable, forbidden territory but still be in the Spirit." Nothing works that way.

The point is to see lusts as the perfect place for continually knowing that they can go nowhere unless deception takes root. Lust sends the pleading message of "I can't live without this; it's too pleasurable and strong." Conceding to this lie means to lose walking in the Spirit. It is amazing what we can live without, however. The Spirit refreshes us and is the emblem of Christ's very life inside—a life complete, not in need of fleshly lusts, but in need of human bodies to express righteousness.

Don't Focus on the Lust

Consciousness comes from opposites. However, an opposite does not have to be known by willed action upon it; it can be known merely by its attraction, which the Bible calls lust. Lust is desire pulled toward forbidden opposites.

Typically, when someone becomes a Christian, lust is assumed as an identity that still exists alongside of our identity in Christ. This creates the sensation of being two persons, whereas people go to heaven or hell based on one identity. A Christian has only one identity—being one with Christ. Everything else is a lie, and once the lie is recognized, the answer to lust is equally recognized.

Satan's ploy is usually to hide and keep the tempted person's focus on whatever lust is stirred up in the moment. Lust is as common as dirt, so Satan tries to make it out to be sin and to stir up fear that it will get out of control. If he can keep the saint focused on trying to manage lust, the saint's focus is off of the Lord's keeping and our true identity. Then, the deceived saint keeps a measuring stick busy to quantify lust and devise ways to shrink or eliminate it. Everything becomes about the lust, and the will is ignored. Condemnation abounds over the lust, and fighting it does the opposite of what one hopes for. It does not shrink but takes over as an obsession.

Heaven laughs at this. Since when could anyone control thoughts and feelings from the soul or body? However, faith is always possible, based on true identity and walking in the Spirit. Rather than trying to manage lusts, look at Spirit. Lust then gets swallowed up, even if it does not feel that way immediately. Delight in the Lord takes over, and lust seems to shrink, not because it is managed on a soul or body level, but because the mind set on the Spirit is life and peace (Rom 8:6). Oneness with Christ and His Spirit becomes our fascination.

Every Perfect Gift

It is a grief when someone appears good but is revealed to be predatory underneath. This is a throwback to the Fall, when the serpent appeared benign but was in fact the destroyer who planted distrust. Learning trust comes with who we are, Christ in us, for Christ is the only one who can deliver anyone from a life of suspicion and fear. Though we are to be aware of the enemy's devices, the major point of faith is God's keeping and protection—knowing that every evil around us is God's calling card to know that we are whole and complete (James 1:4).

The perfect human is subject to temptation just like the lost human, or the carnal Christian. It is fantasy to think that spiritual maturity brings exemption from trials and temptations. If anything, the spiritual battle is more acutely felt since the one tempted is not slumbering away in fleshly lethargy, no threat to the devil.

It is always dangerous to know how wrong things are in the world. The unrenewed mind attacks evil on a surface level, trying to right injustices, only to perpetuate resentment over injustice while refusing the Cross of Christ as God's answer for every evil. Knowing the evils of the world is no less painful to the Christian, but the battle is in the inner man, where the point is getting fixed in Christ's indwelling life by the Spirit. God is who He is, without any "variation or shifting shadow" (James 1:17). He is not like the serpent—appearing good but evil underneath. If anything, God appears evil but is good underneath.

He appears evil because He does not exclude temptations and trials from the perfect life and because suffering is as much a part of God as miracles like healing. Just when a situation looks hopeless and inescapably dark, that is the moment to know that every good gift is ours from an unchanging God who sacrificed Himself completely for our highest good.

God Is in Control

If the world looked like God is in control, no one would need faith because faith flourishes against appearances. Thus, when it looks like evil has triumphed, faith knows that God is in control. Evil is temporary and will not last, God is eternal. The Old Testament prophets cried out to God in anguish when nations far more wicked than their own apostate people held power. In the New Testament era, the same dilemma exists: persecution is expected, and being a conqueror means holding fast to the faith when culture contradicts it.

Life is about getting fixed in the nature of God as the sacrificial lamb who may be ignored, persecuted, or killed now, but who rises from the dead because death can only be on a bodily level for the Christian. To get a wheat harvest, Jesus says, a wheat seed must go into the ground and die or else it exists alone (John 12:24). It dies to what it was above the ground and goes beneath the soil in order to rise a producer of seeds. This is the way of multiplication, death on one level, life on another.

Instead of "I should not preserve myself," faith now says, "I cannot preserve myself." Instead of "I should do others no harm," faith says, "I cannot do others harm." This is what John means when he says that to be "born of God" means that one "cannot sin" (1 Jn. 3:9). Christians start out knowing that when they commit a sin, there is forgiveness. Then they learn how to overcome the evil one and refuse the lie that says, "Christ is not enough." The more deeply the truth of abiding sinks in, the more life in Christ becomes like concrete setting up and drying in the certainty of "I cannot sin."

When a Christian faces temptation to sin, the answer becomes "I cannot do that anymore." It is not a resolution based on merely human internal inventory but upon the keeping power of God, which is based on Christ keeping the one belonging to Him. This is our faith.

October 17

Speaking Back to Feelings of Unforgiveness

A man says, "I can't forgive myself." Pain fills his face as he sits with six other men in a small group Bible study. Although the study is winding down, this man's question is not academic, and everyone turns to 1 John 1:9 except the man who asked the question. He can't find it, so the man next to him helps. Now everyone is on the same page. Someday this man will be helping others find that page. For now, he has opened the door to a new life.

The verse is simple: "If we confess our sins, He is faithful and just to forgive us our sins, and to cleanse us from all unrighteousness." How can this be true when others are enraged and unforgiving, and when the enemy's heavy load of guilt makes forgiveness seem like an impossible dream—maybe possible for some worthy soul full of other virtues to barter for forgiveness?

The verse does not ask for compensatory actions; it is not about making amends. All God asks is confession of the sin, which means agreement with Him. This is not a matter of feeling a certain way or of reasoning about what happened. When God speaks of confession, it is a Spirit induced agreement where the receiver accepts God's valuing of the Cross. It is devoid of anything destructive, having only one intent—forgiveness and cleansing.

God says how He responds: He forgives the one who sins and cleanses him. This is the transaction between God and the one who confesses. Does God do what He says He does? Here is where faith comes in, since feeling forgiven is not the point, and reasoning about forgiveness is not the point. All that is in view is Jesus Christ crucified, buried, and raised—"who loved me and gave Himself for me" (Gal. 2:20). Others may or may not agree yet with God about the sin this man committed. However, he needs one rope to hold onto for now.

October 18

Set Your Mind on Things Above

An old cliché talks about being so heavenly minded that one is no earthly good. The saying implies a dreamer or fool who is not practical—someone who talks about things that do not put food on the table or provide remedies for illness. Yet it is Jesus who says not to worry about food and clothes or to consider earthly life as the main kingdom to be concerned about. In eternity is a throne where the sovereign God rules outside of time and earthly life, yet He also rules over earth.

Both are true, time and eternity, because opposites cannot be eliminated. However, one of them will be our driver, which is why Paul says, "Set your mind on the things above, not on the things that are on earth. For you have died and your life is hidden with Christ in God" (Col. 3:2-3). This does not mean that there are not earthly things, or that they are evil; it means that they are not the source and energy of the universe. Outside of flesh consciousness is the throne in the heavens where Christ is seated at the right hand of God. This is command central for all things in heaven and earth, and no one can access it by the flesh or in any earthly way.

Access is by the Cross, upon which Jesus died, and upon which we died. The effect of that was to hide our life in Christ (Col. 3:3)—hide it not from us, but from those who still define life only in earthly terms. To affirm earth and deny heaven is to shut one's self off from the glory of God (Rom. 1). By the Spirit's aid, we are to press through earthly concerns to get heaven's view of things, and then earthly worries are much lighter and seen for what they are—temporal.

The person who sees this is indeed considered no earthly good by the fleshly mind. However, when earthly means fail, and they always do, only the saint has a pocketful of miracles.

Knowing That You Have Done Enough

Beware of deception when it comes to measuring results. Teams that do not win or businesses that fail to make money fire their leaders and find new ones to produce results. If your identity is centered in this approach, life will remain temporal. Even in education, the focus on test scores and grades treat learning as information apart from wisdom. However, what God cares about is Christ formed in the saint by His Spirit, and only He can do this. No one can feel or reason his way to this result. Only faith works, whereby God authors and humans receive (1 Cor. 3:7).

If you live by faith unto the Lord wholeheartedly (Col. 3:17) and loss or poverty results, you can know that the God who opens doors, can close them as well. However, the inner door—the one to the Spirit—is never closed. One can always be rich in the Spirit and fellowship. The point is identity. The point is life. Paul said that he could abase or abound (Phil. 4:12) and neither touched his identity. He had times of quickened responses from many hearers, but also times of apparent dwindled harvest, yet his identity remained the same. It is God who authors the harvest.

Faithfulness does not change with changing outer circumstances. Our part is to give what we know "in season and out of season" (2 Tim. 4:2). Being who we are is never out of season. Besides, God defines the seasons and their harvests. We do not even know what those are yet. In sports, thrilling victories are forged in the game's late stages. How do we know what the game is, necessarily, or what God's clock is? The point is that on a canvass vaster than we can see, we give our all by the Spirit even when results look slim. What happens from that is God's business.

October 20

Overcoming the Evil One

John writes about children, fathers, and young men (1 John 2). About young men he says, "you have overcome the evil one." Overcoming means knowing the opponent's strategies. In Eden, the serpent used lies. That is basic; sin always comes out of a lie. If Eve, and then Adam had not believed a lie, they could not have fallen.

Not only are we to move past being children who know forgiveness, we are to overcome the evil one and then move into parenting. The big step is becoming convinced that the devil's power is nothing compared to God's power. It is pitiful, though, when someone does not believe in Satan or recognize him. That is delusion indeed.

However, it is sad as well when a saint will not rise up in faith and say, "I don't take it!" when tempted. There is a strange pride that the world and carnal believers take in being too weak to resist the evil one, as if Christ is greater than the devil, but Christ is not greater than the devil in them. Certainly Christ can keep us from giving in to lies and fleshly lusts.

John says, "you are strong." The protest comes, "We have no strength of our own." Yes, a branch has no life of its own, which is why John favors the term abiding. He says, "the word of God abides in you." There is the strength. The Christian merely abides in God, and thus abides in His strength, which manifests as the branch. The branch simply remains in the vine. To be one with Christ means that the vine expresses itself by its branches.

Here is where Satan brings in the lie, inciting believers to say, "I am sinful flesh" rather than "I am a God-made branch, cleansed, and expressing Christ." Unbelief gets perpetuated by lies spoken in first person as if they are merely human thoughts, rather than lies spoken by Satan. Humanly, no one can overcome, but faith overcomes and knows it, not by emotion but by the Spirit-quickened word of faith.

October 21

Recognition

Recognition starts by seeing what will not work. As long as there is hope that wrath will work, a spark of it will start the same old raging fire. "Maybe the fire will not get out of control this time. Maybe there is a just cause for resentment." The worst things a person does to himself are in the name of justice, as if having been wronged makes resentment not poison. However, to not get off of myself and onto the wellbeing of another, means getting stuck in the whirling wheel that has not made it to the Cross, where the miracle is. Rescue can only come from the Cross, not human resources.

The whirling wheel is not evil of itself but turns evil if one does not embrace the Cross, which is to embrace who we really are—the new man. However, the new man is just as helpless as the old man because it is man who is helpless. Knowing who we are does not mean a slip back into "I should be able to figure this out" or "I should feel more love toward that person." To be human always means to be a vessel.

Thankfully, failure has its proper effect. The saint wakes up to what *will* not and cannot *ever* work. The Spirit has made plain what body and soul are, as well as what is from the enemy. It is not that you can say no; it is that you are willing to be delivered. It can even mean being willing to be made willing. "Lord, I am not hoping for permission to light the haystack with that match again."

But what does one say now? Perhaps no clear word flashes on the screen of consciousness. Wait, and it will. Tell the Lord that you do not know what to say and to give you a word. Then repeat after Him. It sounds too simple, but it is proper emptiness, which, in the obedience of faith, becomes the word of God abiding within.

Parable of the Leaven

Jesus told a parable about a woman who hid leaven in 50-60 pounds of flour (Matt. 13:33). That is a lot of flour. Ordinarily, leaven is symbolic of evil, or of bondage, or of hurry to escape; but Jesus uses leaven here as symbolic of His kingdom. Someday, Christ will manifest Himself and confront the world at the apocalypse. In the meantime, our life is "hidden with Christ in God" (Col. 3:3).

It is not that the church's witness is hidden. In fact, it is proclaimed all over the world unless driven underground by persecuting governments. Getting rid of the church is no more possible than getting the leaven out of flour once the leaven is in it. On an individual level, God hides Christ in a person who believes, and the leaven begins its work. Unless one holds onto legalism and religion, the Holy Spirit will permeate every bit of the flour that the human is. Christians begin to manifest Spirit life in ways not even planned or analyzed. By His Spirit, Christ simply takes over—that is unless resistance is encountered when trials come. How long can that resistance last?

The fact is that if you belong to Christ, nothing that comes to you happens to unleavened flour. Christ is all in all in the Christian. This means that no flour is wasted or discarded. It all has leaven hidden in it that cannot be separated out. Wish as you might at times that you had not gotten into the stress of being a Christian, there is nowhere else to go as Peter said (John 6:68). Suffering is the one thing that produces glory, so the only thing to do is to stay focused on the "eternal weight of the glory" and not the temporary pain of the suffering (2 Cor. 4:17). Keep in view the goal.

October 23

Which Problem to Solve

How great it is to discover real problems. In the news, problems get defined by media mostly without deference to scripture. Readers and listeners also bring their own grid to the news about what is important. For one who sees evil as sin based, the news can only be a shallow reminder of a world trying to evolve without acknowledging the Fall that got the human race expelled from Eden.

The same is true with personal issues, family friction, and job stress. Conflict arises from loneliness, greed, anger, lust, etc.—followed by the catch all, "I'm no good," or, "I'm this or that kind of person," meaning independent-self definitions. Since the devil quickly changes the slant on anything, he can keep someone jumping from issue to issue, leaving a person always needing more improvement, followed by resolutions like, "I'm working on myself." Clichés then abound like, "I've got a lot on my plate" or, "You don't understand how busy I am." What was once the ridiculous chase of the dog for its tail is now ennobled by being busy and having issues to identify and work on.

The same is true with family problems: what family doesn't have a load of headaches—or worse, insensitive members making selfish demands. Work can be the same way. It is liberating to discover that God actually means problems to be what they are in order to drive people to Him. The central problem is that all have sinned, and all have been "children of wrath" indwelled and controlled by the "spirit of error" (Eph. 2). Hidden inside was the enemy.

Therefore, God had to put fallen man into Christ's crucified body to separate us from the spirit of error that enslaved us. Then in Christ's resurrection, He put Himself into us as our new master. This is the solution of solutions. Everything else called a problem can only be solved by Christ living in those redeemed from their lost condition into the family of God.

October 24

Travailing Over Others

Galatians is the outpouring of Paul's labor of faith over that church. They had been set free, reveling in their freedom, but they started to cool and slip back under law. Thus he includes a curse on anyone who preaches another gospel—even Paul himself should he do so. Later he fears that he has "labored in vain" and he is "perplexed" (4:11, 20). He says that to go back under law means being "severed from Christ" and "fallen from grace" (5:4).

This is the ultimate agony for Paul—that someone would not "stand fast in liberty" but do something as drastic as fall from grace. This forces him to a desperate stand. What can he, or will he do? Obviously he cannot control them. Even if he could be with them in person, would he legislate, or go and seek out the legalists creeping in and punish them? It would be entangling to try and control others, either those who had experienced liberty or those threatening freedom from without.

All that was left was faith. He moves into confidence in the Lord that they will "take no other view" (5:10). The hook of freedom is in the fish's mouth and will stay there. Somehow, the Galatians will turn things around—cast out the lie and stand in freedom. They had not just tasted freedom and spit it back out. They had swallowed it all the way. Thus, the chilling of their attitude signaled the necessary hell that anyone returns to who has swallowed freedom and then stepped back from it. By walking temporarily in the lie of independent self (which being under law implies) the burden of righteousness falls back on the human, instead of Christ in the human by faith.

Back come condemnation and fear—people pleasing, plus "I should" and "I should have" sweep in with stinging regret and depression. This is excellent conditioning for not remaining there. It is the necessary hell that reveals what hell is and why grace is ever more so delightful.

October 25

The Spirit as the Mirror of Light

Uncertainty is common. Otherwise, no one would ever stop and think. For the Christian, uncertainty means looking into the mind of Christ, instead of, "What do I think?" as if reason can figure things out. The Christian takes no view at first. Paul says this well: "Not that we are adequate within ourselves to consider anything as coming from ourselves" (2 Cor. 3:5). To be human is to have no adequacy, only the capacity for faith, which is a receiving function. Amazingly, God created man to generate action only after 100% receiving—and only from one source.

This is why rules and codes do not work. Those imply "Tell me what to do, and I will do it," with the emphasis on a self that supposedly can. This is why "the letter kills" and it is meant to because God's gift to us is His own Spirit by which we see God and by which we are carried to the action conceived and originated in the Spirit. Everything falls back upon the Spirit. Without the Spirit, there is only the dry letter and the dead imitation according to what the blinded mind thinks is compliance.

Under the Old Covenant, men could not see the Spirit because of a blinding veil (2 Cor. 3:16). The veil was removed by Christ's sacrifice, so that fallen Adam could die, be buried, and rise in Christ to see the Spirit. In the darkest hour of anyone's life, where all is condemning and hellish, the Lord simply says, "Look at Me." The gaze turns from self to God, for "God is light" (1 Jn. 1:5). Although sounding overly simplistic, this command is mirrored in nature. To look for light means then to see what the light shines upon. Then the Bible is understood.

The veil that hid the light was always Satan's lie of independence. We thought freedom was doing our own thing, but freedom is transformation into Christ's image by looking at the Spirit like a mirror, and the light then lights you and becomes your light (2 Cor. 3:18).

The God of All Comfort

Comfort comes from God, and God comforts in all things, for God is the "God of all comfort" (2 Cor. 1:3). It is sad to hear someone say about a tragedy, "That person will never get over it." How hopeless that sounds, as if a wound can be so deep and lasting that God cannot swallow it up in His comfort. That is giving God an evil report.

This does not discount pain. God does not expect that anyone say that pain is less than it is, or that the agony of tragedy is less than it is, yet the deepest suffering becomes the setting for the most glory. No one likes suffering, and God never asks anyone to like it, which is why the Bible uses words like endure and wait. If you like something, it isn't suffering, and there is always plenty to dislike, even for those who do not murmur to the point of unbelief.

God "comforts us in all our affliction" (3:4). He also quickens our desire to share it with others who suffer. Instead of dwelling on "Why did this happen to me?" there is the Godward pull from the Holy Spirit to be for others. Just as there is sharing in suffering, there is sharing in comfort by the one Spirit. In this life, we are constantly weak, which is not sin. Only when weakness is despised does one's attitude turn to sin. Faith is a battle, and it is always good to say, "Thank You God for keeping me."

His keeping is essential: we do not "trust in ourselves, but in God who raises the dead" (3:9). Death is the worst case scenario, but even if death comes, there will be resurrection. Many deliverances from death come to us, keeping the angels busy, but even when it is time to die, there is comfort. Nothing escapes God's ability to rescue from despair and cause us to trust His sovereign purposes.

Mentors Are Ordinary People Too

By appearance mentors look stronger than average folks, as if they are giants untouched by adversity. The immature also picture mentors as not having the same temptations as others, as if they possess super powers to fend off negatives, like one would flick a bug off a shirt sleeve. Truly, mentors are giants, but they did not start that way, and their makeup has not changed along the way. A vessel is a vessel: once a vessel, always a vessel. Our job is to contain Christ, and any old vessel will do.

A Christian appearing as a giant is always the same simple person—someone who has settled into containing the overcomer. We do not become strong humans. Rather, the consciousness of weakness is accepted as not sinful, but rather perfect. Human weakness is normal, as is having constant trials and temptations. They are the daily fare in which faith operates. Negatives are still just as negative, and daily dying is just that—dying.

A vessel has no strength of its own, and the devil never stops doing what the devil does: lie, kill, destroy, and lust. Thus, there is no condemnation for weakness or for going through hard times and solicitations from the enemy. The answer to condemnation is simple: "No thank you devil."

Mentors even look like they do not need our prayers. Why waste a prayer on someone like Paul or on one of the greats in our lives? However, Paul did not see things this way. He did not want to be perceived as having sufficiency within himself, or as if he was a different order of human. He coveted all means of grace, and especially prayers, even from those who had been or were his own carnal children in the faith (2 Cor. 1). The reason is "that thanks may be given by many persons on our behalf" (1:11). Each person stands alone in his own faith, but arrival at that faith is often aided by somebody's prayer, even for those who do not appear to need it.

Doors that Open or Close

Spreading the truth is not like business marketing plans that target natural appetites. Spiritual doors open where there is spiritual appetite, especially desperation to know how a Christian can know adequacy. Paul knew quite well that no one can put pins on a map and then dig up contacts in order to bear fruit. A door must open, and only the Spirit does that (2 Cor. 2:12). This may sound dramatic and sometimes is, where the opportunity to witness was blocked, but a door suddenly opens for the Spirit to flow out by you in witness to a non-believer or in comfort to a believer.

Knowing this makes life easier to understand. When a door is closed, no human willing or muscle can open it, and when a door opens, Satan and hell cannot close it. It may not be clear why at first, but the point is knowing who opens and closes doors, "who opens and no one will shut, and who shuts and no one will open" (Rev. 3:7). Thankfully the door to the heart of one walking in the Spirit is always open. Personally, that is settled, and all work for the Lord after that is the Lord working as He wills and leads.

When not judging by appearances, it is easy to rest in whatever our work is because we are led in it: "thanks be to God, who always leads us in triumph" (2:14). This is a strong verse—not based on anything more than God's faithfulness in leading the one who rests by faith that he is led. The triumph may not have the look and timing as at first hoped, but God knows every part of a recipe and every detail from setup to completion, and how many hands will touch a person's life before all is done.

Paul calls us an aroma. How pleasant that is to those who share in the Spirit, and how unpleasant to those still of the flesh (2:16). Thankfully, a Christian is not the manager of his own self-image or his image among others.

Fragrance

Things in nature have a scent. Some animals can smell food or danger from great distances, long before seeing them. It is odd that people forget that they have a scent too—one not compounded of words necessarily. Words are essential, but note that Jesus Christ was the word (John 1:1). His being was the word, and His words proceeded from who He was. So it is with Christians: they are joined one spirit to Christ, and therefore it is normal that an unmistakable scent wafts out from them. It is the fragrance of Christ Himself, now mixed with you.

As life wears one down, the false belief of being in control gets exposed, and the Christian learns not to resist God's guiding, strange as it often appears. The fragrance grows. Though life seems stranger, it is only because His ways are not our ways, and thus should appear strange. Stranger still is that God "always leads us in triumph in Christ" (2 Cor. 2:14). Triumph does not leave wiggle room but implies a constant walk in the Spirit, not the in and out carnal experience of being in the Spirit one minute but out of it the next. Notice the word "always." Do not settle for less, for your faith needs a target that is total.

Triumph, however, does not mean the common place fleshly resolutions that say, "I can do anything if I set my mind to it." Fleshly positive thinking is just that—fleshly. It requires no miracle or Holy Spirit. Triumph as the Bible speaks of it concerns where you have been defeated with no hope of your own. This is where the devil intimidates those not knowing what triumph really is. Triumph means deliverance—the kind where Christ's fragrance now shows up in restful deliverance every time where bondage once ruled. Jesus has come home in your heart, not just as a vague resident to be called upon now and then for help, but as your very life (Col. 3:4).

Who Is Adequate?

The Christian life becomes so far beyond anything we can do that it is ridiculous to think of ourselves as the source of anything. Until then, life is always Christ plus something, and that something is a pinch of self that does not see the question, "Who is adequate for these things?" (2 Cor. 2:16). What looked humanly possible becomes the impossible, leaving only faith in what God alone can do, even when He does it through you.

Such workings of God in us look egotistical to those who see only flesh, which is why Paul says, "Are we beginning to commend ourselves again?" (3:1). To the person still trusting in the flesh, it looks like God's workings in the Spirit in us are a matter of personal ego. The world runs on personal ego, and so does the carnal church; therefore, to say who you are in Christ sounds like the same. Until all is Spirit, there can only be flesh rubbing against flesh with no resolution except to compare one's self with others and work harder for accolades from others to buoy up a sense of self-worth.

The Spirit person lets God bore all the way down inside to where the heart is no more than a "tablet" for the Holy Spirit to write on (3:3). Anyone can be a tablet. That takes no special gifts, just the willingness of faith. "Here God, write whatever You need to on my tablet." He writes the same basic identity on all, based on all being in Christ's death, burial, and resurrection. Then He writes the orders of the day for each servant in his or her call to serve, and each is not an inscription to compare but a calling of God unto one tablet and a response of one tablet back unto God by faith. Those moving in the flow of the Spirit know their own tablet and the tablets of others, all as letters from the same pen.

Confidence

Confidence is generally viewed in the world as a trait to work on and build. A person gains confidence to act or take on an enterprise, and every small step in a positive direction is the basis for another step. Accompanying this is the belief in human ability to get through adversity, even triumph. However, the Bible asks us to put our confidence in Christ in us, not in a supposed independent self.

The Bible treats man as a vessel, and a vessel simply contains. Properties such as love, patience, and goodness are unique to God and therefore can only be experienced by a vessel if the vessel mixes with its contents in an organic union. This is why the Bible speaks of Christians as branches of the vine or as the body of Christ.

Now one can talk rightly about confidence. Instead of mere self-confidence, one possesses confidence "through Christ toward God" (2 Cor. 3:4). Confidence is in someone—someone who truly is adequate. Paul uses the word adequate as the underpinning for confidence (3:5-6). Where does the adequacy come from? It comes from God "who made us adequate as servants of the new covenant."

Confidence is placed in the adequate One who then makes the person exercising confidence to be adequate by union. Union is not a matter of uniting the intellect with written words on a page but with the Spirit who wrote the words. Apart from the Spirit, the words can never come off the page except to the brain, which leaves the reader where he or she was to start with, except perhaps with more resolutions. Paul calls this the ministry of death (3:7), whereas the ministry of life is the Spirit of life. This is so simple, except to the one who chooses to remain blinded.

The Mystery of the Veil

In 2 Corinthians 3:13 we reach the mystery of why Moses wore the veil. Glory was fading, and the secret is hidden in the Shekinah dwelling above the ark but behind the veil. The Shekinah—God's glory—is a soft, delicate Spirit, gentle and feminine. The veil was her protection from the harsh, legalistic, and lustful gaze of fallen man. God in His mercy would subject His divine wisdom to only so much wrath from man because man's wrathful gaze causes the Shekinah to fade away into hiding.

What would make the Shekinah flame up and burn more brightly? It would be the loving gaze of the perfect man, namely Jesus Christ, whose love would make the Shekinah secure and able to unite with the seed (Christ) and bear offspring, as Paul says when he calls the Jerusalem above our mother (Gal. 4:26).

The glory of God could have rested upon Moses indefinitely and not faded, for he was a type of Christ, and God's glory was God's way of communicating with Moses face to face. Moses was also a type of the new man, who is united to God's glory through the old man having been put to death in Christ's death and then buried. In Christ's resurrection, the self is born again as a new creation man.

But no wonder Moses put on a veil. It was not because the glory would have faded. No, since Moses was at home with the glory, it would only have increased and rested more upon him, for Moses was not really a man under the law. He could walk invited up into the mountain of God that quaked, setting all other men in fear, but which for Moses opened into a holy place of fellowship.

The glory upon Moses felt the lustful and wrathful gaze of fallen man, still under the law and not wanting to come to the end of it yet, and so the Shekinah upon Moses deliberately faded and hid in the face of wrath. Christ frees us to gaze now without wrath and cause the glory to increase and grow in manifestation—in us.

Two Ministries: Death and Life

The Holy Spirit is living and speaks, but there must be a hearer who perceives. No wonder Jesus lamented that people have ears but do not hear. In the beginning, God created man with perfect ears to hear and be quickened by the words uttered by the Holy Spirit. However, the Fall destroyed those ears. God continued to speak and have prophets write down the words. Yet fallen man can only read them by the intellect.

Healing must come for deaf ears to open, and the Cross does this. At first, it can feel like a small start: inside is the nagging of a buried conscience that is a form of God's voice pleading. God reaches out to spark response to His call. Restlessness occurs because when honest, we want more than words on a page that we only read intellectually. There must be fire and life—a burning bush.

We awaken first to the ministry of death. When we were lost, we worshipped the words and our supposed ability to understand and obey them. This was Satan hiding behind the scenes making us think this because he thinks it. Satan's choice is fixed, but the human's is not yet fixed. To the honest hearer comes conviction: "I have not kept this word."

If pursued to agreement with God about sin, awakening is possible to the Spirit behind the words on paper. To know their meaning requires having the Spirit, for only the Spirit knows the Spirit's words. Then they make sense as expressions of a living Person, and our ears open to God's offer of healing through the Cross, which alone is the healing of all things. Christ's resurrection life opens the ears of those continuing from unrest all the way to Christ in you the hope of glory. Thus, life is not you living but Christ, yet as you, as faith looks through the apparent impossibility of this to the relief and joy of it. Argument about it ceases—because it works.

When Condemnation Goes and Glory Comes In

Without the acknowledgement of sin, grace means nothing. God becomes an accessory to approve of the self-life that flesh wants to indulge (refusal to take to the Cross). God is for us, and we are for ourselves—it is us all the way, making glory a shallow, sensual life in a temporal world where intellect and appearances operate selfishly.

To save us from this blindness, God gave the law to shock awake anyone paying attention. When seriously reading the Bible, it becomes devastatingly apparent that the law's requirements are infinitely beyond any ability to measure up, other than shallow self-congratulations over an occasional good deed that does not require serious loving of an enemy. Only by trivializing the law can one find any self-righteousness in what God means as the tool to break down confidence in the flesh, not uplift it.

Paul certainly got the law's intent by the time he wrote Romans Chapter 7: "for the good that I would I do not, but the evil which I would not, that I do" (7:19). No one gets to grace without passing that road, or else the grace is not grace but self-indulgence. The law's ministry is glorious, but it has "no glory" when compared to the ministry of the Spirit—the only glory (2 Cor. 3:8-10). Glory is God Himself by nature, then He made manifest to us, and in us, by His Spirit. The misery and bondage that come to light through the law end in the eternal relief of being joined to the Lord as one spirit (1 Cor. 6:17).

Life becomes glory because it is union with glory. This is what brings "boldness in our speech" (2 Cor. 3:12). Letting the Spirit be our whole life turns loose the imagination and creative powers of God in us. These were first present in the creation of the world and now are again in the recreation of the new world. When Christ rose from the grave, He ascended to make us new creations and reestablish man's regency.

November 4

The Veil and Glory

God's manifested glory in the Old Testament waited behind a veil that no one but the High Priest once a year could pass through without consequence of death. The veil represented hardness of heart, holding onto lawmaking as the means to live. Law—even God's law—is not to be used as a false hope of a higher plane whereby humanity supposedly can behold and eventually rival the glory of God. That is Babel and can only create a race of devils.

God has an answer for Babel—a veil that keeps sin in its own domain until it has become utterly sinful. When a man is blinded by even a glimpse of God's glory, the honest thing to do is to fall stricken and say, "I know nothing of that."

Thus the Israelites were not allowed to pass through the veil of the tabernacle because the old man cannot pass through it. Only the new man can. However, as a foretaste of glory, because Moses was a man of faith, and a type of Christ (and also of the new man in union with Christ), God spoke to Moses face to face. Translations of 2 Corinthians 3:13 convey the idea that Moses' veil hid the Shekinah from what was being "abolished" (KJV), "passing away" (NIV), "brought to an end" (ESV), and what was "made ineffective" (NEB).

What would pass away? The Old Covenant (the Law, with its ministry of condemnation) would pass away and be replaced by the New, in which Christ removes the veil. That is the only safe and true way. All other attempts to remove the veil are subtle forms of self-effort, still in denial that the old man had to die and be reborn to gain admittance. Christ alone removed the veil by His death, burial, and resurrection to birth the new man—the man now one with Christ. This man can look intently at God's glory all the time, while being transformed. He knows that the self is nothing of itself but is perfect and complete in Christ through the new birth.

The Lord Is the Spirit

"The Lord is the Spirit" implies that the Spirit is not a vague essence or impersonal force (2 Cor. 3:17). Only the Fall of man perpetuates such lies to avoid an intensely personalized view of the Spirit. Popular as fantasy tales are, with heroic forces and good ideals, they fall infinitely short of God making us in His image and establishing accountability to Him as Lord. It is insulting and vain to stop short of the God who desires, knows, and wills—and who created us in His image with those same capacities. Satan, however, does not want man to think of God as a person. A non-person cannot be Lord—only a force that one can use like electricity or nuclear energy.

Paul says that man's fall veils the eyes of those still lost or carnal so that they cannot see the glory of God. This is because the glory fades into hiding from fleshly attempts to seize upon it for "pleasures" out of "wrong motives," which is "adultery" against God (James 4:3-4). The Spirit is freedom embodied by the Cross and not license and law-lessness, turning the grace of God into carnality. No wonder God veiled the ark on pain of death until Christ made us safe by His sacrifice to look at the Spirit (Isa. 11:3). Only the new man can look safely because the new man, one with Jesus, looks as in a mirror and is transformed by beholding the divine glory.

To be a Christian means waking up to being the new man, who operates from above, seated with Christ and operating by His wisdom mind. This mind is not the soul or body operating according to the flesh as if independent, while calling that fleshly life Christ. The Spirit radically divides soul and spirit (Heb. 4:12) and teaches the new man to look into the mirror, not at earthly things. The new man lives only by the Spirit and then operates soul and body as safe instruments of the Cross in the heart of God. How wonderful!

Turning to the Lord

When Jesus died, "the veil of the temple was torn in two from top to bottom" (Matt. 27:51). Thus ended having to remain separated from God. The law as a schoolmaster had meant seeking to approach the ark by works of the law—impossible. God can only birth His sons after they have died in Christ to be reborn (Rom. 6). The veil of separation is removed with its bondage to the lie of independence (Rom. 7).

Always looking away from self to God is the key (Rom. 8). In no other way is the veil removed, for not looking only to God means still looking for a remedy from self. It is not evil to be a self; it is evil to trust in the self as the source of life. Christ IS our life (Col. 3). "Whenever a person turns to the Lord, the veil is taken away" (2 Cor. 3:16). There it is, in its pristine purity. One cannot turn to the Lord without turning from self.

This appears to be the annihilation of self, but the reverse is true. Giving up your life is the way to find it (Matt. 10:39). This is proved repeatedly by those who obey in faith. A "mirror" appears, which is "the glory of the Lord." Looking by faith to the glory of the Lord transforms the one looking. To become enamored of looking at the Lord is to find one's self by surprise.

Without effort and without thought of constructs for self-improvement, the beholder is "transformed into the same image" (3:18). A person becomes what he steadily gazes at. Put another way, what you take, takes you. Since the Lord is the Spirit of freedom and the sum of all love, gazing brings transformation into the same image. This is how the new man is manifested—the one who has risen with Christ in His resurrection and ascension. We are literally born of God. This sends to the trash all efforts to mimic Christ. Instead, by having turned to the Lord and remaining turned, Christ lives His life as your life.

Needs

Everyone needs sleep, food, love, and other remedies from the natural creation. Our bodies are made up of the natural creation and therefore have corresponding appetites. This is simply natural fact, but trouble comes by believing a lie about the natural world—that it is our life. Instead, Christ is our life (Col. 3:4) because God defines life as Himself and no other. Only God is life; therefore, the natural world is not evil, but neither is it life. It is created to express life, namely God. No wonder Romans Chapter 1 says that the universe reflects God's glory, even in its perishable state. God did not withdraw all radiance from creation at the Fall, else hell would have manifest in totality. He kept a witness and a cord of mercy, calling those who would look and long for life again.

Adam is our earthly father, and he plunged us into the natural world as if it is life. This is how Satan keeps a hold, for Satan's ploy is simple: keep the fallen race thinking that it is purely temporal and independent, thus bound up only with the senses and the concerns of the immediate, rather than concerns of the spirit and of the eternal.

This can even take a religious form. Paul was alive at one point, at least so he thought (Rom. 7:9). His pride was being fulfilled, and his natural appetites were satisfied, with his career on track, thinking that he was righteous. He fed from nature and from the deception of the enemy, who hid the source of this false satisfaction. Then God opened Paul's eyes to what the law really says. It was devastating but humbling. Everything that was supposed to be life was not, because one thing was missing—Life.

To meet the Lord is to meet life and to contain life. Then, when natural needs are not met, we do not say, "I do not have a life." We say, "Christ is my life," for truly we are in the world but not of it (Jn. 17:14).

November 8

Receiving Mercy

Looking into the Spirit's mirror and receiving mercy go together (2 Cor. 4:1). In fact, mercy cannot be known until we look away from self and "turn to the Lord" (3:16). This is because self-absorption blocks mercy. Such obsesssion with self keeps a whirl of condemnation going after self-commendation has collapsed. Turning away from the Spirit's mirror is what Lucifer did. Consequently, the glory left him—causing him to be naked, destitute, and wrathful because of desire never satisfied. Nothing is ever enough to the self-seeking person because only God is enough. All the mysteries of completeness are fulfilled within the Godhead, and then experienced within the one who receives the Lord.

Thankfully, Adam's fall was not fixed like Satan's. Adam wanted his own way, plus God at the same time. He was in bondage to the enemy but still had the longing to turn back and believe the redeemer's promise—the promise to defeat Satan and buy back Adam and the race out of our slavery to sin and loneliness. In God's great mercy, He receives back every lost son who through the blood and body of Christ wants to return to the Father's house. When someone turns to the Lord and begins to walk in the Spirit, the true self of that man appears constantly in the Spirit's mirror. This is the indirect result of looking to the Lord, for we are never meant to see ourselves directly, but only in a mirror provided by the mind of God.

Then we also know how exceedingly sinful sin was in the past, when we did not turn to the Spirit, yet the awareness of this new knowing is sorrow and repentance without condemnation. Our fall in Adam, continued individually by each lost son, becomes apparent, yet with forgiveness and hope. The miracle of restoration brings thanksgiving and praise—wonder at God, and new-found love of the blood and body sacrifice of Jesus Christ who rescued us from the eternal loss of both God and ourselves.

Not Losing Heart

When mercy is received, one does not lose heart (2 Cor. 4:1). Any sin can be forgiven and cancelled in its effects upon the heart of the believer. This frees us so that no memory of sin can lurk inside, waiting to rear up and steal our boldness when we step out in faith. Instead of losing heart, we stand in God's assurance of forgiveness and freedom to walk confidently in the Spirit without condemning introspection. Anything can be laid before God and forgiven once and for all, producing a clean conscience. Those who do not know this talk about hurts and offenses as if talking heals them, when in fact, without Christ, this only inflames them and leads to endless entanglement, or lies like, "I will never get over this."

Society is confessional to the point of spewing out its shame, with nothing but legalism and resolutions to offer as help. With the blood of Christ, a sin is gone. Its consequences may enrage those without mercy, but God shields the repentant one from condemnation and enemy attacks. Often, those offended demand constant apologies and complicated schemes of restitution that make one long for others to know the depths of restoration in the Cross.

It is also not wise to think that confessing sins like billboard proclamations is a mandate. The Holy Spirit knows how to keep confession holy, and only for the ears of those who need to know. The main thing to know is that when you have made things right with God, you are right. He will notify you of when to confess to others, and how to do it, and when to honor the requests that they make, but no man is to become a prisoner of unforgiving people. This puts man above God, which was why the Fall happened in the first place. Remembrance of a sin by an offender is good practice in seeing the sin under the blood of Christ, and Christ's body as having made the believer's body holy.

Handling the Word

An automatic sense of shame accompanies failure to let Christ remove the veil of blindness (2 Cor. 4:2). This is because the nakedness of the Fall cannot be covered by fig leaves or by any human devices; only Christ can remove it. Resistance to Christ perpetuates shame, and shame never goes away by itself, for it is the enemy's stronghold and false hope of independence from God, whereas God created us for union with Himself through Christ.

We instinctively know that God made us to be clothed with glory, but not self-made glory. The glory is the pure glory of God, God Himself, in His radiance and nature—the Shekinah that waited behind the veil for Christ to reunite man again with glory, for God created us to express His glory. This is Bible 101: God is the giver, man the receiver.

When a man tries to be something on his own, he holds onto the shame of his nakedness and must compensate for it. This leads to "craftiness" (2 Cor. 4:2). Instead of being simple and clear by the Spirit, accepting the role of being a vessel to contain Christ and a branch to express Him, one must conjure up an image to project and imitate to feel better and fool others. This craftiness is witchcraft from the enemy, which Paul "renounced" since in Christ's body death we died to the shame of the "alone I" lie, and rose in Christ as the new man. Plenty of temptation gives us opportunity to confirm the same, and the Bible says to expect this.

Therefore, there is no more "adulterating the word of God" (4:2). Nothing of the lie of independence is mixed in with preaching the word, for the word stands on its own, not needing apologies for the Cross, or for preaching that it took the Cross to free us from sin and Satan so that we could be reunited to God. This is the path to glory—the only path.

Conscience and the Mind of Christ

The word of God speaks to every man's conscience, not his intellect (2 Cor. 4:2). The conscience is the seat of knowing right and wrong (Rom. 2:15). When listening to the word of God, listen with your spirit. Look past bodily urges. Look past emotions. Look past mental reasoning, and listen with your spirit. Though the brain is a beautiful instrument, it is not eternal of itself and is only a data processor, not the organ of knowing. When the Holy Spirit speaks, He speaks as a Spirit and to a spirit possessing conscience, and the hearer can resist, which is to say, misuse freedom.

Much confusion will exist where bodily appetites, emotions, and intellect function as interpreters, instead of conscience. The world is built up on this false way of interpreting, making the resulting world a lie. No wonder John says, "the whole world lies in the power of the evil one" (1 John 5:19). Becoming a Christian is a shock—waking up out of a mass of delusion. It is a birth as a new creature into a new world, the kingdom of God. No wonder Jesus told Nicodemus that only by being born again can anyone see the kingdom of God. It is hidden to flesh, and flesh cannot find it or enter it.

When the Gospel is presented to the unsaved, and they continue to resist, the reason is simple: "the god of this world has blinded the minds of the unbelieving" (2 Cor. 4:4). This is the veil that the natural man cannot see past, and God does not mean for unbelief to see past the veil. No mental calculations can find a solution to penetrate and see past that veil. Only the conscience—which every person has, no matter the intellect—can open the door of faith to receive the word of God and see its wisdom by aid of the mind of Christ. The point is never our mind but the mind of Christ, which takes the place of our mind. All Christians share in only one mind.

Seeing

Blindness to who Christ is does not come from human choice alone as if it is a merely human quality. Unbelief is the result of willingness to remain blinded, incited by an evil agent who keeps the truth veiled and perpetrates blindness: "the god of this world has blinded the minds of the unbelieving" (2 Cor. 4:4). Blindness means darkness; therefore, the need is for light, and "God is light" (1 Jn. 1:5). That personalizes it. Light is a person. Satan uses the natural light of the intellect to fuel pride and deceive those who are blinded. They think that they see, when all they really see is the natural world. Something must tear away the denial that resists awakening to inner darkness and the need for light.

Natural light has its glory. Romans Chapter 1 tells us that even the physical world radiates God's glory, so that God holds man accountable for not seeking to know Him shining through nature. This is a first step toward the spiritual light that saves a man and leads to his new birth and life thereafter in the kingdom of light. Light shines from God to show the glory of His image, and those who follow through learn that the final revelation of His image is Christ. The son is eternally His image and has been made manifest as both God and man (John 1). This is the supreme meaning of being human: God expressed as man, first and foremost in His only begotten son.

Being the family man that He is, God's plan is a vast family of sons created in Christ, who is the seed that impregnates the divine womb to produce sons born of God. They are not born independent to be like God but are born *of* God—His very own children through the Cross. Without the Cross, the heavenly womb cannot bear children but would remain barren. Thank God that Jesus did go all the way for us so that we could be redeemed from slavery to the enemy by dying in Christ, and be born new creations whom He has sanctified (Heb. 10:14).

Hidden

Given the choice to look at ourselves or to look at God, Satan's enticement is toward self-worship. This is all we knew from birth because of sin's author hiding within. Just as our life is "hidden with Christ in God" (Col. 3:3) beginning with conversion, it was hidden in Satan before the new birth (Rom. 5:12; Eph. 2:2). The present earthly senses mask reality, and the enemy wants to keep people slumbering in spiritual death while feeling alive otherwise. Comfort becomes the enemy of conviction. Even the carnal Christian needs a similar awakening. Though joined to Christ spirit to Spirit, the flesh keeps its appeal until the cycle of sin and condemnation has conditioned the saint to walk in the Spirit instead.

Lust, loneliness, and unresolved anger do their work until the worn out Christian dies to efforts for change, which delights God, because God has already caused us to die in Christ. Then it becomes pleasant to look at the Lord. It becomes unpleasant to see the self in any way other than an image mirrored back to us from the Spirit. We take no view of the self that does not come directly from looking at the mirror, which is the mirror of freedom, for "where the Spirit of the Lord is, there is liberty" (2 Cor. 3:17).

The person preaching self-improvement is opposed to the Gospel (4:5). It is not that we are not selves, even gloriously born again selves, but the point is the One who created us new, and with whom we are enraptured. Lovers are not in love with themselves but in love with another. What the lost or carnal mind calls love is infatuation with one's own self, triggered by a convenient, flesh-happy prop. When the object of infatuation stops feeding narcissism, so-called love is quickly dispensed with for a new quest. But when love means preaching Christ Jesus, the one loving accepts the role of "bond-servant" to others for "Jesus' sake" (4:5). This alone is freedom.

Light Shines out of Darkness

There is darkness, and there is light. God made the eternal decision to be light. Confronted with the choice to be self-for-self or sacrificial love, He forever swallowed up the choice to evil by saying no to it. Therefore, evil to God remains in Him impossible since the Cross is fixed in His heart. He considered and rejected evil so as to fix Himself as self-for-others love. His capacity for choice defines personhood for Himself and humanity, for if God did not choose, how could we correspond to His image?

Man, however, by the agency of Adam, chose evil. However, this choice was not a fixed choice from his spirit center, and thus God, by grace, offered His only begotten son as a sacrifice so that this present life becomes a proving ground for anyone willing to call upon the name of the Lord and be saved (Rom. 10). Anyone who chooses Christ becomes a saint who enters a battle not waged against flesh and blood, but against the enemy (Eph. 6). The darkness no longer abides within us but comes against us, pretending to still be the master in us.

The world is still full of darkness, but for a believer, light shines out of darkness. Darkness itself never produces light. That is impossible because the absence of light cannot produce light. But where darkness opposes and threatens us, faith makes its jump to look to light, to God's glory, manifested in the face of Christ (2 Cor. 4:6).

As a believer stands by faith amidst the hopeless darkness of the present evil age and the devil's false assertion of victory, light shines from the face of Christ to accomplish the plan for heirs that God set in motion before the world began, for those who believe. Evil can never stop that. For the believer, darkness is only the setting from which light shines. Darkness does not create light, but darkness prompts light's miraculous occurrence, as glory swallows up its opposite. Thus Paul says, "Death works in us, but life in you" (2 Cor. 4:12).

Life out of Death

It does not work in the natural realm for life to come out of death. Death is death—final on the natural level. Accordingly, those who see only flesh, know only corruption and mortality. They either see evil as irreversible and become bitter, or they compensate by good works to try and outweigh the evil. However, even with their good works, evil never loses its sting, to get swallowed up by glory. The Gospel provides for infinitely more than the pitiful situation of the Fall. In Christ, suffering is transformed into glory.

Our salvation began by God putting us to death in Christ so that we would rise as a new creation. Christ lives within! True, our mortal bodies are still mortal since it is God's plan to have "treasure in earthen vessels" (2 Cor. 4:7). All that is life and supernatural comes from Him at the same time we hide the mystery in clay containers. It is not hidden to faith, but it is hidden to all else. Despite mortality and enemy attacks, Christians look to the Spirit to see and declare who we are as new creations. When our intercessions are finished, pointing others to salvation and then maturity, God calls us home to await the manifesttation of the new body, already ripening within, that will correspond to the new heaven and earth.

Meantime, constant opposition is expected, which Paul calls affliction (4:8). This is disturbing and painful as the enemy tries to "crush" the going forth of the word and beat down enthusiasm by scorning it into retreat. God says, "Don't take it!" We do not have to take it. By looking to the Lord and not getting tangled up in arguing with evil, light comes from our spirit union where the treasure is always the treasure. Evil does not redefine anything about God or about those in whom He is the treasure. No matter what death does in its assaults, it does not alter life. In fact, the suffering that death causes, results in life all the more manifesting for others.

Perplexed but not in Despair

Being perplexed can include feeling torn up in your mind. When the truth is presented, and others ignore it or treat it in a superficial way, it is perplexing that what you see as clear, and as rescuing light, is treated by others as something of little consequence. They say, "That's good for you, but I believe what I believe." This is painful since we know that the issue is not hundreds of topics that no one can be certain of, but is the one topic that concerns a person's eternal fate, based on receiving Christ as our identity and life. When Jesus calls Himself the vine and we the branches, that is a oneness not to be ignored. Being attached to the one who is life itself and the lamb slain for us is the utmost good news, but it is treated with resistance ranging from indifference to scorn to persecution.

No wonder the joyful saint who has seen his burdens lifted and his debt cancelled in Jesus cannot fathom everyone not wanting the same relief. Why we held onto condemnation, anxiety, and works of our own as long as we did perplexes us, and finally when we see how easy it is to know deliverance, it seems equally easy for others as well. Can they not learn from our experience? This is a mystery. It tears us up inside to see others doing the same futile things we did, and we long for their deliverance. If they do see, it is maddening if they fall back from freedom.

We are perplexed but "not in despair" (2 Cor. 4:8). Despair means giving way to hopelessness: "That person will never see." This insinuates a final, disastrous verdict. On the other hand, hope takes a stand of faith, first, that regardless of others' resistance, God works in His way and time, bringing to faith those He lays on our hearts to intercede for. We stand firm in our own faith for the truth, and for ourselves, and for particular ones for whom we believe. They must die and rise like we did.

Faith Is in Another

Faith is not vague as if to say, "Just have faith," and therefore others will be comforted. Faith means being taken by something or someone. Bill Bright said, "Putting faith in faith is like casting the anchor inside the ship." Notice that "Abraham believed God, and it was reckoned to him as righteousness." His faith was in another. This is stressful: God means appearances to be contradictory and a normal, daily dilemma—a negative backdrop. This sets the stage for glory's positive breakthrough to swallow up what to flesh is impossible.

Do we get used to the gap between appearances and Spirit? Shock and consternation are common when any wave of appearances hits. It would be easy to take guilt: "Where is my faith?" Norman Grubb said, "I never start with faith." This sounded weak and contemptible coming from a man known for great faith. But he knew to embrace the negative, not expecting himself to be strong since God's strength is made perfect in weakness.

Courage is courage because it is received from the Spirit while feeling fear. Love is love because it is received from the Spirit while feeling hate. It is a lie to identify ourselves only as our emotions and mental reasoning, falsely supposing courage and love to be qualities humanly mustered up. Courage and love are what God expresses in us, even while we feel the opposite.

True, we desire soul and Spirit to line up in harmony. However, there is no condemnation when they do not. My wife, Tandy, told me of a friend who said that we should manifest the Spirit's fruit. Her friend, however, thought this meant trying to imitate Christ. "But it is the fruit of the *Spirit*," Tandy replied. A branch bears the orange. It doesn't make the orange. Jesus modeled this in His humanity by saying that He could do nothing of Himself (Jn. 5:19). Neither can we. "Apart from Me, you can do nothing" (Jn. 15).

November 18

Persecuted but not Forsaken

Persecution interrupts comfort. If we didn't care about comfort, persecution would be no problem. Who would care if excluded from a special group or if targeted for hateful treatment? Having goods taken unfairly or being physically harmed would not cause one to flinch. But we do struggle with these, and the Bible does not say that things will change during this life. So what is the answer?

God uses these to fix His sons in knowing who they are in Christ. When old responses pull and beg to be expressed, a miracle occurs to the one willing to see Christ manifested instead. The pull to old responses does not mean that the old man is still alive, but that the same old flesh responses can occur if not recognized as a lie. When persecuted, we need support, and the Lord unfailingly is that: we are "persecuted but not forsaken" (2 Cor. 4:9). To be forsaken is to be alone—not understood—but God does not leave us there.

No one wants to go through hard things alone. Yet there is an alone walk with God that must be embraced to trust in God, not man. Even in this, however, comfort appears through others sent by God to comfort us (2 Cor. 1:6). This is the great mystery, that God Himself can comfort us directly from the throne without others, or by messengers. When the comfort is brought by messengers, we appreciate them while marveling at the voice of God through other suffering humans.

Whereas comfort used to be primary, rendering comfort is more precious now. Christ never forsakes witnessing to us that we are His very body; thus, we never go through anything alone. There may be a season when no other human being is our comfort, but this gives way to the comfort of the Lord, first from Himself, and then recognized in those He sends to us. In them we hear the same voice that we have learned to recognize as the faithful shepherd.

The Furnace Door

Injustice sparks anger. While anger can be a motivator leading to justice, anger can also get misused and become self-for-self in a rising rage that does more damage than the injustice that provoked it. This is serious business. Without right anger, there is no fire, no passion.

Only the Cross transforms anger into its proper form. The mystery of the Cross is that God returns sweetness, gentleness, and mercy to those with whom He is angry. Though a day of vengeance is coming for those who are not won over to the love of God in Christ, only God Himself understands and carries out vengeance. Our role as believers is not vengeance, but impartial justice. Our role is priestly and merciful. We absorb many wrongs, which only the Cross in us can do.

Proverbs 12:16 puts it like this: "A fool's anger is known at once, but a prudent man conceals dishonor." This is a riddle: it would not seem correct to conceal dishonor. Therefore, what dishonor is concealed?

The devil likes to throw insults at our faces. He will goad us with irreverent and blasphemous taunts from the world, or carnal brethren, to provoke overreaction. His goal is to move the believer away from God's grace to ignore certain affronts. The devil wishes to get the believer fighting evil with evil—to trick the believer into wrong use of anger that is a wrong judgment and recedes from the Spirit of wisdom.

James says that Wisdom is always available, that God generously gives Wisdom to anyone not doubleminded. There is no need to remain unwise and let the devil keep his earthly, sensual, demonic hold in our members. The sweetness of Wisdom is always there to close the furnace door to fire that should stay in the furnace so that the warmth can radiate.

When Turmoil Attacks

Christians and non-Christians know the swirl of troubling thoughts about problems and urgencies needing attention. With that comes the consuming fear of not getting everything done, or not being able to change the world for the better. This is temptation to external anxiety and frustration, as if it is the individual Christian's job to fix a host of problems or even a single overriding problem.

Neither Jesus nor the apostles operated like that. Their way of changing the world began with the new birth and subsequent transformation of one wayward person at a time. James says, "he who turns a sinner from the error of his way will save his soul from death and will cover a multitude of sins" (5:20).

Change of institutions and laws can only be as effective as the sanctification of those governed by the institutions and laws; otherwise, the laws will get rewritten by the wicked and for the wicked; and institutions will eventually rot and crumble. The one true institution is the church, the body of Christ; and it is a living body with Christ as head, not an institution in the ordinary sense. Of course Paul wrote Timothy and Titus detailed instructions for the leadership and governing of the local church, but the church can rise no higher than its grasp of the living Lord indwelling believers and keeping His own laws.

What good are laws if we cannot keep them? First we discover that we cannot keep them and that God always knew that we cannot. He never designed humans to do so. To be human does not mean a separate self who tries to keep the Lord's way by imitation. What God means us to imitate is faith—faith in the one abiding in us who does keep His own commandments.

When turmoil attacks, say, "God, nothing can wither my leaves or hurt my fruit. Nothing can keep my sacrifices from prospering" (Psalm 1). I am on time.

Struck Down but not Destroyed

Life is full of harsh and unexpected happenings. They come to everyone, both those who believe and those who do not. The difference is that those who believe, or who come to believe, have hope. Hope does not mean that God fixes everything a certain way right now. What it means is that nothing that strikes us down can destroy us: "struck down but not destroyed" (2 Cor. 4:9).

Lots of things strike a person down: an icy stare or word, an act of betrayal, or an outright assault. Included are family disasters, disease, and financial upheavals. Paul calls it "constantly being delivered over to death for Jesus' sake" (4:10). He did not interpret the things that struck him down as happening for no reason. He may not have known the reason, but he knew for whose sake he suffered.

He did not go it alone, and neither does any child of God. What happens to you happens to the one who owns you, lives in you, and is joined as one to you. Christ continues to suffer because though the atonement is complete, the intercessory suffering of Christ's body is still in progress. Our suffering is equally His. In fact, it is more comforting to see it as His than ours because it removes the suffering one from questioning, "What did I do to deserve this?"

Here is what destroys the world: an evil comes about, and the evil screams that it has the power and that God cannot mean it for good and bolster the victim to stand in that. The shock waves hit, and the world says, "A person cannot get over this." God says, "Watch Me turn this into glory—into life for others for Jesus' sake.

Jesus called it seeing with the single eye (Matt. 6:22). When darkness attacks and claims victory, do not minimize the darkness. It is exactly what it is, evil in all of evil's terrible forms. However, in the face of that, state, "God is bringing good out of this. He is doing it." Stand on that.

November 22

More Life out of Death

Death has come near us many times, and we have escaped. Someday, in God's perfect time, each child of God is taken home. Faith says, "God, Your timing in my life is perfect. You have the perfect timing and pace for my daily living, and not one heartbeat is unplanned." This is the sovereignty of God. Jesus knew that He could not go before His time, and neither can we. This brings peace and is a stay against recklessness and hurry.

Where antichrist is, physical danger accompanies the Gospel, and Paul lived with this constantly (2 Cor. 10-12); he also knew the constant evil pressures of the world that produced taking up his Cross daily so that he could say, "death works in us, but life in you." This is always the remedy for death. It means knowing that to believe is to be a "living sacrifice" (Rom. 12:1).

Such expectation makes all the difference, in contrast to a sleepy, carnal life. It lends itself to a "spirit of faith" (2 Cor. 4:13). This has the sound of cultivated practice, making faith not mysterious and remote but rather concrete and practical. Faith is in a person, and in this case, it is in the person who lives in us and who brings life out of every attack by Mr. Death—the enemy.

Paul says, "I believed, therefore I spoke" (2 Cor. 4:13), which refers to the Psalmist's words, "I believed when I said, 'I am greatly afflicted'" (Psa.116:10). Even though a faith person cries out that he or she is afflicted, that very cry is still made in faith, not to inform the Lord as if He does not know, but to affirm the depth of the present suffering in which the cry is made, and to equally affirm that God has it. It is the same to say, "Lord, it really is this bad, and You have it!" Deliverance from physical death may result, or "precious is the sight of the Lord is the death of His godly ones" (116:15). There are no mistakes.

November 23

The Offense of Grace

It is annoying to hear grace mentioned superficially as a means bypassing a holy life. One would almost think that grace is a lightly perfumed spray to apply over carnal ways to circumvent the necessity of transformation. It sounds indulgently like the "forgiven sinners" consolation that acknowledges sins but never dispenses with them by living from the power of another—namely the Holy Spirit.

Grace should be so dangerous that it baffles works-minded people, leaving them to wonder why there is not retaliation when others are insensitive, mean, and backstabbing—or when they think that grace means being out of touch, a bit mentally tipped, or like a fairy godmother, or perhaps even too simple and pure to see evil going on to do anything about it. When others see grace ignore insults, forgive offenses, and seek the good of those who do not deserve it, grace is evident, even if people think that you are crazy for being that way.

Grace is also evident when the measuring cup of self-performance does not dominate your thinking—the "How am I doing?" obsession. Instead, you see the Christian life as Christ living it, while marveling at the constant miracle of Jesus doing in His children what is impossible to humans. Paul speaks of the "grace which is spreading to more and more people" (2 Cor. 4:15). To understand what he means by grace, look at the preceding verse: "always carrying about in the body the dying of Jesus, so that the life of Jesus may also be manifested in our body."

The risen Lord cannot die again: "Christ, having been raised from the dead, is never to die again" (Rom. 6:9). His work of salvation is complete, not needing a repeat. Regarding interceding for others through His body on the earth, He takes the assaults of death and evil against us in this world, and by union with us, expresses grace back to others. We see evil as evil and feel its impact, but we sink into Christ's nature for our responses.

Your Harvest Is Certain

No matter what the circumstances are of our physical death, "He who raised the Lord Jesus will raise us also with Jesus" (2 Cor. 4:14). Without that conviction, life is short and sad. Striving to make a better world sounds noble but is pitifully arrogant. We do not try to make a better world; we announce a new world—the kingdom of God and Christ as king, we ourselves born of His seed as royal sons to reign forever with Him. This is grace—that sin did not destroy God's plan for a race of humans to manage His universe. The means is union with the Godhead through Christ's resurrection, whereby God expresses Himself by His children. Thinking about this is invigorating since daily we see mortality, as well as the prevalence of evil.

Yet Paul chose to look at "the grace which is spreading to more and more people" (15). We too take a leap and believe in the harvest no matter how meager it looks at present. Abraham was promised offspring more than the stars, and we no less. Without a leap we could only lose heart, especially as we move closer to RIP on a tombstone (even though we won't be there). Yes, the physical body "is decaying" (16), "yet our inner man is being renewed day by day."

This is astonishing; no one naturally feels this way. Evidence from what the mental, emotional, and physical self sees only declares our efforts to be in vain, deserving the mocking and scorn of unbelievers. But what world do they see? They see only the outer one, so how can they understand the Spirit's quickening miracle never running out? It's a marvel. The Holy Spirit is never less in the cup. The vine's sap is never less in the branch. If Elijah's widow never ran out of oil, why would we not see the Spirit renewed daily (1 Ki. 17).

Feelings of exhaustion and emptiness are normal. Dread of futility is a common temptation. Brush them aside as lies.

Difficult Things

Difficult things feel like they will last forever, too heavy to endure. Troubles are just too hard and last too long. No wonder the yoke of Jesus is restful to receive. His yoke is light and His burden easy (Matt. 11:29-30). No human yoke is like that, and certainly not the devil's yoke. Time alone cannot bring relief. When depressed, it seems to take forever between the ticks of the clock. The pain of affliction feels consuming. In the little book of Habakkuk is a big thought. God calls the prophet to get up high on a watchtower for an encompassing view. The news was not good. Things were going to get worse before they got better. However, Habakkuk saw that "the just shall live by his faith" (2:4).

Faith is in the "things which are not seen" (2 Cor. 4:18). The Fall closed Adam's spiritual eyes, and the Cross reopens them for those who believe. Another world comes into view, that of the kingdom of God. Jesus told Nicodemus that to see the kingdom of God one must be born again, which means literally that. Until a new birth, this world looks to be the only one except for maybe a vague sense of heaven in the future, but with the new birth, heavenly things become more real and feed a person more than earthly concerns.

This does not mean that earthly trials are not severe. It means that we learn to measure them against eternity and glory. This is why, no matter how oppressive a thing is, it comes under the category of "momentary, light affliction" (2 Cor. 4:17). Nothing but faith carries us over to that view. In earthly terms, such talk is sheer madness and insanity, but in faith language, it is the release into seeing wonderful purposes accomplished that will bring memories lasting forever. Taking up the Cross daily does not mean that we like suffering but that our true love is for what is eternal and glorious. What appears a waste now is eternal treasure.

November 26

Living in an Earthly Tent

It is nice to live in a house, but regarding our bodies, Paul calls them "earthly tents" (2 Cor. 5:1), which makes more sense as we age. Grief makes itself known, and people get their bucket lists going of things to do and experience before mortality wins the inevitable battle. There is no reason for stoicism here. Paul sure was not a stoic: "in this house we groan, longing to be clothed with our dwelling from heaven" (5:2). He even calls us naked in our present condition.

We instinctively want to be clothed with more than the earthly. Something is missing, and it was lost in the Fall when our first parents let their heavenly clothing get away from them by cutting themselves off from the sevenfold Spirit as their clothing (Isa. 11). Man's body, both male and female, had flourished in a gown of Light. This was the perfect union of the glorious God and the human. No darkness, sin, or fear gripped man in his body, soul, or spirit in any way. Only by forcing a separation did intruders take hold and leave us naked and ashamed.

Salvation brought a newly born spirit, and now the new man lives in an old body. This body is washed with "pure water" (Heb. 10:22) and therefore not defiled, even though still mortal. Now the body is a cleansed and fit instrument for the Spirit to manifest Christ's life in the present world (Rom. 6:13). Still, though, it is a tent life and a mortal body, one in which "we groan, being burdened" (2 Cor. 5:4). The reason is simple—to learn the life of faith, first for ourselves, and then walk kept from sin by God's keeping so that we can witness to others how to find this for themselves.

How, in a mortal body, can one walk free from sin and in hope of a new body, while beset with old lusts that keep knocking on the door, and a devil who lies continually? This is the miracle of faith in our Keeper walking about as us in these tents.

Home in the Body, Absent from the Lord

It is odd to say that we are one spirit with the Lord (1 Cor. 6:17) yet "absent from the Lord" while "at home in the body" (2 Cor. 5:6). No Christian wants to be absent from the Lord. The very word *absent* brings up memories of absences from school and classmates, or from family. Absence implies pain. However, union with Christ gets us through life's messes and tragedies. Without the presence of Christ's resurrected and ascended life in us, we would give way to discouragement and eventually despair. Yet we are absent from the Lord while in an earthly body.

How interesting that the Bible reckons being present with the Lord to mean absence from the very body that He uses as His presence on the earth to call others into the body of Christ for salvation and fruit-bearing. In other words, we grow to maturity while we are absent from the Lord. What a concept. It is extraordinary.

Evidence for the rightness of this is added by Jesus telling His disciples that He had to go away so that He could send the comforter (John 14:28). Clearly from Pentecost and the explosion of the Spirit into the lives of the disciples and the expanding church, God means to get a lot done while we are absent from Him. The good news is that the absence is temporary and is for our solidification in how to "walk by faith and not by sight" (2 Cor. 5:7). God works from the inside out, getting us settled in Spirit life against every imaginable appearance.

This explains Paul using the word *courage* twice (5: 6, 7). Life is built on opposites, one swallowing up the other, so the exhortation is to let the Spirit swallow up fear so that we move on with the plan. Every good soldier fears his commander more than the enemy, and so the beginning of wisdom is never outgrown, namely "knowing the fear of the Lord" (5:14). This checks the temptation to rash claims that God doesn't know what He is doing. The old saying is true: Father knows best.

The Beginning of Wisdom

Love casts out fear, right? Yet "the fear of the Lord is the beginning of wisdom" (Prov. 9:10). There is fear that shrinks back in unbelief, and there is reverent fear that takes action. Wrong fear promotes disrespect, recklessness, and cowardice, whereas proper fear is bracing—the foundation of sobriety and alertness.

To have proper fear means to wake up, attentively recognizing that life is not a big, indistinguishable blob but instead is a series of dangerous challenges that only wisdom can guide us through. Thus, the God-lover is the one who knows enough fear to recognize that every word and action are being recorded for future review at the "judgment seat of Christ" (2 Cor. 5:10). The Gospel does not mean lack of accountability; it means Christ's merciful judgment of His own to divide what is of Him from what is to be discarded—not carried over into eternity. It is a program of waste management, and the stakes are high since waste is sorrowful.

Paul used his fear of the Lord to "persuade men" (2 Cor. 5:11) but not with fleshly rhetoric of mere politics or commerce. It was his fear of God on behalf of others who were wasting away in a sleepy state of denial. We are not to think, "I should speak to that person" as if driven by guilty compulsion. Rather, silence is rare and precious; but, when the fear of the Lord comes over us, overshadowing us to persuade others, we know it because the prompting is evident in us where our spirit hears from the Spirit. We know, and God knows, that the motive is pure (2 Cor. 5:11).

Hopefully, the hearer hears from the same spirit-to-Spirit center; otherwise, we will be misinterpreted as arrogantly trying to control things. That is a risk one must take when our conscience is clear and known to be guided. Fear of the Lord means seeing the inner radar, not the outer one of appearances. Trust it.

November 29

The Craziness of Love

Love drives us all. Worldly poets and musicians know this in their deluded way; the love celebrated is temporary and sensual—at best a mutually self-serving pact. For the Christian, love drives him because "God is love" (1 John 4:8). All creation can be no other than love either in a rightly used or misused form; but make no mistake, love in self-centered or sacrificial form drives us.

In the lost and carnal, the hurts and pains of love gone wrong lead to all addictions and forms of retaliation that make up what the Bible calls sin. In Christ, however, love takes the form of the Cross; and in Christ, and He in us, love can be nothing other than the Cross. Really, heaven is no more, no less, than the Cross manifested in the children of God and all redeemed creation.

Love itself makes the difference, not the appearance of love. Appearance oriented people think that others all play the same game since they cannot imagine any other way. Thus, carnal onlookers thought that Paul had to be self-centered just like they were, and furthermore out of his mind for insisting that he was only for Christ and for others (2 Cor. 5:12-13). That is how it works: when finally in your right mind in Christ, the fleshly thinking of others is seen for the grief and insanity that it is—satanically driven, supposedly enlightened self-interest. The Cross is a wisdom all its own, making no sense to those not born of being crucified with Christ as their only hope.

Paul says that to be out of one's mind is unto God, i.e. out of the natural mind and into the mind of Christ—a sound mind that is for others (2 Cor. 5:13). To be considered out of our minds is hard to take. It forces us to the mind of Christ (Wisdom) to know that we *are* of sound mind—still for others despite how they see us.

Reconciled to What?

Seeing ourselves or others according to the flesh can only produce frustration without resolution. Actions and supposed motives will remain hidden and dark, without clarity, and only lead to either soul/body indulgence or to legalistic attempts to control the self and others. Under either deception, Christ may be the savior to a believer but not much more than an example from history to imitate. Mental assent to the historical Christ makes Him a real person but not a living one in believers now. Why would Christ have appeared on earth with such power and revelation only to be a moral example of conduct, another code? Why would He have appeared only to have been a one and only of its kind, a vine with no branches or a head with no body? Did He not intend to come back to earth in everyone who is born again?

The surface church does not see this and hides behind resolutions and human failings that seem good reason to shrug the shoulders and trudge on in the same old way with a life not infused with miracles and astonishing turnabouts from sin. Worse than particular sins is the baseline lack of seeing that Christ by His Spirit draws us to His faith, saying, "Come along with Me. Say that I am keeping you."

The Gospel is that a believer is "a new creature" (2 Cor. 5:17). As light pours in on this, clarity comes by revelation that the old man was not an independent, flesh person, but a satanically driven, old man who was dead in sin. This man had to be crucified, not reformed.

To be "In Christ" means being in His crucifixion, resurrection, and ascension—putting us in His ongoing life. You look the same and have the same personality, but now there is light shining out of you. The man in the mirror has the same earthly form, but the Spirit within radiates that "old things passed away". When Paul said, "Be reconciled," he wrote a church that did not yet see who they were (5:17-20).

December 1

What Does Your ID Card Look Like?

There is no mix of old and new in a believer. Though a Christian experiences a mix of old and new, it is only from not seeing the truth yet. God does not see a believer as a combination of old man and new man; He only sees the new man—even if the new man is still uninformed about being a new creation. Birth and identity are everything, making all else a lie and a passing deception as revelation takes the place of appearances.

This is God's word and work, not man's. He says so (2 Cor. 5:18). If you were sitting face to face with God, He would say, "I have caused your old man to pass away and made you a new man. I did this in Christ. Christ is the reconciliation. Tell others the same." Where trespasses continue, the new man still believes the lies that accorded with the identity as the old man. But they do not fit now.

I used to think that when Paul says, "be reconciled to God" that he intends nonbelievers (5:20). The verse looks like an appeal to be saved. Certainly, the Bible is read by anyone, and a verse like this can speak to an unsaved person. However, Paul is writing the Corinthian church. You would not think that the Bible would say "be reconciled" to Christians, but the reason is that the recipients of the letter were not reconciled in their minds yet to what God is reconciled to in His mind about who we are.

The thrust of the passage is for Christians to move on, not to something deep and for a few great saints, but to what anybody's ordinary ID card would say, for example a driver's license or access card to a privilege. ID cards are common, and they make us feel special, but the notion of identity is as common as citizenship. Hardly a worse fallacy has beset the church than that of a Christian having two natures. God says we have one—His.

The Threefold Cord

Fellowship is supernatural, whereas relationships are the specialty of this world, but ill done and sickly on a human level. The scripture says that one cannot stay warm alone (Eccl. 4:12), implying a deep mystery. Ecclesiastes speaks in human terms, the result being vanity. However, when looking beneath the surface, the divine mystery comes to light. No one can stay warm with just human company; it gets shallow and turns into vanity. But "a threefold cord is not quickly broken" (4:12). The Spirit is the third cord that turns relationships into fellowship. Apart from the third cord keeping each of the other two warm individually, the two cannot relate to each other without falling into carnality.

Thus, if you are a Spirit person, it is foolish to think that a non-Spirit person will understand you. A human cannot know you. Only God can know you, and then another can know you through God. Paul illustrates this repeatedly to the Corinthians, who thought that Paul was too outspoken even though he describes himself as an "ambassador" who will "appeal" and "beg" for his carnal readers to "be reconciled to God" (2 Cor. 5:20). Notice that the urging for reconciliation is to God, who then sorts out fellowship issues. When a Corinthian Christian reconciled to God, he or she then saw who others were as well. The mirror of carnality by which we judge ourselves and others is replaced with the glorious mirror of the Spirit.

The sticking point in reconciliation is seeing that a Christian is the righteousness of God in Christ. It is right to acknowledge and confess sin. That is not in dispute. However, the Christian life is a life—Christ's—in us. Sins get forgiven so that life can go on. The point is life. Christ became our sin so that we could become His life (2 Cor. 5:21). He was ever spotless but became sin, so that He could crucify it (and us) in Him and resurrect us in Him as righteous.

December 3

Christ Did not Sin but He Was Made Sin

Paul concludes his appeal to be reconciled with an overwhelming piece of evidence, one that he details in Galatians 2:20 and Romans 6 but nails here with one of the most remarkable verses in the Bible: "He made Him who knew no sin to be sin on our behalf, so that we might become the righteousness of God in Him" (2 Cor. 5:21). We will spend forever digesting on Jesus as the spotless lamb, and that God made Him to be sin on the Cross.

This requires seeing underneath the sins of a broken law. More profoundly, our lost condition was such that each human, other than Jesus, came from Adam, and was an "old man" before becoming a "new creation." The old man was the sin man, meaning the self who was joined to the old master, namely sin—yes, even Satan. This was hidden from our knowing at that time since a lost person can barely take it that he has sinned, much less that he was enslaved by sin itself in the form of the enemy. We were the incarnation of sin.

Therefore, for Jesus to totally take our place, He had to be made who we were. God unzipped Jesus on the Cross, put us into Him and zipped Him back up. This is why Galatians 2:20 says, "I am crucified with Christ." Our union with Christ started by Him taking our old man into Himself in such a way that it made Him to be sin. Then when Christ rose, since He had taken us into Himself in His death and burial, He made us the righteousness of God. This is what the Bible is asking every Christian to believe, for in eternity, there is no other option, so why wait and remain carnal, when eventually we will reconcile to God about the full work done by Christ.

God does not ask us to be reconciled to part of what salvation is; He appeals to us to be reconciled to the totality of our salvation. Anything less means hanging onto an old ID card for a new creation.

Taking on a Calling

We do not think up our own calling. The Spirit does the calling, and we respond. The Spirit will show a place of darkness, into which we speak restoration. After the initial inspiration, comes the tedium of slow change or no change, with the darkness appearing more intense than ever. Satan stirs fury and hell against the messengers of the Cross. Though the Bible says to anticipate this, and when it happens, theoretical knowledge is suddenly real and practical. Early victories give way to a more entrenched realization of a longer war to be won, which is why the scriptures place emphasis on endurance and patience.

The weariness of day after day, the shocks of dryness and waste in others' responses, plus their misinterpretation of what God wants, can cause the messenger to question, "Am I really supposed to stand here? Was I overzealous in what I thought was the call?" This continues as the sense of weakness becomes more evident. Resources get used up, bringing the acknowledgment of complete weakness, which was always true but is perceived gradually until the meaning of being a vessel grows clearer and is embraced with ever more sweetness and thankfulness.

The victory that God said He would win, He will win, but not in the manner first thought. Temptation comes to give up, quit—to even reject the very ones that God sent us to. It becomes easier to understand Jonah. But just as God knew how to swallow Jonah and let Jonah think for a while until he came to his senses, God knows how to send His fish to find us. Once the Cross is embraced, the messenger goes back to *catching* fish, not needing to be swallowed by one.

The agonies that twisted us and magnified the devil and evil take a resurrected turn toward seeing that what others mean for evil, God means and uses for good. Where misery had triumphed earlier, the same situations now occasion our ecstasies born out of the Cross.

The Secret of Loving a Bride

The secret of loving a bride is that it is a miracle. It does not come from our flesh, for that is impossible. No man can do that, or woman either. One goes straight to the Holy Spirit as Galatians makes so clear. The world does have those who in marriage find compatibility through flesh means, but that is a hindrance to what God means. God means marriage to be incredible suffering in which the two, each individually, die to anything but the all sufficiency of Christ as being our only life. This is the complete man or complete woman.

Thus, whereas we start by thinking that marriage should be fun and it should complete us with the other gender, God means marriage as the pathway to finding out who we are, which then becomes our outreach to the nations. When one of the two in a marriage does not see this, the believing one has the opportunity to take a faith stand for the other, which means much waiting and endurance. This is the way of the Spirit.

It is not a law. It is simply the nature of Christ formed in us (Gal. 4:19). No man wants to do this. I knew a man who went to the lawyer's office to discuss getting a legal separation since his bride and he were separated. He wanted to force the issue, but God checked him and showed him that this was not the way to know God and get through. Little did he know that his suffering (really Christ's sufferings, Col. 1:24) were just beginning. He rebelled for a season, but the darkness—the lack of Light— was the very thing God used to press him to see Christ as his life—Christ plus nothing. He realized that he had never loved his bride apart from self-interest.

It was not an awakening of condemnation but one of amazement at seeing the difference between soul and spirit and how God loves others through a human vessel. This is heaven's goal for every son of God.

Flesh View Gives Way to Spirit View

It is always the day of salvation (2 Cor. 6:2). Paul exhorts Christians not to see from the flesh, as if people are just people, not controlled by a master—the masters being either sin or righteousness (Rom. 6). Neither master is just a property or principle. One is the spirit of error, and the other is the Holy Spirit. This puts flesh in a different light. When Adam fell, the race plunged into the dark abyss of judging all life by emotions, mental reasoning, and bodily sensations—none of them intrinsically wrong, but all of which are no guides for life.

The Spirit man stands apart from his earthly properties and appetites, judging them by the Spirit. He does this by the Spirit joined to his own spirit, for that is what the new man is. He can see himself apart from himself, seeing the Spirit view of the would-be flesh man when temptation comes to see the self as helplessly led by earthly stimuli. Adam fell into the pit of darkness where he believed the lie that he was of his humanity alone, not merely inhabiting it. He thought he was of the world, not merely in it.

We inherited the same fall (Rom. 5); therefore, God has to regenerate the human spirit out of spiritual death for a person to see the difference between flesh and spirit. When seeing only flesh, flesh judges by all it knows, which is more flesh. Unpleasant emotions seek to find an answer by changing them to stimulating, pleasant ones—the same with thoughts, and of course bodily appetites.

The real problem is spiritual, and Paul told the Corinthians that the day of salvation is always today because he wanted them to wake up to the Spirit, not just as particular gifts and experiences, but as the fountain of life itself and the producer of fruit beyond the pale of emotions, mental reasoning, and physical appetites. Then, a man operates from Spirit/spirit clarity and discernment. Flesh becomes the servant and is the instrument of Spirit manifestation.

Today if You Hear His Voice

Since the word of God is living and active (Heb. 4) it is always speaking. The *Logos* never rests from speaking. Hearers just take ill-advised rests from listening. In the world, a saint tires of human voices that never shut up and vainly babble. With God, however, the voice is soft, continuous, and life-giving—not tiresome to hear. It may be costly to listen, and it may lead to excruciating things to endure, but the voice itself is always a shepherd, or nursing mother, or loving father, or quickening spirit.

Paul says, "Now is the day of salvation" (2 Cor. 6:2). We are accustomed to thinking of salvation as a process whereby a person needs to get ready. We say, "That person is not ready yet. That person cannot hear yet." The Bible does not recognize this. With being born again, walking in the Spirit, and guidance, the scriptures present God as having done everything on His end. Paul quotes Isaiah 49:8 where the people had entreated God, and God replied with all that they needed. This does not mean that prophecies requiring historical manifestation take place immediately, but it does mean that faith in the prophecy itself is God's answer for the now.

The Corinthians kept acting like God needed to do more to solve their problems, whereas Paul replied in the spirit of Psalm 95:7 and Hebrews 3:7, "Today if you hear His voice," meaning that when God has totally done what He is going to do, the solution on our end is faith that He has. Through Christ's blood and body, and the provision of the Spirit, God has done all that there is to do concerning our salvation no matter what our circumstances are.

All inner needs at our core have been satisfied by abundant provision accomplished on God's end by the Cross. When we protest that God has not as yet done something pertaining to an outer dilemma, He says first to see completeness within.

Looking Away from Self and unto God

People often ask each other, "Do you like what you are doing?" The world turns on liking something, whereas those born of God turn on faithfulness. Liking is fickle; it comes and goes. To live according to likes usually means immediate soul or body pleasure, whereas to live by faith means suffering. Norman Grubb began a talk on suffering years ago with, "Suffering is what I don't like." Everybody suffers. The glorious opportunity in suffering is to turn suffering into redemptive purpose for others.

Even when you like your skills and their utilization, you cannot like them enough to avoid suffering. The natural can never compensate for spiritual lack, resulting from making self the center of everything: "Why is this happening to me?" God unglues us from ourselves as the reference point and invites us to look at Him. It sounds vague for God to say, "Look at Me," but the beginning of freedom is looking away from the self and looking at God. In Him "are hidden all the treasures of wisdom and knowledge" (Col. 2:3). They do not reside in us but in Him, and Christ is the "mystery" of God (2:2).

To look at God reverses the flow of our spiritual thoughts away from the self and unto God. One operates by faith from the mind of Christ, which includes consciousness of the tree of life and its fruit—the fruit of the Spirit (Gal. 5). By faith a man says, "I am looking at You, God, not myself; and I am walking in the fruit of Your Spirit."

This is the essential ministry. Whatever task God calls a man to is measured not by numbers and commerce, but by faithfulness as a servant. The faith man says to God, "I am here to serve, not to be served." How else can one be more than a conqueror in the endless, grinding tasks of life that feel thankless and routine? The Spirit of God can only be freshness, even while persevering through appearances one more minute.

What Makes a Thing Hard or Easy?

Salvation looks hard from the outside like it is too complicated. Think about how many words are given to theology and how bewildering the Bible appears to the mind not reading it with the mind of Christ. That is because the Bible only makes sense within the mind of the one who wrote it. Therefore, to try and interpret the Bible rationally without the Spirit can only reduce the Bible to the level of the one reading it. Light only comes when a man lets go of his own mind and accepts the invitation to revelation not possible except as a gift from another sphere.

The block to this comes from the lie that freedom comes from doing. Thus, preachers in that mode excel by piling more requirements of doing upon themselves and upon the hearers. This is a heavy load—very hard. Suppose your preacher has loaded you with ten things to do, and the yoke of them is very hard. Then two men come along the road, and one of them puts upon you a yoke of only one thing to do. The other tells you not to do anything. Which is easier?

To the old mind, the one thing is easier to do. It is ten times easier than the former load, and it keeps you in the mode of doing. There is still something you can do as a work in your salvation. The one who told you to do nothing is perceived as infinitely harder because the offense is that you are taken out of the equation as a contributor to your salvation. This is the hardest message of all. To the fleshly mind, it means giving up; Christ has done all there is to do for justification and for sanctification as well. One only now need walk in Christ and His Spirit.

The fleshly mind will opt for the one thing as a false picture of grace. The mind set on the Spirit will find peace and delight in doing nothing and surprisingly find itself energized by the Spirit to cultivate a whole new world.

When Others Disappoint Us

It is inevitable that others will disappoint us. It may come from sinful decisions or simply just different preferences or leadings. If we have not disappointed ourselves, hurts from others will be harder to resolve. Thinking "I would never do that" will keep us blinded. Romans 7 is a place of learning that the self is not in control when it comes to sin, just as the self is not in control when it comes to righteousness. This is the lesson of being a vessel—a container expressing a master.

Every wheel has a hub for the spokes, and the hub of life is "I would do any sin if You weren't keeping me Lord, and thank You that You are." It helps to visualize that I would do exactly what that other person has done who disappointed me. I tell people, "If there is a sin that I have not done, it is only because of receiving the keeping before I got to that sin. Apart from the keeping, I could just as well be on my way to that sin as any other."

God uses crushing disappointment in our lives, both with self and others, as opportunities to know Christ as our life (Col. 3). One day working in 1993, I felt so depressed that I wished I could die. Immediately, a little, still voice said, "For you have died, and your life is hidden with Christ in God" (Col. 3:3). This made no sense, but the verse got filed away until just the right moment of seeing, "So that is what that means!" Things had to get bad enough before they could get good enough.

God scripts the lives of His own to bring them home inside to who they became at conversion. Through all the bitter disappointment, we learn to say, "God, if that is what it took for me to see, it was worth it." Then we stand and watch God do this for others too, turning our faith to the goal that they will come through.

Tiresome Tasks and People

Everyone tires of the same tasks and the same irritating people. The progression goes from getting tired of it, to being sick of it, to loathing it, to wanting to get away from it, to making a decision to stay or go. This is how God enlarges our capacity for suffering. We think we can put up with a lot, even tolerate a lot, but eventually, everyone reaches a limit: "That's it! I've had enough."

How can you know when it's time to quit, time to leave, time to move on? This is a Holy Spirit matter. Life's vexing issues bring to the surface the difference between the vessel and the one who lives in the vessel. Where the burden to put up with things lies on us, we will not wait or endure in believing God for something or someone. Where the burden is shifted to God against appearances, fresh springs of living water are at the door.

God is a God of extremes. This is His passion, and He made us to function in the extremes. That is the law of opposites because the most difficult and thorny problem becomes the occasion for the easiest and sweetest solution. That's right; the answer is hidden in the middle of the problem. To push the problem away hoping for a geographical solution only means a similar problem in a new setting with different people—but really a rerun of the old script.

My friend Scott Pearce tells a story about years ago when he drove to the end of his driveway planning to head off and leave the stress of his marriage. The Lord said to him, "You can leave, Scotty, but you'll just take your problems with you."

This is not just a marriage story; it is a universal story. Everywhere we go, what is in us is the same. When things are unbearable for one more second, what if we say, "God, Your fresh life and renewed interest are here in the moment?" What if staleness is the false lid hiding the freshness that faith calls forth?

Living Waters

Jesus said that believing in Him means the flow of "living water" from within, out of one's "belly"—one's innermost being (John 7:38). No matter what the need, the supply is living water. A fountain cannot give forth water both bitter and sweet (Jas. 3:11). The Cross is a fountain of sweet water only with no threat of poison to others, yet the sweet water can only manifest from an earthen vessel that sees itself as a water conveyor and not a water producer. You can bottle the water, even pour it, but you cannot make it. This is good to know.

Getting the water to flow takes understanding that it flows by faith. Trying to make it flow is not the same as letting it flow. The point is that faith simply receives and is more than saying that God can do a thing. Yes, it is imperative to know that God *can* act; however, this is not yet the word of faith that He is doing a thing. Faith moves from saying to God, "You *can* do it" to "You *are* doing it."

Going by appearances will never work. The focus will turn back to the self in its emotions and thoughts, plus the earthly body. These are not the door into the invisible. We must start with the invisible to see the invisible made visible, which sounds backwards, but to God, our former approach was backwards.

At first, we might think, "A little water would be good" or "If only some drops would pop out now and then." Jesus talked about the thirsty man who wants to put his mouth into the river and totally quench a deep and profound thirst (John 7:37). Once the water goes in, it comes out. The picture is even humorous—water coming into the mouth and exiting the belly: river in, river out.

You can never drink too much. The world celebrates a big thirst when it comes to its beverages, but more importantly, the Bible celebrates the person who thirsts for living water, is filled, and then flows out with it. Drink up, flow out.

December 13

Some Rudiments of Intercession

When going through excruciating trials with others, it is easy to think, "Why me? Why did I have to be affected by this?" That is a fair question. It would seem easier not to know people than to risk the pain. But faith rescues us from a despairing view of life. Just as the sun in the sky burns constantly and gives life, a loving and just God is our refuge when negatives overwhelm us. It is comforting that there is no need to figure out why things happen. Just trust in God who does know and who does not make our keeping dependent on having to figure things out.

The sun shines its same light and warmth, regardless of the weather. God is the same when hurt and pain are our weather. Ours is the eternal anchor of knowing that, and that Christ lives in us. We can go forward loving others and believing the good that life is, now and forever. Apparent enemy victories make us reel temporarily but do not change God's nature. Neither do they vary the faith and purpose of our lives. The most excruciating thing becomes the setting for the greatest glory.

Remember that the first fruits go to the altar. What looks like defeat is only the first sacrifice for a greater harvest later. Jesus Christ did not die as the intercessor for defeat but for victory, and for a sweeter victory. Yes, for many others, there will be "a garland instead of ashes, and the oil of gladness instead of mourning" (Isa. 61:3).

We would like to think that people we believe for will not cross boundaries that lead to horrible consequences, but they do (as we once did), and our intercession looks to be a failure. It is not, for no intercession is ever wasted or returns without fruit. Instead, God expands our vision to see fruit even greater than what we first believed for.

December 14

God's Unchanging Love

How we fare with the universe depends on the nature of God. If He is fickle or mean, we are in trouble now and forever. If His favor depends on what we do, we experience the frustration of our efforts to be like a God who cannot be imitated. God makes all of this easy, however, because He does not base salvation on what we do but upon His own nature. Even repentance is not something we do; it is receiving what He did in Christ. God undertakes the whole thing Himself and does it all, leaving us to rest in His finished work. This is what the Sabbath means. It is the place of rest, entered into by those wishing to rest. Without faith, one remains on the outside. Without faith, one remains unreconciled even though God reconciled Himself to us through Christ.

God never changes. William Law, the 18th century English writer, likened God to a bell. No matter what strikes a bell, the bell can only make the sound of a bell. Likewise, William Law says, the sun in the heavens can only do what the sun does, which is to be heat and light. Similarly, no matter what humans do, there is always a Cross in the heart of God. That is all that God can be, and we just respond yes or no to how we will spend eternity relating to that.

The Cross means that God has made the eternal choice to be self-for-others. For us, this life is about our getting fixed in our choice in what we think of that. God had always known that Adam would fall, knew all of our sins that we would manifest, and knew His plan to redeem those who wish to be redeemed. Strangely, not all choose to recognize love's way and that love can only be through the Cross. To rebel against the Cross is to remain in works, and to remain in works is to resist grace, and to resist grace is to work on forever as a slave of sin.

There Is Nothing More for God to Do

In Christ's blood, there is complete washing from sins. That gift stirs the writing of hymns like "There is a fountain filled with blood." Communion bread then speaks of the new man, because the old man died in Christ, was buried with Christ, and is raised with Christ as a new creation (Rom. 6 and 2 Cor. 5). In the new birth, God transforms a person into a new creation that did not exist before, one that human effort cannot bring about. There is no need for trying to be like a composite picture made up of Christian heroes not understood according to their faith.

Hebrews Chapters 9 and 10 unfold how God did a complete, saving work that God will never do again. It does not need anything further: Christ accomplished our cleansing and wholeness. Those chapters stand immovable against human pleading for God to do something else to meet the human need for peace and self-acceptance. It is sad to keep thinking that Christ is not enough, when God says that Christ makes us complete.

Communion acknowledges that Christ washed us and birthed us supernaturally as God's sons. Others may not understand why we can relax about ourselves and why our drive is now for others to know. In contrast, the devil-driven world and the carnal church live in turmoil, with resolutions to perform, as if resolutions can perfect the self and make it be loving and charitable. This presses to intercession believers who have been to the bottom of that lie. They intercede to make up what is lacking in the sufferings of Christ (Col. 1).

Christ has done everything to perfect the individual. Now by His body the church, He completes the forming of that body through the intercessions of those already in the body. "Therefore, we are ambassadors for Christ, God making His appeal through us. We implore you on behalf of Christ, be reconciled to God" (2 Cor. 5:20).

December 16

The New Isn't the Old Fixed Up

No one gets victory by resolutions or by desire to be different. Yet, desire is a key because faith is meaningless unless deliverance from sin is available. Then a seeker can desire it, take it, and be taken. No one does this, however, without desperation, for desperation drives transformation. Additionally, there must be something (*someone* really) available, or all is hopeless. Desperation eventually comes about by holding on to an Old Covenant mentality, as if the Law is still needed as a schoolmaster (Gal. 3:24). The Old Covenant schoolmaster, however, could only operate on a fleshly shadow level—never bring about a new creature—and those of old who were righteous, were righteous only because of faith in God's promises.

This is the beginning, and it is exciting, even while the suffering saint appears awful and unchanged, for desire can lead the desperate person to take the new birth, which goes beyond being saved (conception). The new birth is living as the new man (delivery). It means sins washed away surely; without that, there is nothing. But also comes understanding of Christ in you (Col. 1:27), which is more than inviting Jesus in as an addition to, and helper to, the same old failing self. This is where the new birth, seen for what it is, proves radical. The old self had to die. Yes, it had to die in Christ, not just be faint or weakened, but dead. There had to be a funeral, whereby the old self died and was buried, never to be again the old man (Rom. 6).

Now comes the miracle of resurrection. A totally new creation is birthed from the heavenly womb, which can look confusing, for there you are in the same mortal body, with the same personality, yet you are not the same person operationally as before. The transformation comes not of you, for you are born not of the will of the flesh or of the will of man but of God (Jn 1:13). You have let God bring you out of the womb into the kingdom of God—from conception to delivery.

December 17

The Righteousness of Job: Part 1

Job's suffering grew so intense that even the "trash" of society derided him, scorners who had fled society to live as wild men in the wastelands, feeding on roots and braying like animals. They were not even employable on a level to work with the dogs that ran with Job's flocks to protect them. Not only did Job's friends torment him with reproof, but outcasts from society mocked him in their songs (30:1-11). Job laments at this and states his purity, having kept himself from sexual lust, and as to good works, being a man of unconditional charity. Chapter 31 concludes, "the words of Job are ended" and perhaps heaven sat relieved. The three friends even refrain from further sermonizing to Job, "because he was righteous in his own eyes" (32:1).

Then appears the younger Elihu, who deserves study since God never reproves him like the three tormentors. Elihu says that Job justifies himself rather than God (32:2). Elihu repeats Job's summation that he stands innocent and without iniquity (33:9). Then Elihu brings up God's ways of dealing with what the Greeks later called "hubris," meaning pride or a fatal flaw. Job risks letting pride trip him. Elihu warns, "What man is like Job, who drinks up scorning like water?" (34:7). If pride takes root, sin must follow. Job's assertion, "It profits a man nothing that he should delight himself with God" (34:9) bursts headlong into enemy territory. Elihu then affirms the justice of God, for which Job himself previously argued until his afflicttion. Since Job has put God on trial, Elihu says of Job, "he adds rebellion unto his sin" (34:37).

Job does not realize yet that his case against God only hurts himself, or as Norman Grubb continually said, "The wrath is in man." Job's budding pride and vanity only threaten to destroy himself. Thankfully, Elihu, as God's spokesman, stands strong against Job's pride to point him away from it and back toward faith.

December 18

The Righteousness of Job: Part 2

God intends redemption for Job, not final judgement. Elihu, God's messenger, says, "and if they be bound in fetters, and be holden in cords of affliction; then he shows them their work, and their transgressions that they have exceeded [...] that they return from iniquity" (36: 8-10). God will provide a "ransom" (atonement) (33:24).

Elihu concludes by preparing the way for God's word to enter. Elihu begins to praise the majesty of God in His incomprehensible works in Nature. Thankfully, Job does not argue with Elihu or with the ensuing whirlwind of God's voice. He softens and repents in dust and ashes. The wisdom and sovereignty of God have prevailed. Job does not have to understand. He just has to worship and believe.

Job's story foreshadows the Gospel era, for "there is none righteous, no, not one" (Rom.3:11). Job knew this, and his hope had always been in God's grace. But he feared that his past sins were now the cause for his trials, and he slipped dangerously toward the precipice of pride and accusing God. But Job's redeemer was alive, and ours as well. Norman Grubb said it like this: "Quick sin, quick cleanse, quick out, quick in." He always warned against the second sin, the sin of wallowing in condemnation.

Thankfully, Job accepts reproof and rises in Christ. Job learns to see suffering as the foreshadowing of Christ's intercession through us (Rom. 8)—beyond the question, "What about me?" Instead of an endless wheel of self-justification, blaming God and others, the one undergoing trials says, "God, how are You using my sufferings to 'fill up that which is lacking in the afflictions of Christ in my flesh for His body's sake, which is the church'" (Col. 1:24)? No longer is the focus one's past sins. They are gone. The point of suffering has become the members of the church that Christ will be formed in through our present intercessions.

Bodies Washed with Pure Water

Hebrews 10:22, says, "Let us draw near with a true heart in full assurance of faith, having our hearts sprinkled from an evil conscience, and our bodies washed with pure water." Two astounding thoughts are expressed. One is the gift of a conscience made clean. This is a wonder—the perfect conscience we possess in Christ as His gift through His blood. By this we refuse the accusation of the devil and do not base our identity on thoughts and feelings. The Spirit tells us what is true.

We refuse the sin consciousness of being condemnation-minded and continually guilty with nagging torment and continuous questioning of our motives. As new creations joined to Christ, we experience plenty of such assaults from Satan, but live clean in conscience unless foolishly defiling it by sin by letting temptation's enticement move to lust's conception (James 1:14). If we do sin, the Holy Spirit convicts us according to the particular offense, affirming us as sons, and never with that vague, general, "I'm no good" pit of shame.

The second great thought of Hebrews 10:22 is "bodies washed with pure water." The Holy Spirit has washed our bodies. He not only cleansed our consciences, but removed the lie, "We have these sinful bodies, this evil flesh." This is sanctification of the body. Therefore, we accept in Christ the restoration of our appetites and faculties. To repeat, James says that only when lust conceives does sin birth. Our bodies are dead (mortal) because of sin, but quickened by the Spirit (Rom. 8).

These verses remind us of the God-made goodness of our humanity. The only problem was that Satan stole it at the Fall, but Christ restores it to us even now as we await the glorified body that will swallow up this mortal body at the last trumpet. Christ liberates the body—it is His instrument for righteousness (Rom. 6)—a cleansed body for a cleansed conscience.

December 20

The Ordinary Saint: Part 1

You cannot know who you are by trying to be unique through self-effort. Trying is the hallmark of Romans 7 and the block to restful living. In Romans 7, Paul describes failure to gain deliverance from sin, and sin is not a popular subject, which is exactly why the Bible talks about it, because we would never get to it on our own, and so God had to bring it up or we would have wandered in deception forever without a mirror to puncture our happy ignorance, if indeed it is happy.

No one can know God apart from a desperate struggle with sin. Often, talk of sin sinks to minimizing it by calling sin a mistake, an addiction, or a disease. This robs sin of its biblical vigor. The opposite problem, however, is taking sin seriously but continuing to obsess in condemnation over it. Neither extreme reveals the solution.

Minimizing sin is futile, for sin means failure to keep God's law while living under Satan's lie that a creature can be independent. Denial hides nothing and cannot do any good. But neither will obsessing over acknowledged sin, which only keeps a person sin conscious. Christ's blood is our only expiation, so there is no point in efforts to expiate ourselves. Trying or good works will not work, for neither one can assuage conscience. Taking condemnation rebuts Christ's sacrifice.

Once sin becomes known via the law, this paves the way for receiving God's gift of forgiveness in Christ. That is the first part and wonderful. The second part is walking in the Spirit (Gal. 5) because that is the only way to be kept from the frustrating pattern of sin-forgiveness-sin-forgiveness, etc. Hopefully, those not free from sin will meet people not living in defeat, and covet what they have. Usually we think the kept ones are special and not ordinary folks like us. Surely they have some elevated status. However, they are just like us except that they believe.

The Ordinary Saint: Part 2

When meeting people who do not live defeated, we either try to imitate them, or else we think, "That person is special. I could never know the same life of rest." Imitating them without success leads to thinking that select others are entitled to the magic, but we are not, when really, the magic is simply grace that is offered to all and equally a-vailable to all.

Once exhausted from imitating and trying, collapse can occur. The human mind fails and good that it does. Finally, it is refreshing to walk in "the mind set on the Spirit" (Rom. 8). By this time, you don't care about discovering yourself but want relief from yourself. This is not a denial of the self; it is the birthing of the true self—the one that is really you expressing Christ, in your members. You are not unique in how you come to it (details differ, but faith is faith). You are unique in that you are the only human you. The wonder of this comes from two things: we do not create the new self, and we do not try to keep it. God does both, having crucified us and then raised us in Christ. Faith agrees with that. Then the Spirit makes us know that we are originals. Truly, you are you, and you know it. This is the wondrous work of the Cross.

The Cross is everything. It is in our hearts because it is the heart of God, for it is death to self-for-self in the heart of God that leads to His light and love, which manifest in those who repent from their lost estate and begin living by the mind that was in Christ Jesus (Phil. 2:5).

This might sound too hard, but there is the dark side of the Cross and the light side of the Cross. The dark side only Jesus could embrace as our savior. The light side of the Cross is the resurrection and ascension side, whereby we operate in the heavenly mind and essence, even in situations of daily dying. This is the secret formula for knowing your uniqueness. It is not necessary though to keep it a secret anymore.

Christ in Us When Tempted: Part 1

Christ did everything for our salvation in the whole human—spirit, soul, and body. However, until we see this, Christ living in us can seem small, like a broom in a broom closet or like a jewel in a jewel box—precious and holy, but hidden away except for occasional viewing or handling. But what if Christ in you is not only for special occasions (or crises) but for all of life, and even temptation? We especially need to know who we are when the devil introduces guilt and questioning of motives, as if we are unworthy to say who we are when bombarded with soul feelings and evil thoughts that the devil would like for us to interpret as of us and not merely his pulls upon us. Do not be surprised, do not take condemnation, and do not think that you are your temptations.

Temptations never cease in this life. When they come, we hear the voice, "This is really sweeping me away. There must be something wrong with me for even feeling drawn in this direction." This is Satan's voice speaking in first person. Refuse condemnation and reply, "I *would* do that, Lord, for there is no sin that I wouldn't do if You didn't keep me, and thank You that You are keeping me." The "I would do any sin" reflects understanding that to be human is to be powerless. The life of being kept means being kept by a master. The "if You don't keep me" part is important, along with the "thank You that You *are*" because that is living by faith. But faith cannot save you apart from its object. Bill Bright said, "Do not put your faith in faith; that is like casting your anchor inside the boat." For us, faith is in a person, namely Christ.

God's keeping operates by the union of Christ and you—Christ living in your human form. Though this does not look supernatural, it is, because the quality of life that radiates is divine, for we are "partakers of the divine nature" (2 Peter 1:4).

Christ in Us When Tempted: Part 2

Christ *is* your life, and He lives it in an ordinary but miraculous way: "As He is, so are we in this world" (1 Jn. 4:17). This means even in my clay pot that looks ridiculous sometimes. However, I answer, "I didn't think of it; You did—that's not my idea, it's Your idea." I am not looking at myself much of the time anyway. Is He now me? Yes! Am I God? That's a silly question. We should not even have to deal with that question. "But what about all of my crazy thoughts? What about all of my crazy feelings?" So what! I used to complain to my mentor, Norman Grubb, about all of this. Oh boy, was he ever Mr. Sympathy.

I caught him one day between talks, and to my horror, he sat beaming as I poured out my travails. That outraged me because I was jealous and thought, "I want what you have. What is it? How do I get it?" As I poured out my pressures and temptations (not yet aware that everybody has them), his face beamed. He lit up, "Wonderful! Very healthy! Good practice!" I wanted to choke him.

Another time, I called up my friend Sylvia Pearce and complained, burning the wire with woe and lament, only to hear her say, "Brian, this is so good for you." I wanted to arrghhh! I mean, how about when something hits you and it is true, but you just want to choke that person at the same time. I could not get any sympathy.

So I went to Mimi, my mother-in-law, saying, "You know, I did this and I did that." She said, "You couldn't have done anything different." I was purple with anger. I said, "What do you mean, I couldn't have done anything different?" "You couldn't have done anything different." "I should have done things differently. I could have done them differently." "Well, you couldn't have done anything different." I didn't get it. Finally one day, I got it. Failure is one hundred per cent until the keeping is not our job.

December 24

Don't Be Surprised at the Strength of the Negative: Part 1

The strength of the negative should be no surprise. Fleshly lust pulls and the allures of enemy are powerful, tempting us to think, "This is stronger than ever" or "I can't resist this day after day." To appoint a convenient agent for our temptations and trials, God chose an enemy powerful enough so that we can know that we are weak and powerless. God already knows it because He created us that way. We are the ones who need settling in, that to be human is to be dependent when facing all onslaughts, small or great. To be weak and powerless is not sin!

Trusting in God corresponds to need, so to know the need for constant and total keeping, God must undercut our false self-dependency. Only by trying and failing do we learn that the enemy can't be defeated apart from a keeper. Until then, the nagging sense of frustration is worrisome that we are not free—that passions and unbecoming attitudes lurk beneath a kind exterior and all too often burst forth despite efforts to restrain them.

While living in the devil's lie of self-dependency, one thinks, "I wish that lusts would decrease or that the devil would retreat." That doesn't happen. It is a healthy tonic to say instead, "I hope the feelings and thoughts get worse!" Shocking as that sounds, it is a good antidote against fear and a chance to affirm that we do not live by a thermostat that can be set to avoid discomfort.

In Christ we have died to sin and to law, and this death is not just a positional truth written in a faraway ledger kept by angels. Knowing that we are dead to sin and law—and thus free always to refuse condemnation—is the everyday truth of how to deal with the passions and assaults of the devil. To take his bluff means a slip into thinking that our bodies, emotions, or attitudes are more powerful than the Holy Spirit who governs them. Not so.

Don't Be Surprised at the Strength
of the Negative: Part 2

God actually means for us to laugh at negatives and see them as an everyday thing, felt in all their fury, but then replied to with, "Oh, this is just garden variety lust," or, "Oh, this is just the enemy's lie again, and he is stomping his feet in a rage to bluff me."

In Romans 6, Paul says that we were baptized into Christ's death so that the body of sin might be destroyed. Sin does not get to operate in our bodies anymore because Christ's body death cut us off from Satan and sin. At that same time, we died to the law since sin's power is derived from the law. The Christian life is lived by the power of the Holy Spirit and walking in the Spirit.

Therefore, when the negatives entice, the first thing to know is that God means them to. Take no condemnation for their drawings. That only puts one back onto trying. Further, do not try to manage any of this. Just go on with ease in knowing that by faith you are living in the Spirit's effortless flow despite the intensity of Satan's bluffs.

The devil is a big cry baby and cannot take it when a Christian does not get as fussed up as he does about all that is wrong in the world as if God is not sovereign and good. The devil is also a coward when a Christian does not capitulate to his urges to respond with complaining. James says that the devil will flee from us (4:7). It does not take much for him to flee, just a little faith, a little love.

It is true that this life is excruciating a lot of the time. There is no point in adding to that by fear and useless trying to manage the battles. As you rest in the Lord, refusing intimidation, walk on in the Spirit, and fruit will abound on your branch—then in those who want what you have. That makes it worth it.

From Slaves to Friends: Part 1

The Bible calls us slaves and then friends of God. The slave level comes first because of God's call to obedience. At first, this sounds like the opposite of freedom. However, our obedience is faith, and faith means receiving. Anything else is Satan's lie of independence. Believing the lie confuses freedom with independence, whereas the only free person in the universe is God, so only in union with God through Christ can we experience freedom.

Since Adam sinned by seeking freedom in supposed independence (really, misused freedom), everyone born of Adam has lived as sin's slave. But now, we who believe live as slaves of righteousness. Note that we have always lived under an owner and master (Rom. 6). No one can decide to escape Satan's slavery and just move out from under it (2 Tim. 2:26). Christ first had to be made sin.

He had to become Satan-indwelled humanity on the Cross and die as that to free us (2 Cor. 5:21). Only then can we say, "I am crucified with Christ; nevertheless I live; yet not I, but Christ liveth in me" (Gal. 2:20). Freedom, in this case, means the freedom in God to see and choose this.

Choice is faith, and faith means taking something, in this case someone, then being taken by Him. What you take, takes you. This is how faith works. Life operates the same way, down to sitting in a chair. Is the chair available? Will it hold me? Down I go, losing control, until taken by it. Likewise, faith in the Spirit's fruit.

Then follows the next level, friendship with God. Jesus begins to call His disciples friends instead of slaves because of their obedience of faith. He shares with them His ways (John 15:14). As friends of God, we dare to be bold toward God because we do not seek our own interests anymore. Instead of just observing God's acts without His wisdom, we know His ways that relate them to a purpose outside of ourselves—for others (Ps. 103:7).

From Slaves to Friends: Part 2

God's life is always for others, as are God's friends—those in union with Him. When Israel rebelled by making a golden calf as an idol in the wilderness, God told Moses His plan to destroy the nation and start over with Moses. Moses wouldn't take it, appealing to the inevitable scorn from the Egyptians. He appealed to God's covenant with Abraham, Isaac, and Israel. Seeking atonement for Israel's idolatry, Moses said, "But now, if You will, forgive their sin—and if not, please blot me from Your book which You have written" (Exod. 32:32).

Abraham appealed to God as a friend when God told him the plan to destroy Sodom. Though fully aware of himself as dust and ashes, he persisted in appealing that God spare Sodom if it had even ten righteous people. A friend takes bold liberties that a slave won't. A friend steps boldly into the inner counsel of the Lord. Thus, Jesus calls His disciples friends, "if ye do whatsoever I command you" (John 15:14). What is His command? He had already told them earlier about the primary command—to abide in Him to bear fruit, and now He tells them that He no longer calls them servants, but has shared with them everything that He has heard from His Father.

"According to your faith be it unto you" (Matt. 9:29). Refuse the sin consciousness that Jesus died to release us from, Satan's seesaw consciousness of self-commendation and self-condemnation—those evil twins. Dragging around with a nagging sense of unworthiness and sin keeps a person self-focused, trying to get worthiness already ours through the Cross. He made us worthy in one, never-to-be-added-to sacrifice. A nagging sin consciousness means thinking that God will do something additional for us, when Christ did it all, not to be repeated. Accept His verdict and go on as friends and sons of God. If a specific sin occurs, receive specific forgiveness, and get on as God's friend.

December 28

What Is Choice?

Choice is what we love and what we hate. If we don't think we have choice, we believe that a dictator has stolen it. If we possess it, we feel swamped by the tension of alternatives. If God had created us without choice, we could plead being made helpless automatons. We crave to dispense with disturbing thoughts, scary feelings, and pressure-packed temptations. How good would it be, though, to exist merely as inert ooze in a predetermined way without freedom? Thankfully, the statement, "I hate this tension" can become, "This is the perfect opportunity for faith, and God is getting me through this."

The way many talk about choice sounds like self can independently perform its own good or evil. Those who live from Galatians 2:20 recognize this lie right away, knowing that choice in the end is about what spirit operates in us. Walking in the Spirit (Gal. 5) means walking free of Satan's sin-consciousness and being kept from sin. Even if a Christian temporarily chooses not to walk in the Spirit, leading to sin, repentance restores Christ-consciousness. Satan's bluffing sin-consciousness is now recognized and refused. Christ's blood and body are the complete work.

But what about the non-Christian, by definition in "the snare of the devil, having been held captive to do his will" unable to choose to escape by self-effort (2 Tim.2:26)? Freedom is only in Christ, and choice is of one's master. The non-Christian's one, God-granted freedom is to walk in the path toward receiving Christ, not the freedom to act independently.

God is the God of choice, reveling in it. And in us that means nonstop opportunities for faith as we contain Christ and express Him in this life. Only with faith can we bear the idea of choice and then live as more than conquerors in responding to the constant pressures daily upon us. Those pressures do not feel fun a lot of the time, but we count them all joy. Even tragedy must serve us, not we it.

December 29

What Is Work and What Is Rest?

Which reality determines whether Jesus violated the Sabbath by healing on it (Jn. 5:9)? What Jesus did appeared like work to His opponents, but was it? Jesus said, "He who speaks from himself seeks his own glory; but He who is seeking the glory of the One who sent Him, He is true" (Jn. 7:18).

This redefines work. The Pharisees lived by their own perceived ability to keep God's law, which *is* work, so they were actually the ones working on the Sabbath, whereas Jesus lived from rest all the time. Jesus then says, "Judge not according to the appearance, but judge righteous judgment" (Jn. 7:24), which parallels "We walk by faith and not by sight" (2 Cor. 5:7).

As we rest, we know by faith in the moment that the mind of Christ has taken over the job in us of our speaking and doing. What a relief. However, be prepared to be misunderstood, as if when you are resting, others think that you should be working, and when you are working, others think that you should be resting.

The point is not to mandate that you stay home from work today; externals are what they are. Rather, the point is to work from rest, and also to rest from rest. Rest is a person, namely Christ, and rest is known by witness of the Holy Spirit, based on Christ's sacrifice. A person who does not know this can sit in a recliner all day as if resting, but be under works on the inside with the heavy load of assessing things according to outer posture. A person who sees the revelation of rest can appear to labor and yet be coming from rest on the inside—living in the eternal Sabbath (Hebrews 4).

Work, as Satan and the world operate, means endless trying to become somebody by outer measurements and definitions. Rest is impossible; nothing is ever enough. Work from rest in who you already are in Christ implies completion already.

Distressing Thoughts and Feelings

We all need rest. That is a fundamental of the Bible, for God created the world in seven days and then rested. We are exhorted to rest from our own works and enjoy what Christ completed. This starts by not taking condemnation for feelings and thoughts, even though that looks like the only safe way to keep a rein on self.

No one is exempt from distressing thoughts and feelings. They tempt everyone—even to the point of wondering if relief will ever come again. No formula exists to predict these times, and sin is not necessarily the reason for them. Yet God means for us to experience without self-pity everything that comes to us. Satan doesn't take this without a fight to keep accusation as appearing correct. His worst attack comes in the form of his own evil mind.

However, "We have the mind of Christ" (1 Cor. 1:16), while at times feeling like we have the mind of Satan. This occurs because God lets Satan attack us with the lie that his mind is our mind. Though this is unpleasant, there is no need to fall for it. When assaulted, we possess tremendous faith weapons: first, we don't panic, but relax. When we were inexperienced, we saw the enemy and began to look at self. This led to self-loathing and obsessing, saying, "I'm so bad."

Second, we do not give in to the urges for fight or flight. We used to tense up and become combative, or else we tried to outrun the devil when we thought our defensive efforts would not hold out. But now, instead of fighting or running, we relax and do nothing, even saying, "This whirlwind of inner evil thoughts can go nowhere. It has nothing in me, and I will not be bluffed." At the perfect moment, the Holy Spirit bears witness after faith has stood.

The Christian life is easy, for Christ lives it for us. We do nothing but believe. Yes, Satan does attack, but there is an ease of faith, even in the middle of temptations that we once saw as irresistible.

Fret Not

Disagreement with others stirs up stress. It can be from what we consider wrong in the world, or wrong in our brethren. It helps to know that the devil is the prince of this world, and the tempter of the saints as well. If he tempted Jesus, be sure that the sons of God are not exempt.

However, God is in charge and means all disagreeable situations for good, despite horrible appearances. Jonah, for example, knew that Nineveh was an evil empire, but Jonah's commission was to preach repentance. That's just the problem; Jonah knew God's mercy, and that fretted Jonah to head for a ship going anywhere else. If Jonah could have taken vengeance, he would have run to the task.

We get a daily dose of the same, for it is common to man—this predictable temptation to want punitive justice without mercy. And sometimes, God will not even send us to preach mercy, just have us believe for it in silence. We may not be called upon to interact at all. God may just give us a word of faith to stand on and believe without external intervention.

This sounds like doing nothing, even irresponsible, but God is not concerned with humanistic versions of responsible action to change things. Rather, He is about the obedience of faith. Habakkuk 2:20 says, "Let all the earth keep silence." What is frustrating is if you are called to be the first one to do it.

Stand in faith that the word God gave you is done. No one wants to do that at first. We do not have to want to. If we do what the Spirit of God directs, peace will reign inside, and we will enter intercessory travail that God can use to transform others, whether seen immediately, or whether others even know whose faith helped lead to their transformation. Like Jonah, we die to initial revulsion and then miraculously stand in the love of Christ that wins others we would not have guessed as recipients of our calling.